JUNG AND AGING

JUNG AND AGING

POSSIBILITIES AND POTENTIALS FOR THE SECOND HALF OF LIFE

EDITED BY
LESLIE SAWIN
LIONEL CORBETT
MICHAEL CARBINE

Spring Journal Books
New Orleans, Louisiana

Published by:
Spring Journal, Inc.
New Orleans, Louisiana, USA
Website: www.springjournalandbooks.com

Cover image: Detail from *Remember What You Long For* by Pat Silbert © 2011. Acrylic on handmade paper & canvas w/gold leaf. www.patsilbertpaintings.com

Editorial and production assistance:
Drummond Books, drummondbooks@gmail.com
Cover design, typography, and layout:
Northern Graphic Design & Publishing
info@ncarto.com

Text printed on acid-free paper

Library of Congress Cataloging-in-Publication Data Pending

CONTENTS

PART IV

FINDING MEANING:

SPIRITUALITY IN THE SECOND HALF OF LIFE

FOREWORD

S wiss psychiatrist C. G. Jung called the period of older age the "second half of life." But when does "aging" begin? When we enroll in a Medicare plan? When we retire from the workforce? When our bodies begin to show signs of wear and tear? How can we age "well"—and creatively? How is spirituality helpful in later life? What services does our society offer to help those in physical and emotional need? All these questions, and more, were part of the discussions in an outstanding and enlightening conference, *Jung and Aging: Bringing to Life the Possibilities and Potentials for Vibrant Aging,* presented by the C. G. Jung Society of Washington in collaboration with the Library of Congress and the American Association of Retired Persons (AARP) Foundation. The discussions held at this conference form the impetus for this thoughtful book, which includes presentations from the conference as well as new material from others engaged with the issues of aging.

The years beyond midlife have the potential for being one of the most productive and satisfying periods in our lives. Although these years hold many challenges, including health concerns and physical aging, perhaps the most important challenge we face is finding or continuing to find meaning in our lives. We have many choices: we can focus on loss, disappointment, perhaps becoming depressed or, alternatively, we can transform this period into one of profound psychological and spiritual growth. This transformation requires a rebirth—a new way to live and be in the world. We need to reassess and prioritize our interests, our passions, and seek ways to pursue meaningful and intimate relationships.

For C. G. Jung, aging was not a process of inexorable decline but rather a time for progressive refinement of what is essential. Research suggests that the human brain can remain active, creative, and highly functional during our later years. Too often, we forget that our mental and spiritual health is less a matter of fate than of choice. We can either shrink from life or enlarge it by engaging the passions of our soul, mining the rightness of our true Self, and living the life we are truly meant to live. This book provides wise direction in this process.

The start of the turning point toward aging may begin slowly and quietly. One starts feeling a kind of unease. Many of the activities we enjoyed before are not as pleasurable. The challenges don't quite excite us the way they previously did. Boredom and impatience with spouses, family, friends, and colleagues can begin in a slight, subtle, and barely perceptible way. It is like listening to one's heartbeats and breathing, and for most of us it creeps up on us and happens sooner than we expect.

However, we need to recognize that aging is an important transitional period of life and learn to understand and honor it as such. To borrow from Jung's favorite quote about the presence of God, invited or not, for all of us, aging is either coming or already here.[1] And this transitional period, this time of physiological and psychological change, can easily turn into a crisis if ignored. Or it can be a time to start balancing where our energy should be—a time when we connect with and honor our true priorities for the final stage of life.

Aging ushers in a new set of tasks and questions. What is the meaning of our life? What has it been, and what will it be? More than anything, these are issues that Jung struggled with in his life and work, and they are addressed in the various approaches taken by the contributors to this book. Jung understood that as we age, we come to realize that there is more to life than what we have experienced in the first half of life. As he understood it, the latter stages of life move us to search for personal meaning to supplement what we have achieved and accumulated during the first years of adulthood. This search for meaning may come in the form of reviving earlier dreams and hopes or, for some, simply reviving silenced inner fantasies. As Jung might have put it, developing a career, having children, are illusions compared to that one thing, that your life is meaningful.

While many schools of psychology claim that personality development basically takes shape between birth and adolescence, for Jungians, it does not remain fixed there for the rest of our lives. As we age, those parts of the personality that we may have rejected earlier

---

[1] The full quote is "Vocatus aut non vocatus, Deus aderit," "Invited or not invited, God will be present." C. G. Jung, *Letters: 1951–1961*, edited by G. Adler, A. Jaffé, and R. F. C. Hull (Princeton, NJ: Princeton University Press, 1975), p. 611.

return with a vengeance. As Jungians see it, the important point to remember is that life does not continue as it was as we age. We must be ready to make changes and adapt.

For Jungians, shedding light on the importance of spirituality and self-reflection is paramount—points well developed and amplified in chapters written by leading Jungian analysts and authors, along with contributions from the non-Jungian professional world. Those who provide services to the aging and geriatric physicians who deal with the realities of everyday life reveal the complex and overwhelming challenges faced by professionals working with older adults. Their chapters enable us to understand what has been done, and what still needs to be done, to help our aging population. The insights they provide in this book are invaluable.

Aryeh Maidenbaum, Ph.D.

∼ Introduction ∼

On March 28, 2012, the Jung Society of Washington, in partnership with the Library of Congress and with the generous support of the AARP Foundation, convened a symposium at the Library of Congress. Entitled *Jung and Aging: Bringing to Life the Possibilities and Potentials for Vital Aging,* the symposium addressed C. G. Jung's ideas about ongoing human development across the lifespan and how these ideas could help change our view from that of aging as a time of withdrawal and relentless decline to aging as a time of active engagement in and contribution to society.

The program goals were to examine the current understanding of aging and the services that support the aging process, to enhance our understanding about the psychological and spiritual aspects of aging, and to identify potential uses of Jungian tools to promote optimal and vital aging. Jungian and Freudian analysts, as well as representatives from social work, medicine, and the creative aging movement, spent the day discussing Jung's groundbreaking ideas about psychological and spiritual growth during the second half of life and how these ideas could be used by those working with older adults to promote productive and vibrant aging. They explored the potential of Jung's concepts about growing older in light of current best practices in the field of aging.

The symposium was moderated by Aryeh Maidenbaum, Ph.D., director of the New York Center for Jungian Studies. Lionel Corbett, M.D., professor and core faculty member of Pacifica Graduate

Institute, delivered a plenary talk entitled "A Jungian Exploration of
the Possibilities and Potentials for Vibrant Aging." Three panels then
discussed the key points in Corbett's presentation from the points of
view of their respective disciplines:

Panel 1: Productive and Vibrant Aging from a Psychological Perspective

Panel 2: Gerontological Views of Productive and Vibrant Aging

Panel 3: The Role of Spirituality in the Second Half of Life

The symposium would not have been possible without the
generous financial support of the AARP Foundation. The Library of
Congress recorded the symposium, and the webcast is available at:
http://www.loc.gov/today/cyberlc/feature_wdesc.php?rec=5505 (first
part) and http://www.loc.gov/today/cyberlc/feature_wdesc.php?rec=
5506 (second part).

This book closely follows the symposium organization. Most of
the presenters at the Library of Congress have amplified their
presentations here, and we have added a few new chapters that offer
additional insights and perspectives on the aging process.

Part I, "The Second Half of Life: A Time of Growth and New
Meaning," contains two chapters: chapter 1, "The Case for a
Jungian Viewpoint of Aging," by Leslie Sawin, and chapter 2,
"Successful Aging: Jungian Contributions to Development in Later
Life," by Lionel Corbett. Sawin's chapter outlines C. G. Jung's
perspective on the second half of life and how it can enhance and
support successful aging. Corbett's chapter, which is based on his
plenary address at the conference, lays out a model for successful
aging, offers mechanisms for maximizing individual potential, and
points the way toward a model of aging that encompasses the whole
person. Using these papers as a starting point, successful aging is
then examined from several points of view.

Part II, "Psychological Perspectives on Navigating the Second Half
of Life," provides psychoanalytical perspectives on aging. Three
psychoanalysts discuss specific aspects of the second half of life. In
chapter 3, "Emergence and Longevity: Some Psychological Possibilities
of Later Life," Jungian analyst Joseph Cambray discusses the lifelong
development of the psyche, including the notion of emergence and
its relationship to personal longevity. He also discusses the role of
wisdom and folly in the second half of life and their important
contributions to the aging process.

Jungian analyst Michael Conforti writes about developing new meaning in chapter 4, "Intimations in the Night: The Journey toward a New Meaning." Using Ernest Hemingway's powerful story, *The Old Man and the Sea*, Conforti offers an example of how the development of new meaning comes about through one man's personal struggle with the acceptance of growing older.

Psychoanalyst Robert Langs concludes this section with chapter 5, "An Adaptive Perspective on Aging." His discussion of how an adaptive perspective on aging includes death as a natural process rounds out the important psychological components for successful aging.

Part III, "Gerontological Perspectives on Successful Aging," is comprised of four chapters written by people working in the field of aging. The authors discuss the state of aging research and policy and present specific recommendations for useful tools and approaches to best support successful aging and adaptation to the second half of life.

In chapter 6, "Opportunities for Ongoing Jungian-Gerontological Partnership," Michael Carbine discusses programs and services for those who are aging and identifies opportunities for partnerships between the aging services field and the Jungian community. He suggests that the Jungian community possesses unique insights and perspectives in four areas that could enrich and strengthen efforts by aging services professionals to help adults navigate aging-related transitions: the value of curiosity, the power of creativity, the importance of spirituality, and the critical role of meaning in the ability to transcend suffering and accept death. He encourages the two communities to begin discussing collaborations around these four areas.

Kelley Macmillan, in chapter 7, "The Whole Person Services Model and the Second Half of Life," reviews the concept of the whole person services model and its application to the breadth of aging services and examines this model in terms of how an individual can benefit from this approach. He then discusses the interfaces between the whole person model and the Jungian model of the second half of life.

Gay Hanna, in chapter 8, "The Central Role of Creativity in Aging," offers a viewpoint on creative aging and the importance of creativity in the second half of life. She provides an overview of the nature and theory of creativity and offers examples of how it is used to enhance wellness in later years. Her discussion highlights the importance of creativity in the second half of life and how the Jungian perspective supports creativity as an asset in later years.

In chapter 9, "Some Thoughts on Aging Well," Mary A. McDonald offers the perspective of a geriatric physician on the process of aging. She identifies four essential elements in a recipe for aging well: engagement, resilience, hope and spirituality, and a sense of humor. Using clinical vignettes, she illustrates the central role these four characteristics play in how people adapt to the aging process.

The final section of the book, Part IV, "Finding Meaning: Spirituality in the Second Half of Life," expands on one of the critical elements of the experience of aging: spirituality and its role in redefining meaning for the second half of life. The concept of turning inward and finding meaning and a personal spiritual perspective is at the heart of both the Jungian perspective on the second half of life and successfully meeting the challenges of growing older.

Melanie Starr Costello addresses the issue of a personal spirituality as an integral part of growing older in chapter 10, "Conscious Aging as a Spiritual Path." She inquires into the nature of symbolic life, psycho-spiritual development in later life, and the nature and role of resilience in responding to change. This perspective is enlarged in a section on literary and mythological formulations. The chapter concludes with biographical sketches that portray qualities that can be found in individuals who have been able to become conscious of the spiritual potentials of aging in depth.

Jerry Ruhl and Roland Evans discuss relationship in chapter 11, "Spirituality and Relationship in Later Life." They argue that spirituality and relationship are deeply connected and that relationship can serve as the container for profound inner growth during the second half of life. They identify the need for a significant other, what they call the person with whom we share our life. Building on this premise, they discuss the nature of intimacy and primary relationship from a historical perspective, its importance in the individuation process, and the role of relationship in later life. They analyze the basic nature of relationship from the immature to the transformative and offer data from interviews that help define the nature of a transformative relationship.

James Hollis offers a challenging perspective on self-examination in chapter 12, "For Every Tatter in Our Mortal Dress: Stayin' Alive at the Front of the Mortal Parade." Starting with a quote from Yeats, he focuses on five paradoxes about the "problematics of aging": the fullness of life versus the necessity of loss, our inability to fully imagine the future as an aging person, our desire to retain youth and health, our inability to live in the face of our mortality, and the role of the "fool" in old age. He then offers some ideas about aging: embracing curiosity, asking the right questions, and recovering "personal authority." He concludes with important questions that, when asked, enlarge our perspective and help redefine meaning.

Lionel Corbett concludes this section and the book with a summary of the importance of personal spirituality and meaning in aging successfully and of living the second half of life fully and creatively. In chapter 13, "A Jungian Approach to Spirituality in Later Life," Corbett discusses numinous experience and its role in spirituality, individuation as a spiritual process, and the formation of meaning as an important mechanism for acceptance of old age.

We hope this material contributes to the ongoing discussion of the creative potentials of later life.

~ PART I ~

The Second Half of Life:
A TIME OF GROWTH AND NEW MEANING

~ CHAPTER ONE ~

The Case for a
Jungian View of Aging

LESLIE SAWIN, M.S.

C G. Jung is regarded as one of the leaders of modern studies
of adult development because of contributions such as his
1930 paper "The Stages of Life."[1] He believed that
psychological and spiritual growth is possible at every age and often
continues into very old age. So to think of aging as a period of
relentless decline is a mistake. In fact, much current research
supports the possibility of continuing growth and development
during old age and, therefore, the premise that one can grow into
old age rather than sink into it (p. 20). For Jung, old age was a
summons to internal growth and personal development, and it
provided the opportunity to enrich life, deepen spirituality, and
define a new sense of purpose or meaning. He wrote that we would
not live to old age if longevity had no meaning for the species.[2] Hence,
the later part of life must have an inherent significance.

The *Jung and Aging* symposium was convened to bring together
psychoanalysts and specialists in gerontology and spirituality to explore
the potential of Jung's concepts about growing older and the second

half of life in light of current best practices in the field of aging. Its goals were to examine the current understanding of aging and the services that support the aging process, to enhance our understanding about the psychological and spiritual aspects of aging, and to identify potential uses of Jungian tools to promote optimal and vital aging.

Rather than defining "successful aging" as the absence of disease and disability, a recent and more comprehensive definition suggests that successful aging should be measured by a person's perceived satisfaction with his or her ability to adapt to physical and functional changes over time while maintaining connections to others, interdependence, and a sense of meaning and purpose in life (p. 22). These characteristics embody a theory of both adaptation to and transcendence of limitations.

Jung's Stages of Life

Looking at Jung's "Stages of Life" through the lens of the symposium raises two questions: (1) What does the second half of life, as presented by Jung, have to offer older people? and (2) What does the engagement process inherent in the Jungian approach to that stage offer for finding meaning in later life and integrating death as part of living?

Jung wrote in some detail about the stages of life and the particular role of the second half of life in two volumes of his *Collected Works*: volume 7, *Two Essays on Analytical Psychology* and volume 8, *The Structure and Dynamics of the Psyche*. "The Stages of Life" is also included as a chapter in *Modern Man in Search of a Soul*. We applied his concepts of the second half of life as the organizing focus for the discussion. This chapter will examine the concept of the second half of life as applied to aging, beginning with Jung's metaphor of the sun.

The Journey of the Sun

I must take for comparison the daily course of the sun—but a sun that is endowed with human feeling and man's limited consciousness. In the morning, it rises from the nocturnal sea of unconsciousness and looks upon the wide, bright world which lies before it in an expanse that steadily widens the higher it climbs in the firmament. In this extension of its field

of action caused by its own rising, the sun will discover its
significance; it will see the attainment of the greatest possible
height, and the widest possible dissemination of its blessings
as its goal. In this conviction the sun pursues its course to
the unforeseen zenith—unforseen, because its career is
unique and individual, and the culmination point could not
be calculated in advance. At the stroke of noon the descent
begins. And the descent means the reversal of all the ideals
and values that were cherished in the morning. The sun falls
into contradiction with itself. It is as though it should draw
in its rays instead of emitting them. Light and warmth decline
and are at last extinguished.[3]

Jung uses this metaphor to describe two stages of adult life, early
adulthood as the rising of the sun and the second half of life as its
descent after achieving high noon. The period of ascendance can be
characterized in several ways. It is the time when a young person may
fulfill the biological demand to continue the species, protect his family,
and construct a presence in the outer community, what Jung calls the
natural aim.[4] Morning is typically a time of expanding and growing
with a minimal sense of limits.

The values that govern this period of life are outward-looking. The
adaptive personality is geared to achievement, acceptance, and
providing what society rewards. This is often accompanied by a loss
or diminution of important elements of personality, such as
introspection and personal development. This period can be
summarized in two ways: "The first half of life is biography," when
most are driven to achieving goals which position them in the outer
world.[5] It also can be viewed as a time when many of these governing
complexes are unconscious and, because we are other-directed in our
vision, philosophies and belief systems support the natural aim and
external orientation. It is a time for building and expanding, when
meaning is generally obtained and typically measured through
achievement. It is a time both for fulfilling biological imperatives and
relating to the rest of the world.

High Noon

The term *midlife*, if nothing else, implies a period of time
between the events of the first half of life and the very different

imperatives of a second . . . . One of the distinct contributions
that Jung has made to the field of psychology is his
understanding of development as an epigenetic process that
takes place over an entire lifetime . . . . Each stage of a person's
life is marked by its own developmental tasks and goals.[6]

Midlife is a well-recognized phenomenon in Western culture
and represents the moment when the shift toward the second half
of life begins. The midlife transition happens at a different time
for each of us. It marks the confluence of three events in an
individual's life: (1) the zenith of accomplishment in terms of career,
community standing, and personal accomplishment; (2) the time
when the family network begins to change, children leave home,
retirement approaches, family responsibilities begin to shift; and
(3) the appearance of a subtle and quiet dissatisfaction with current
values and sense of self as these changes happen and progressively
a yearning for a new sense of self.

The midlife process is both deeply psychological and also strongly
social, in disparate arenas, ranging from work to biological and
emotional shifts. For Jung, the period of high noon marks the end
of the natural, biologically and socially driven aim and the start of
a new developmental phase. It is often a turbulent and stressful time.
As James Hollis writes,

the agenda of the first half of life is forged from suffering
demands of all kinds and responding to the blows, challenges,
and seductions of life, while the second half of life has more
to do with wrestling with the aftermath: guilt, anger,
recrimination, regret, recovery, and the possibility of forgiveness
of self and others.[7]

These phases of the sun, morning and high noon, represent
distinct developmental stages that each of us will experience, each in
his or her own way and time. As Satinover and Bentz describe it:

Just as a biologically timed maturational sequence is set into
play at puberty by the release of hormones, the experience
of disillusion and ennui at midlife triggers the onset of a new
maturational phase. We are moved to explore those aspects
of the psyche originally set aside by ambition and desire in
the establishment of career and family. In fact, Jung believed

that the pursuit of meaning is properly undertaken *only* in the second half of life.[8]

Thus, the first moment of midlife, or high noon, marks a moment of transition that Jung felt was a natural developmental landmark. It invites one to take the next step in the process of development when the time is right and the natural internal process occurs. It provides an opportunity to turn away from the external and to begin the journey of turning inward. At this point, the sun starts to turn inward, to illuminate the inner life. What is the work of this inner illumination?

The Second Half of Life

> The second half of life presents a rich possibility for spiritual enlargement, for we are never going to have greater powers of choice, never have more lessons of history from which to learn, and never possess more emotional resilience, more insight into what works for us and what does not, or a deeper, sometimes more desperate, conviction of the importance of getting our life back.[9]

For Jung, richness and meaning in life is found only through acknowledging and working to achieve the relationship between consciousness and the transpersonal levels of the psyche, through understanding and embracing our dual nature, the ties between consciousness and our unconscious life, and the need for each aspect to connect with the other. He writes that

> our psychic processes are made up to a large extent of reflections, doubts, experiments, all of which are almost completely foreign to the unconscious, instinctive mind of primitive man . . . . Instinct is nature and seeks to perpetuate nature, whereas consciousness can only seek culture or its denial.[10]

In a way, one half of this dual nature is exemplified by our conscious, rational thoughts and the other by our dreams and symbolic thinking. An overarching goal of the second half of life is to understand and embrace the meeting of pairs of opposites within the personality, such as thinking and feeling. Just such a pair is the two halves of adult life: one arising from the needs of nature and the other in service to the expansion of consciousness that builds culture.

The work of the second half of life frequently demands wrestling with internal tensions, images, and concepts and trying to become conscious of the repressed or neglected dimensions of one's own soul. The goal of this process is to individuate, expand consciousness, achieve balance, and progressively embody the unique individual that is each of us.

To do this we are asked to hold the values of the morning of life with those of the evening so that we can reconcile and integrate them. We often enter a period of contradiction of and challenges to our own beliefs and philosophy. One of Jung's important mechanisms for such change is to develop the opportunity to explore otherwise undeveloped aspects of one's personality, such as one's emotional life, interpersonal values, and imaginative powers.

According to Jung, "after having lavished its light upon the world, the sun withdraws its rays in order to illuminate itself."[11] This process of internal illumination can lead to several important results:

1. finding meaning and direction for the second half of life through the process of grappling with opposites that can lead to relativization of the ego, to individuation (the process of reaching our full potential and achieving wholeness), and to expanded consciousness and a new meaning for life;
2. bringing that wisdom and a greater sense of self and consciousness to bear on a cultural vision; and,
3. developing a relationship to the spirit and to the transpersonal Self that shifts the seat of personal identity from the physical sense of self to the transcendent Self— and enables the potential integration of the inevitability of death as another developmental milestone in life.

This expanded sense of vision, consciousness, and a new relationship to one's ego can bring both a new relationship to communal interactions and community and a deepening of one's connection to the life of the spirit. Jung felt that people in the second half of life have a duty to undertake this inner illumination. He saw this process as a way to attain a new relationship with the spirit as a necessary preparation for accepting the final stages of life and meeting the unknown.

The image of a natural turn inward and a process of inner illumination is beautiful. For Jung, this process and its light is the vehicle for the unknown spiritual journey to come. As the body declines, the inner light and expanded consciousness provide a different form of strength. Just as youth and physical strength support the morning of life, inner illumination and a new connection to the transpersonal support life's evening and the soul's journey toward physical death. The inward turning of the light illuminates a different source of strength and creativity.

Meaning in the Second Half of Life

> But it is a great mistake to suppose that the meaning of life is exhausted with the period of youth and expansion . . . . The afternoon of life is just as full of meaning as the morning; only its meaning and purpose are different . . . . Man has two aims: the first is the natural aim . . . . When this aim has been reached a new phase begins: the cultural aim.[12]

Examining the tension of opposites and the specifics of internal work can lead to an understanding of how a self-examination process could result in a new definition of meaning, a renewed sense of creativity, and the awakening of a curiosity about and attraction to internal illumination. This potential for those entering the second half of life is summed up by Satinover and Bentz:

> This is really the heart of the question: the wisdom inside . . . [having] a sense of meaning triggers an inner process that relativizes assumptions about life, which are necessary to the fulfillment of the biological imperatives . . . . The sense of meaning, for many of us, reaches awareness only when we realize its absence. It appears to serve as a kind of inner compass that guides us along the direction in harmony with the formation of character—even though we may not have any conscious or articulated sense of just what that is . . . . Put simply, to the extent that any action furthers the development of character, we will experience a sense of meaning . . . . It is fair to say, however, that the final goal of life, as Jung understood it, was not to accomplish certain things, or to experience life broadly or to have dreams or visions or, for that matter, friends or family. When viewed from the perspective that all of these things will ultimately be lost, it

becomes clear that they are not ends, but means—the means
by which we set up a platform from which character launches
the next phase of its own development.[13]

The Jungian perspective has a great deal to contribute to the
understanding and optimizing of the aging process. The search for
direction and the struggle to find meaning in the aging process fit very
well with Jung's perspective on the second half of life. Jung's focus on
the role of spirituality in the second half of life supports and enhances
a critical element of what is known about successful aging. Best
practices in aging—a focus on relatedness, creativity, community ties,
and establishing a meaning that helps one look forward to the journey
toward old age and death—are all outcomes that follow the inward
illumination process.

Many of us long to have a balanced sense of self—integrating both
the spiritual and the rational aspects of ourselves. The perspective
that Jung offered about the second half of life and its tasks shows
that he is a man for our time in terms of both understanding the
need to integrate aspects of ourselves and coming to terms with
aging. This book expands upon Jung's principles for the second half
of life and offers specific strategies and tools for using those
principles to enhance the process of aging and to live the second
half of life with openness and meaning. It builds upon Jung's
principles of finding meaning in the second half of life and offers
insights, tools, and guidance for that journey.

Jung and Aging Symposium

The symposium identified two core principles at the heart of
successful aging: (1) psychological and spiritual growth are possible
at every age, with new challenges at each period of life, often continuing
into very old age; and therefore, (2) that to think of aging as a period
of relentless decline is a mistake.

As discussed above, Jung proposed the idea of different
developmental tasks for different stages of life, although each individual
may come to these tasks at any time depending on his or her personal
development. One current model of aging as a natural process (the
whole-person services model) naturally builds on Jung's perspective.
The symposium offered several growth-enhancing possibilities that

are available during the second half of life, including: the development of unused potential; the opportunity to explore otherwise unexpressed aspects of one's personality, such as emotions, interpersonal values, and imaginative processes; the maintenance of self-esteem; and the exploration of new roles and opportunities, including new family, social, and civic roles.

The symposium identified important connections between one's spiritual life and successful aging. Jungian psychology is particularly helpful in this regard since it allows one to develop a spirituality that is independent of any particular religious institution or set of doctrines or dogma by focusing on meaning. That is, one's spirituality can be based on direct experiences of the sacred, a permission often denied in the religious or cultural formation of many people in earlier periods of their lives. Jung also valued creativity, which he believed to be one of the most important of human instincts and a vital ingredient in healthy aging. In fact, research suggests that creativity is essential to both physical and psychological well-being and vitality in the second half of life.

In addition, symposium presenters offered several growth-enhancing possibilities that often present themselves during the second half of life that are also built directly on a Jungian perspective. It is our hope that readers will find much of value in this book to help them and those they work with as they undertake their journeys into and through the second half of life.

NOTES

[1] C. G. Jung, "The Stages of Life," in *The Collected Works of C. G. Jung*, vol. 8, ed. and trans. Gerhard Adler and R. F. C. Hull (Princeton, NJ: Princeton University Press, 1960).

[2] C. G. Jung, "On the Psychology of the Unconscious," in *The Collected Works of C. G. Jung*, vol. 7, ed. and trans. Gerhard Adler and R. F. C. Hull (Princeton, NJ: Princeton University Press, 1953), § 114.

[3] Jung, "The Stages of Life," § 778.

[4] Jung, "On the Psychology of the Unconscious," § 114.

⁵ Pittman McGeehee, lecture presented at Saybrook University, Houston, Texas, on January 11, 2013.

⁶ J. Satinover and L. T. Bentz, "Aching in the Places Where We Used to Play," *Quadrant* 25, no. 1 (1992): 22–23.

⁷ James Hollis, *What Matters Most* (New York: Gotham Books, 2009), p. 251.

⁸ Satinover and Bentz, "Aching in the Places Where We Used to Play," p. 23.

⁹ James Hollis, *Finding Meaning in the Second Half of Life* (New York: Gotham Books, 2006), p. 10.

¹⁰ Jung, "The Stages of Life," § 750.

¹¹ *Ibid.*, § 786.

¹² Jung, "On the Psychology of the Unconscious," § 114.

¹³ Satinover and Bentz, "Aching in the Places Where We Used to Play," pp. 25 and 27.

CHAPTER TWO

Successful Aging
Jungian Contributions to Development in Later Life

LIONEL CORBETT

We could date the beginning of the aging process to middle age, which is often when people begin to ask questions such as "Is this all there is?" "Where am I going?" "What do I really want from life?" People start to think about death more often—not only physical mortality but also the death of the youthful illusions or myths by which they have been living. In Jung's metaphor for the life cycle, he uses the image of the sun rising to a zenith and then at midlife gradually beginning to set. This begins a transition towards what Jung referred to as the "second half of life," which he believes to be the beginning of a process of introspection, a search for meaning, and a deepening of spiritual life. A new level of identity becomes necessary.

This article first appeared in *Psychological Perspectives,* Volume 56(2), pp. 149–167, 2013, and is reprinted here with the kind permission of the Jung Society of Washington.

Current Social Perspectives on Aging

The sheer number of people who are now living into old age suggests that we need to understand more about the potential for growth and development at this time of life—which, for many people, is as long as childhood and adolescence combined. *Successful* aging is a very subjective matter, involving individual values and social constructions. We therefore have to be careful not to impose a norm or standard for all older people by insisting that they all should be healthy, sexually active, creative, and spiritually evolved; to insist on such norms would constitute a prejudice that is simply the opposite of the ageism prejudice. Many gerontologists stress the importance of keeping active in later life, because doing so helps to preserve physical and mental health. But we must be careful not to judge an older person as aging successfully only if he or she maintains midlife levels of activity that are socially conventional. To do so would claim that aging itself does not have a legitimate tempo and legitimate types of activity. This kind of prejudice reflects our contemporary relentless search for endless health and it ignores social constraints; we have to take into account lack of opportunity based on income, education, social status, availability of social support, and other factors that affect people's ability to make choices. This point might be particularly relevant for people who are marginalized, for minorities, and for elderly women living in poverty after a lifetime of caring for others.

Stereotypes about Aging

One of the traditional, negative stereotypes of aging tends to see aging itself as a disease. However, age, by itself, does not tell us much about the state of a person's health; many aging people are relatively free of disease. It is a mistake to see later life as a period of inexorable decline in health and vitality. What we actually see is often a long period of relative equilibrium, during which health changes occur slowly in such a way that the person can adapt, followed by a rapid period of terminal decline—and this ability to adapt to gradual change is important for satisfaction in old age. During the long period in which vitality is maintained, considerable psychological and spiritual development can occur. Our society has only recently recognized that increasing numbers of older people remain highly competent and able to continue education and work.

A great deal of research has shown the negative stereotype of aging to be untrue: It turns out that many individuals are aging well. However, we also must discern and respect the specific developmental tasks of old age and not see it as nothing more than the perpetuation of middle age. Ageism, or the devaluation of old age, is often due to the projection of what we fear lies in store for us.

Roles and Social Status

One of the problems we face as part of the aging process results from our tendency to be socialized into particular roles at different times of life. As we age, we feel we have slipped into roles that may be seen to have a reduced status, such as *retired* or *widowed*. These roles can lead to a sense of diminished self-esteem after retirement, especially for people who have reached positions of prestige and authority—who are at the summit of their professional or business lives—and are then expected to accept a devalued social role in which their skills are suddenly no longer in demand. Older people who accept the negative stereotype of aging believe that decline is inevitable and therefore feel limited and do not achieve the potential that old age may bring. Because our culture does not value old age, there is often an unconscious assumption that for as long as possible, the older person should try to behave as if he or she were young, and this assumption postpones efforts to deal with the specific late-life developmental tasks.

The transition into old age has no clear demarcation and, like any liminal period, may trigger emotional distress. We do not have adequate social provisions to help with this transition; there are no rituals of initiation or rites of passage that would socially validate the transition for the individual. Jung pointed out that difficulty meeting an important developmental task—a fear of taking the next developmental step along one's path of individuation—is an important cause of emotional disturbance. It is therefore important to consider adaptation to old age.

Recognizing and Understanding Successful Adaptations to Aging

The negative stereotypes about aging are a social fiction based on misunderstanding of the behavior of the elderly. For example, some older people deliberately reduce their social interactions, which can be interpreted as a loss of interest; but this shift is actually an adaptive strategy designed to conserve energy for valued activities and relationships. Older people seem to lose control over their lives, but in fact they often enlist the aid of others for activities that become difficult with age, while at the same time maintaining a sense of overall control. Older people can adapt their goals and their sense of self to their physical limitations; they can compensate psychologically and spiritually for biological decline.

Until recently, successful aging was often defined, using a purely medical model, as the absence of disease and disability. More recent views suggest that *successful aging* refers to a person's perceived satisfaction with his or her ability to adapt to physical and functional changes over time, while maintaining connection to others, interdependence, and a sense of meaning and purpose in life. It is important to focus on the individual's personal perspective; an older person with physical limitations and chronic illness may still experience satisfaction with his or her ability to cope, if life is otherwise meaningful.[1]

Learning in Later Life

There is a great deal of current interest in continued learning in later life, and there is now a developing field of educational gerontology. Advantages to learning in later life include a number of factors, such as being able to choose a topic purely out of interest, without it being tied to a career, and having ample time to study after retirement. Programs such as Elderhostel, the Osher Lifelong Learning Institutes, and the University of the Third Age (an international organization dedicated to the education of retired people) are valuable. In addition, retired people have accumulated a lifetime of experience and a vast amount of knowledge that they can pass on to others. Older people often want to spend their time doing something meaningful, and there seems to be an inherent human imperative to keep learning. Fortunately, current brain research supports this possibility: at least until the late seventies dendrites, which are important for new learning, continue to grow in the cerebral cortex. An increase in the density and length of dendrites can compensate for the loss of brain cells in later life. There is even some evidence that frequent brain stimulation in old age reduces the risk of Alzheimer's disease, but the evidence is not yet unambiguous, because it may be that people with healthy brains are more likely to engage in mentally stimulating activity.[2]

Personality Development in the Second Half of Life

Many older people create a life in which they resist social ageism, cope with the difficulties of the aging process, and continue to grow and learn. This attitude is likely to become increasingly common as the "baby boomer" generation ages. Successful adaptation to growing older is influenced by the level of personality development achieved earlier in life. A lifelong personality disorder does not bode well for happiness in later life, but in general, aging provides an opportunity for continuing development of the personality. The traditional stereotypes of older people are either that they are stubborn and afraid to take risks, or sometimes that they are graceful and dignified. In fact, different psychological characteristics show different developmental paths as we age—some personality traits grow, some stay stable across the lifespan, and some traits fade away. New traits may also appear; financial difficulties in old age may produce a level of anxiety that has never been felt before, and this can have a major impact on the older individual's personality if it persists. Genetic factors in personality development become less important in later life; as identical twins age, they become less similar in their gene expression—a finding that suggest a the importance of environment, diet, occupation, and life experiences.[3]

A consistent life environment, such as holding the same job over a long period, tends to encourage consistency of personality across the lifespan. A social role that requires authority increases the individual's level of interpersonal dominance, whereas jobs that require empathy increase that ability. Retirement from a high-status job may lower self-esteem, whereas retirement from a job one does not like may produce new levels of contentment. With increasing age, the complexity of emotions and the ability to elaborate emotions increase, and older people may get better at expressing and regulating emotions. Some research suggests that older people learn to minimize negative feelings and maximize positive feelings.[4]

Many older people function well psychologically; they have a complex inner life, intact cognitive abilities, good control of impulses, flexibility, and the ability to take in new ideas and experiences. Thanks to a lifetime of accumulated experience, older people often develop resilience in the face of losses and adapt with some equanimity. This ability is particularly important if one feels a gradually less potent sense of self, a decrement that can be a source of narcissistic injury in the absence of alternative sources of self-esteem.

Various factors have been identified as important for development in late life, such as relationships with others; the lifelong pursuit of learning; good social connections; and an attitude of acceptance, optimism, and caring for oneself and others. Various qualities of personality have been found to predict positive aging: These are equanimity, gratitude and hope, joy, wonder, curiosity, humor, optimism, and positive self-perception. Other valuable factors include a stable marriage, a healthy lifestyle, exercise, not smoking, not abusing alcohol, and the use of nutritional supplements and prescription medications to deal with genetic predispositions to illness. Personal satisfaction in life and engagement in work that gives meaning and purpose are also important. Another valuable factor is internally guided behavior—the ability to listen to an inner voice and rely on it. Most studies indicate that spirituality, rather than traditional religion, is positively associated with successful aging, health, and psychosocial functioning in late life. Somewhat surprisingly, some of the factors that are not necessarily correlated with positive aging include money, political affiliation, the longevity of one's forebears, stress, and ease in social relationships.[5]

Development in late life has been characterized in various ways. In ideal circumstances, the elder is less driven by ego concerns such as personal ambition and is more interested in his or her larger community and culture. Rather than despairing, the elder develops what Erikson called *integrity*—he or she comes to terms with his or her life, understanding it in the context of life as a whole, and is at peace with life as it is.[6] At this stage of development, the person is able to face the inevitable difficulties of this period with some equanimity while maintaining a sense of meaning and purpose in his or her life. In the Eriksons' later work they suggest that one has to maintain vital involvement with life while, at the same time dealing with, the necessary reduced involvements of old age.[7] In this final stage, a life review may occur in which old issues are revisited from a new perspective, ideally leading to a new resolution. The sense of a coherent identity can be threatened in old age and may lead to despair. The alternative is the development of wisdom and a sense of self-transcendence, so that one can be involved with life in the face of death. Incidentally, Erikson's wife Joan, in her additions to a later edition of Erikson's *The Life Cycle Completed* (1998), offers a critique of his earlier theory, saying that old age may be different to what she and her husband had imagined; the old person may not feel wise at all. She advocates an additional stage in which the task is to develop an attitude of retreat in relation to the world, and an increasingly spiritual perspective that is also described by the theory of gerotranscendence, to which I will return.[8]

The second half of life can be a time of renewed meaning. Because one knows oneself and has confronted one's own shortcomings and shadow aspects, the use of projection often decreases and is replaced by more mature defenses. Many studies show that, compared to the sometimes black and white or overly idealistic thinking characteristic of adolescents and young adults, in older people reasoning becomes more complex and nuanced, subtler and more contextual. One can develop a new way of thinking about oneself and one's identity in various ways: by reinterpreting the past, by reformulating one's philosophy of life, developing new values and goals, and seeing one's life story in a new light. One can radically change one's interpretation of earlier events in one's life; one's subjective sense of the meaning of one's life changes over time, and life can be seen from different perspectives as one ages. Self-transcendence becomes more important than the ego; ideally, one becomes less egocentric and more open to working for the good of society. One becomes less concerned with social norms and inhibitions. We often hear older people say "I'm too old to worry about what other people think." Maslow noticed that self-actualizing people, in his study of people over age fifty, were often spontaneous, free of social conventions, and combined a kind of childlike innocence with sophisticated judgment.[9] The stereotype of the old person as selfish, rigid, and envious of the young actually results from a *failure* of development; these personality traits can be found at any age.

Developmental Tasks of Later Life

I would now like to return to Jung's 1930 paper "The Stages of Life."[10] In this paper, Jung proposes the concept of different developmental tasks at different stages of life, although today we do not think in terms of fixed stages because we recognize that the same developmental tasks and challenges may occur to people at any age. Jung believed that youth is a period for the development of personality and the establishment of a career, a place in the world, and a family. He believed that the next opportunity for major change starts at what he calls the "noon" of life or the midlife period. He believed that serious attention to individuation naturally begins at this time, initiating a developmental process that extends to the end of life. Much of the following is taken from Jung's approach to development.

Given factors such as reasonable economic circumstances, health, educational opportunity, and a social network, a variety of developmental possibilities still remain for individuals in the second half of life.

1. The *development of unused potential.* During the average working life, only a part of an individual's potential can be actualized because of the demands of work and family. But unused aspects of the personality and creative talents remain dormant. An ability such as art, music, or writing may have been started in the first part of life but not pursued; this activity can now be rediscovered. One of the advantages of a broad early education is that it sows seeds that can be reaped in later life. The older person may discover surprising new abilities.

2. *Type development.* Psychological functions that have never been developed may become important in later life. Without going into too much detail, a few examples will illustrate how this works

developmentally. The older person who is a feeling type, good at relationships and interested in harmony and warmth between people, now could develop his or her thinking function by studying a discipline that requires rigorous or abstract logical thought such as a science. Conversely, the person who has always excelled in areas that require good thinking, such as law or science, who may not have paid much attention to his or her emotional life, may seek out an activity, such as volunteer work in a hospice, that requires the development of the neglected capacity for feeling. The sensation type, practical and down to earth, may enjoy the development of the intuitive function by exploring religion, literature, or mythology. The intuitive, imaginative individual who has always been immersed in the imagination or spiritual pursuits may discover the joys of hands-on work such as gardening or sculpting. One caveat here is that the pattern of type development as we age may be different for each psychological type, but this has not been much studied. Some research tends to support Jung's idea that there is a tendency toward increasing introversion or interiority with age, although this is not a universal finding.[11]

3. *The development of the contrasexual aspects of the personality.* Jung described the importance of a man developing his femininity and a woman her masculinity, in the interests of wholeness. This is a controversial topic because it involves stereotypes of masculinity and femininity that fortunately are now diminishing. In its classical form, stereotypically masculine men, starting in midlife and certainly in later life, were said to need to become more receptive and nurturing, whereas their female counterparts needed to develop assertiveness and other stereotypically masculine traits. Interestingly, some empirical research does, in fact, show that older men tend to subjectively experience increasing sensitivity and passivity, and older women experience more assertiveness and independence, although these shifts do not always translate into behavioral changes.[12]

4. *Maintenance of self-esteem.* Until we retire, our self-esteem and self-image have been consolidated by lifelong career achievements, financial success, appearance, athletic ability, and the development of talents and abilities. Obviously these may be less available in later life, so that one then needs new sources of self-esteem. These might be one's friendships, family, humor, wisdom, and one's fund of knowledge

and life experience. Nevertheless it is sometimes difficult to maintain
self-esteem in the face of significant economic and health problems,
or if one feels powerless in the face of ageism. Here, one's ability to
accept the deficits and challenges of aging while capitalizing on the
assets and benefits associated with aging becomes important.

5. New roles and responsibilities. Late life brings alternatives in
family, social, and civic roles.

Family roles. Relationships with grown children change in later
life and a degree of role reversal may occur as children assume the role
of caregiver. One then has to allow mature dependence on others. The
role of grandparent can become developmentally important for
children and elders alike. Grandparents who tell stories of their own
childhoods are living historians of the family, connecting the
generations and providing a sense of the family's continuity.

Social roles. As old friends and family members die, there is a
tendency for the older person's world to shrink, so that it is essential
to retain the ability to form new friendships, even though there can
be no real restitution for the loss of lifelong relationships. Sexuality
can be maintained until late in life, but the unavailability of a
partner, ignorance of the normal age-related changes in sexual
functioning, and social prejudice against late-life sexuality may
contribute to its cessation. At this time of life sexuality is less a matter
of urgency and more an expression of love, affection, loyalty, the
pleasure of touch, and closeness.

Civic roles. Maggie Kuhn, the founder of the Gray Panthers
movement, suggested a list of new roles and responsibilities for
elderly people whose time is no longer fully committed but whose
energies and abilities are intact (personal communication, 1983).
These include:

- Educator and transmitter of knowledge of the past
- Social critic and historian—the elderly may know
  about past mistakes and how to avoid repeating them
- Advocate for people without power or voice
- Worker for social change—a lifetime of dealing with
  our social system enables older people to become
  effective advocates for causes they believe in
- Monitor of public bodies—a watchdog role

- Ethical counselor—one who articulates the conscience of the culture with less risk of being accused of serving one's own career
- Futurist—a long life points beyond itself, so that older people can be concerned with the well-being of future generations.

Perhaps the most important developmental achievement in later life is the development of one's spirituality, to which I now turn.

Spirituality in Later Life

In this section I make the usual distinction between *religion*, as an organized set of beliefs proffered by a historical institution, and *spirituality*, as a personal sense of connection to the sacred or to ultimate reality and as the pursuit of meaning and purpose. There is a variable relationship between religion and spirituality; sometimes religion allows one to develop one's spirituality, whereas sometimes religion gets in the way of one's spirituality. One can be very spiritually oriented with no interest in organized religion. Some aspects of one's spirituality remain stable throughout life, but there are specific changes associated with the challenge of aging, such as coming to terms with death, losses, and illness. In these situations a spiritual perspective is particularly important. Perhaps the main question is whether the losses of old age will produce only bitterness and grief, or whether they can produce a personal deepening—a sacrifice or surrender of the ego in the service of something larger. Will one's own experiences of loss, pain, and the prospect of death produce only despair, or will these experiences cultivate compassion, empathy, and selflessness towards others? Can we let go of the things that have to be released, even embrace our diminished physical situation, but see aging as a spiritual process, so that we retain and develop the spiritual core of the personality? Doing so may require a major shift in priorities and the development of new values.

This is an area where Jungian psychology is particularly helpful, not least because it allows one to develop a spirituality that is not dependent on any particular religious institution or set of doctrines or dogma. Instead, one's spirituality can be based on direct experience of the sacred, as I've tried to show in a series of books.[13] In brief, this means developing a relationship between the ego and the transpersonal levels of the psyche. For Jung, later life was a time when one naturally becomes introspective and interested in cultivating the inner life. Greater acceptance of paradox and ambiguity, disillusionment with rational thinking alone, an open attitude toward all religious traditions, a willingness to give up the centrality of oneself, and the development of universalizing values are all more common in older people.

Spiritual concerns often increase in later life, although many older people feel no such interest because their philosophy of life is largely humanistic. In one study of 150 American men ages fifty-eight to ninety-three, the researcher found that they sought meaning through the pursuit of youthfulness and considered spirituality irrelevant.[14] The researcher thought that this response was a product of American culture. However, her questions were somewhat narrow, largely asking about belief in an afterlife and a supreme being, and did not necessarily evoke what gave these men a sense of meaning in life. Nonetheless, this study suggests that cultural influences and life experiences may radically affect one's spirituality.

In general, after midlife many people become interested in identifying the meaning of their existence and their relation to the wider world. There are many possible components of late-life spirituality, which may or may not include a formal practice such as meditation or attendance at a religious community. Sometimes the deepening of one's spirituality in later life is subtle and not deliberate; it occurs naturally as a result of the physical, social, and psychological processes of aging. Indeed aging has been described as a "natural monastery."[15]

Later-life spirituality has been described as *gerotranscendence*, as noted earlier.[16] This term refers to the older person's experience of a shift in his or her perspective from a materialistic, role-oriented, and pragmatic one to a more transcendent approach to life. Life, death, space, and time are seen as involving mystery and are perceived against the backdrop of eternity. This development can be promoted or diminished by social factors such as opportunity and education, and may also occur early in life in response to serious illness. When it happens, one becomes less self-centered and less concerned with possessions and physical appearance. One finds meaning and joy in simple things; one is more introspective, less interested in meaningless social interaction, and has a greater sense of connection to the world at large. One senses an affinity with past and future generations and a longer view of history. One develops an increasingly broad understanding of oneself and the universe, and one comes to terms with death, loss, and sorrow.[17] The concept of gerotranscendence may seem a bit unrealistic, but some empirical studies support it as valid. Tornstam assumes that this development is an innate process, but he does not suggest its source—which, for Jung, would be the promptings of the Self. Where it does exist, gerotranscendence may also be affected by life experience, by religious beliefs, and by cultural influences. In one group of nuns, gerotranscendence was not found, in Tornstam's sense, but a deepening of their existing beliefs and faith was reported.[18]

For Jungians, later-life spirituality has various aspects; one of these is to let go of the dominance of the ego. As Jane Wheelwright put it, preparing for death is "like preparing for a journey to a foreign country where one doesn't know what to expect, but where one knows somehow that it is necessary to cut down on the sheer quantity of one's 'baggage' in order to make that trip a success."[19] The typical concerns of the ego involving ambition and conflict often become less important as one ages; one learns acceptance and feels freer to become more deeply oneself. According to Jung, in the second half of life it is important to be in touch with the transpersonal Self; one has to find the way the numinosum appears in one's life and find a way to relate to it. Here are some other important Jungian approaches:

- *The discovery of meaning in one's life.* By reflecting on the main themes of one's life—the periods of achievement, success, suffering, struggles, and sacrifices—during a life review, one may discover a sense of destiny, as if one has been guided in a particular direction. (However, a systematic life review is not always advisable and may cause distress for some. The caveat here is that it is often difficult to find meaning in the face of loss, and serious loss can disrupt longstanding systems of meaning such as religious beliefs.)

- *The discovery of mythic or archetypal themes in one's life.*
  Such a discovery allows one to place one's life in a
  larger perspective.
- *The discovery of new values.* Jung believed that people
  would not grow old unless longevity had some
  meaning for the species.[20] For him, meaning and
  the expansion of consciousness are the fruits of
  psychological life, and the meaning and purpose of
  the second half of life are that we contribute to the
  culture—a fecundity of spirit rather than of
  biological fertility.
- *The emergence of wisdom.* When development succeeds,
  one has gained wisdom about human nature based
  on life experience, a process which helps with
  adaptation in later life. Wisdom has many facets and
  is not quantifiable. It is a mixture of knowledge, life
  experience, emotional maturity, discernment, mature
  judgment, and insight into human nature. The
  Psalmist tells us that wisdom takes a long time to
  acquire: "So teach us to number our days that we may
  get us a heart of wisdom" (Psalm 90:12). Jung wrote
  that the natural end of life is not senility but wisdom—
  a state of mind that is hard to define.[21] He believed
  that on a personal level wisdom means aligning one's
  consciousness with the stream of images arising from
  the unconscious in dreams and visions, developing the
  wholeness of the personality, and individuating—to
  become more and more the person one really is and
  to incarnate more and more of one's potentials. He
  points out that wisdom comforts suffering. For Kohut
  wisdom means that we accept the limitations of our
  physical, intellectual, and emotional powers; we
  renounce unmodified narcissism and develop an
  attitude toward life comprised of intellect, humor, and
  acceptance of our transience; and we develop a firm
  sense of values.[22] Erikson believed that wisdom is the
  detached yet active concern with life in the face of
  death; it conveys the fullness and integrity of life's

experience and a sense of its having been worthwhile.[23]
Wisdom allows us to respond to the needs of
oncoming generations; it emerges out of the attempt
to balance despair against a sense of integrity.

Several writers agree that the gifts of later life are spiritual
development, inner growth, and the exploration of one's creativity and
wisdom.[24] However, although it seems to be true that a long life can
bring spiritual maturity, some research suggests that it is not clear that
spirituality really does deepen in old age; although this is the common
assumption, it is largely anecdotal. George Vaillant, director of the
Harvard Study of Adult Development, concluded that spirituality does
not predict successful aging and is not necessarily associated with
successful aging.[25] Part of the problem here is that it is difficult to define
spirituality rigorously; but broadly speaking, it involves meaning,
values, compassion, the sense of a larger order in the universe, the
understanding that the ego is limited, and a connection to the sacred,
to something beyond oneself. Many authors have pointed out that
the more deeply we understand ourselves, the better we understand
others.[26] As we age, we can affirm the value of life in spite of its evil,
pain, loss. We have lost our youthful certainties and some of our
idealism, but we may find new truths and new meaning. All these
gifts can be passed on via education, ministry, various forms of
leadership, to future generations.[27]

There is a good deal of research available in the field of religious
gerontology—the study of the role of religion in old age. By and
large, research shows that participation in religious services increases
in later life, and daily prayer and home religious activities tend to
increase.[28] There appears to be some benefit to physical health from
regular spiritual practice and participation in religious institutions,
although findings in this area are mixed. The benefit may be due
to older people's remaining active and involved in their community,
combined with the fact that members of a religious community
are likely to be helpful in caring for the elderly. The person involved
in religious life is given a sense of order and meaning that buffers
stress and enhances self-esteem. Religion offers forgiveness and hope
for change and healing when one is ill; it offers meaning when one
suffers and the promise of life after death—all of which are helpful

coping strategies. Spirituality also offers people hope during depression, which is common in later life.

The spirituality of old age does not necessarily involve taking instrumental action in the world or trying to influence events in the world; it may be more a process of changing one's sense of self to adjust to the situation—what has been called *passive mastery*. This does not mean simple conformity; it means a shift toward wisdom, a change in one's heart and mind, and empathy, and sensitivity toward others, rather than trying to change outer events. One caveat here is that spiritual development and the interiority this may require in old age can be used as a retreat or a defensive escape from responsibility.

Jung on Creativity

Jung placed great stress on creativity, which he believed to be one of the most important human instincts—he suggested that the person who does not build will demolish and destroy. Creativity is essential to psychological well-being and aliveness, and it is no less important in old age than at any other time of life. People with creative vocations tend to be satisfied with life; participation in activities such as art, dance, music, and literature encourage successful aging.[29] There are many examples of amazing creativity displayed by older people.[30] Examples are Michelangelo, Titian, Edison, and Picasso, not to mention Gandhi, who was seventy-two when he led the movement for Indian independence, and Bertrand Russell, who fought for nuclear disarmament into his nineties.

For spiritually oriented people there is an important connection between their creativity and their spirituality, because creativity seems to arise from the transpersonal dimension—many people experience it as a divine gift, and some writers even equate creativity with the divine itself. (In contrast, classical psychoanalytic writers tend to see creativity as a sublimation of and restitution for destructive impulses.) Creativity can be a form of spiritual practice; it opens us to whatever wants to emerge, trusting that there is something there that wants to be heard; it liberates meaning, renews life, and often allows us to uncover our unlived aspects. Creativity helps to "relativize" the ego, so important in Jung's writing; there is a growing sense that the ego participates in a larger reality, and creativity allows surrender to this expanded awareness. If nothing else, the creative process makes one feel alive and leads to self-discovery.[31] Creativity often emerges as a response to serious loss, trauma, or the collapse of meaning. In later life creativity provides a means of mourning loss. There seems to be an important link between death, creativity, and transformation—sometimes we create as a way of facing death.[32] Grief at a major loss often forces us to choose between going on living and giving up on life.

Facing Death

Our relationship to death has an important effect on personality development, especially in late life. Some older people are very anxious about their approaching death, whereas others accept that they are powerless to prevent it, and this acceptance actually liberates them to enjoy their last years. Thoughts of death often increase as we age, as does dream imagery that refers to death, such as dreams of packing for a journey from which one will not return, or a marriage to an unknown figure. Von Franz has provided a valuable description of the dreams of dying people.[33] Jung thinks these kinds of experiences are actually a preparation for death. In his paper on the stages of life, Jung stresses the importance of death as an essential constituent of life—he says it is psychologically healthy to discover in death a goal and a fulfillment of life's meaning, and not to think of death as a meaningless cessation.[34] For Jung, "from the middle of life onward, only he remains vitally alive who is ready to *die with life*."[35]

Closing Thoughts

We could conceptualize successful aging in many ways. My own feeling about this question is that we should ask the elderly about how *they* feel about it, and not try to impose a theoretical model onto them. There is at least one study that suggests that elders have their own perspectives on what aging well means to them, and in that study very few elders could not define successful aging for themselves.[36] We must make research in the area of successful aging center around the elderly themselves, because what elderly people consider to be successful aging may not coincide with the ideas of any particular theorist or researcher.[37]

I would define successful aging in terms of whether the elder is satisfied with his or her subjective quality of life. Using this criterion, successful aging may have a variety of characteristics. It does not necessarily imply physical health; we cannot use a biomedical model to measure success. A disease-free old age is unlikely, so the successful elder adapts to physical limitations by means of psychological and spiritual growth and by maximizing his or her resources, especially qualities such as self-efficacy and resilience. Whatever model we use, we are moving away from a pathology-based perspective on aging to a model that emphasizes life satisfaction, self-esteem, feeling in control, having a purpose, active engagement, and maintaining a sense of belonging and support.[38] These factors strengthen one's will to live.

Jung's model is valuable for older people because it stresses the psychological and spiritual dimensions of later life, which are extremely important at this stage. Jung's approach to psychotherapy and the individuation process has always been seen as most helpful in the second part of life because of its focus on meaning. According to Jung, at this time the ego becomes less important; attention to the unconscious becomes paramount, and there is an internal pressure from the transpersonal dimension to pay attention to one's unlived life for the sake of becoming a more complete personality.

As a society we desperately need to develop a more positive affirmation of old age. As Thomas Cole put it, as well as supporting good health in late life, we have to find the moral and spiritual significance of decay, dependency, and death.[39]

NOTES

[1] See A. Bowling and P. Dieppe, "What Is Successful Aging and Who Should Define It?" *British Medical Journal* 331 (2005): 1548–1551; M. Flood, "Successful Aging: A Concept Analysis," *Journal of Theory Construction and Testing* 6, no. 2 (2002): 105–108; L. W. Poon, S. H. Gueldner, and B. M. Sprouse, *Successful Aging and Adaptation with Chronic Diseases* (New York: Springer, 2003); and J. W. Rowe and R. L. Kahn, "Successful Aging," *Gerontologist* 37, no. 4 (1997): 433–441.

[2] S. Buell and P. Coleman, "Dendritic Growth in the Aged Human Brain and Failure of Growth in Senile Dementia," *Science* 206, no. 4420 (1979): 854–856; http://medscape.com/viewarticle/558929.

[3] K. Hayakawa, K. Kato, and K. Kadota, et al., "The Osaka University Aged Twin Registry: Epigenetics and Identical Twins Discordant for Aging-Dependent Diseases," *Twin Research and Human Genetics* 9, no. 6 (December 2006): 808–810.

[4] D. Y. Yeung, "Emotion Regulation Mediates Age Differences in Emotions," *Aging and Mental Health* 15, no. 3 (2011): 414–418.

[5] G. E. Vaillant, *Aging Well: Surprising Guideposts to a Happier Life* (New York: Little, Brown, 2003).

[6] E. H. Erikson and J. M. Erikson, *The Life Cycle Completed* (New York: Norton, 1982; republished 1998).

[7] E. H. Erikson, J. M. Erikson, and J. Kivnic, *Vital Involvement in Old Age* (New York: Norton, 1989).

[8] L. Tornstam, *Gerotranscendence: A Developmental Theory* (New York: Springer, 2005).

[9] A. Maslow, *Toward a Psychology of Being* (New York: Wiley, 1998).

[10] C. G. Jung, "The Stages of Life," in *The Collected Works of C. G. Jung*, vol. 8, ed. and trans. Gerhard Adler and R. F. C. Hull (Princeton, NJ: Princeton University Press, 1960).

[11] B. L. Neugarten, "Personality Change in Later Life: A Developmental Perspective, " in C. Eisdorfer and M. P. Larson, eds., *ThePsychology of Adult Development and Aging* (Washington, DC: American Psychological Association, 1973), pp. 311–335.

[12] B. L. Neugarten, "Age-Sex Roles and Personality in Middle Age: A Thematic Apperception Study," *Psychological Monographs* 72 (1958): 1–33.

[13] L. Corbett, *The Religious Function of the Psyche* (New York: Routledge, 1996); L. Corbett, *Psyche and the Sacred* (New Orleans: Spring, 2007); L. Corbett, *The Sacred Cauldron: Psychotherapy as a Spiritual Practice* (Wilmette, IL: Chiron, 2011).

[14] H. K. Black, "'Wasted Lives' and the Hero Grown Old: Personal Perspectives of Spirituality by Aging Men," *Journal of Religious Gerontology* 9 (1995): 35–48.

[15] See http://mepkinabbey.org/wordpress/wp-content/uploads/2012/07/MonasteryAging-2-1.pdf.

[16] Tornstam, *Gerotranscendence: A Developmental Theory*; L. Tornstam, "Gero-transcendence: A Meta-theoretical Reformularion of the Disengagement Theory," *Aging: Clinical and Experimental Research* 1, no. 1 (1989): 55–63; L. Tornstam, "Gerotranscendence: The Contemplative Dimension of Aging," *Journal of Aging Studies* 11, no. 2 (1997): 143–154.

[17] Tornstam, "Gerotranscendence: The Contemplative Dimension of Aging."

[18] S. P. Melia, "Solitude and Prayer in the Late Lives of Elder Catholic Women: Activity, Withdrawal, or Transcendence?" *Journal of Religious Gerontology* 13 (2001): 47–63.

[19] J. Wheelright, "Old Age and Death, " in L. Mahdi and S. Foster, eds., *Betwixt and Between* (Peru, IL: Open Court, 1987), p. 389.

[20] C. G. Jung, *Modern Man in Search of a Soul* (New York: Harvest Books, 1933), p. 109.

[21] Quoted in H. Ellenberger, *The Discovery of the Unconscious* (New York: Basic Books, 1970), p. 712.

[22] H. Kohut, "Forms and Transformations of Narcissism," *Journal of the American Psychoanalytic Association* 14 (1966): 243–272.

[23] Erikson and Erikson, *The Life Cycle Completed.*

[24] See E. Sadler and S. Biggs, "Exploring the Links between Spirituality and 'Successful Aging,'" *Journal of Social Work Practice* 20, no. 3 (2006): 267–280; and Z. Schachter-Shalomi and R. S. Miller, *From Age-ing to Sage-ing: A Profound New Vision of Growing Older* (New York: Time Warner, 1997).

[25] Vaillant, *Aging Well.*

[26] See, for example, G. Allport, *Becoming: Basic Considerations for a Psychology of Personality* (New Haven, CT: Yale University Press, 1955).

[27] H. R. Moody, "Getting over the Denial of Aging," *Hastings Center Report* 37, no. 5 (September 2007): 44–45.

[28] S. C. Ainlay, D. Smith, and D. Randall, "Aging and Religious Participation," *Journal of Gerontology* 39, no. 3 (1984): 357–363.

[29] B. Wilkstrom, "Older Adults and the Arts: The Importance of Aesthetic Forms of Expression in Later Life," *Journal of Gerontological Nursing* 30, no. 9 (2004): 30–36.

[30] R. Kastenbaum, "Creativity and the Arts," in T. R. Cole, R. Kastenbaum, and R. E. Ray, eds., *Handbook of the Humanities and Aging* (New York: Springer, 2000), pp. 381–401.

[31] M. Goldsmith, "Frida Kahlo: Abjection, Psychic Deadness, and the Creative Impulse," *Psychoanalytic Review* 91, no. 6 (2004): 723–758.

[32] R. R. Gordon, "Death and Creativity: A Jungian Approach," *Journal of Analytical Psychology* 22, no. 2 (1977): 106–124.

[33] M.-L. von Franz, *On Dreams and Death* (La Salle, IL: Open Court, 1999).

[34] C. G. Jung, "The Soul and Death," in *The Collected Works of C. G. Jung*, vol. 8, ed. and trans. Gerhard Adler and R. F. C. Hull (Princeton, NJ: Princeton University Press, 1960).

[35] *Ibid.*, § 800.

[36] B. J. Fisher, "Successful Aging, Life Satisfaction, and Generativity in Later Life," *International Journal of Aging and Human Development* 41, no. 3 (1995): 239–250.

[37] E. A. Phelan and E. B. Larson, E. B. "Successful Aging: Where Next?" *Journal of the American Geriatrics Society* 50 (2002): 1306–1308; and E. A. Phelan, A. A. Lynda, A. Z. LaCroix, and E. B. Larson, "Older Adults' Views of 'Successful Aging'—How Do They Compare with Researchers' Definitions?" *Journal of the American Geriatrics Society* 52 (2004): 11–26.

[38] Bowling and Dieppe, "What Is Successful Aging and Who Should Define It?"; A. Bowling and S. Iliffe, "Psychological Approach to Successful Ageing Predicts Future Quality of Life in Older Adults," *Health and Quality of Life Outcomes* 9, no. 1 (2011): 13–22; and R. Schulz and J. Heckliausen, "A Life Span Model of Successful Aging," *American Psychologist* 51, no. 1 (1996): 702–714.

[39] T. R. Cole, "The 'Enlightened' View of Aging: Victorian Morality in a New Key," *Hastings Center Report* (1983): 34–40.

~ Part II ~

Psychological Perspectives on Navigating the Second Half of Life

~ CHAPTER THREE ~

Emergence and Longevity
Some Psychological Possibilities
of Later Life

JOSEPH CAMBRAY, PH.D.

Introduction

At the Library of Congress symposium *Jung and Aging*, Lionel
Corbett provided a succinct yet sweeping synthetic overview
of the current models of aging and recommendations for
optimizing an individual's aging process. In his presentation, Corbett
embodied the capacity for reflection and wisdom associated with
maturation in later life. By highlighting aspects of Jung's theories that
explicate a psychology of the second half of life, he demonstrated the
contemporary relevance of this approach to the American psyche in
its growing encounter with aging, especially among baby boomers.
As the first psychodynamically oriented adult developmentalist, Jung
was indeed a pioneer, and we have yet to mine his contributions in
this area fully. In this chapter I will build on Corbett's paper by
separating out several threads that may help move our thinking from

Jung's explicit writings to the psychology behind them, which can be amplified and extended by the increased understanding of the human psyche gained in the last century.

Gerontology as a field of study of the multiple dimensions of aging, including psychosocial, cultural, and biological forces at play, was founded in the United States by G. Stanley Hall (an American psychologist and the first president of Clark University), among others. In 1922, near the end of his life, Hall published *Senescence: The Last Half of Life,* in which he prophesied a crisis of aging resulting from people living longer but tending to become more isolated and cut off from public life.[1] (He also was one of the first psychologists to identify adolescence as a distinct phase in the life cycle.) His compassionate call for more comprehensive study of the aging process is, I believe, finally being realized. In addition, there is a direct link here to the symposium's main topic, for Hall not only had been a student of William James, whom Jung greatly admired, but also during his tenure as president of Clark University, Hall brought Sigmund Freud and Carl Jung to America in 1909 for a psychology conference in celebration of the university's twentieth anniversary. This conference was attended by many early luminaries in the social sciences—in the front row of a famous group portrait from this event are Franz Boas, Edward Titchener, William James, William Stern, Leo Burgerstein, Stanley Hall, Sigmund Freud, Carl Jung, Adolf Meyer, and Herbert Spencer Jennings (see figure 1). Indeed, Jung was able to meet and speak with William James in person, cementing their friendship, as a result of this event.

Nineteenth-Century Biological Thinking and the Psychology of Aging

Hall drew heavily upon contemporary biological ideas for his model of the development of the mind over the life span. In this quest he sought to apply genetics and evolutionary theory to formulate his views on lifelong psychological maturation. While he was not wholly successful in this, as his theories were incomplete, he nevertheless was a pioneer in opening up the application of biological perspectives to human development.

Figure 3.1: Psychology Conference Group, Clark University, September 1909. Beginning with front row, left to right: Franz Boas, E. B. Titchener, William James, William Stern, Leo Burgerstein, G. Stanley Hall, Sigmund Freud, Carl G. Jung, Adolf Meyer, H. S. Jennings. Second row, C. F. Seashore, Joseph Jastrow, J. McK. Cattell, E. F. Buchner, F. Katzenellenbogen, Ernest Jones, A. A. Brill, Wm. H. Burnham, A. F. Chamberlain. Third row: Albert Schinz, J. A. Magni, B. T. Baldwin, F. Lyman Wells, G. M. Forbes, E. A. Kirkpatrick, Sandor Ferenczi, F. C. Sanford, J. P. Porter, Sakyo Kanda, Hikoso Kakise. Fourth row: G. E. Dawson, S. P. Hayes, E. B. Holt, C. S. Berry, G. M. Whipple, Frank Drew, J. W. A. Young, I. N. Wilson, K. J. Karlson, H. H. Goddard, H. I. Klopp, S. C. Fuller.

In particular, Hall employed Darwin's concept of evolution together with Ernst Haeckel's biogenetic hypothesis (that ontology recapitulates phylogeny) to look at human psychological development both on an individual basis and as a species. In his model, the child recapitulates over the course of its maturation the historical developmental pathway of the species (a type of psychological phylogeny). These ideas have been shown to be far too simplistic a model of human development to be truly useful. But they were part of an important initial attempt to link the disciplines of biology and human developmental psychology. Hall's work did have an impact on both child psychology and educational theories of the day.

Jung and Freud each in their own way wrestled with incorporating these same concepts into their developmental models, though each man came to different conclusions, especially with regard to the role of spirituality in maturation. Freud imagined an ancestral past in which modern forms of psychopathology were seen as previous way stations along a phylogenetic path leading toward modernity. For him, spirituality was reduced to an unconscious residue of the attempts to mollify the anxieties and conflicts from earlier times, as discussed in various of his texts, for example, *Totem and Taboo, The Future of an Illusion,* and the unpublished manuscript which was only brought to light in 1987 with the publication of *A Phylogenetic Fantasy: Overview of the Transference Neuroses.*[2] By contrast, Jung explored unconscious patterns of a collective nature that emerged in contemporary individuals and could serve as sources of creativity holding the possibility of renewal of the personality, as found in his theory of archetypes and the Self. For the interested reader, a useful comparison of their views was made by the late eminent evolutionary biologist Stephen Jay Gould.[3] Hall's views also likely had some influence on Jung's 1930 essay "The Stages of Life," though they were not cited.

Emergence and Longevity

While the biological theories of the origins of the mind from the sciences of the late nineteenth and early twentieth centuries have been superseded by more sophisticated models, the more general problem of the mind-body relationship in the human psyche is something still actively under investigation in the contemporary world. Developments in the field of neuroscience have lent weight to what is referred to as an emergentist perspective on the relation of the mind to the body, with implications for the aging of mind and body.

A brief introduction to systems theory is offered here to help understand the concept of emergentism. General systems theory stems from the work of biologist Ludwig von Bertalanffy beginning in 1936.[4]

Bertalanffy studied groupings of interacting elements with attention to the behavior of the whole entity or system and subsequently categorized a number of these systems based on their properties. In systems where there are many parts that interact, various kinds of behavior can result. The sum total of interactions may lead to a complicated result, for example, all of the gears in a watch that combine to produce a device for measuring time. Although complicated, the functioning of such a device can be understood directly as a summation of its parts—it is a closed system that is independent of its environment for its functioning. However, there are also systems in which the interactions are open to and influenced by the environment. This type of system tends to adapt to the context in which it is found and yields not only a complicated outcome but something wholly new and unexpected, not to be explained solely in terms of its part. These open systems are considered complex, and the new unanticipated properties are termed *emergent*. For example, the collective behavior of flocks of birds, schools of fish, and swarms of insects all manifest phenomena not found in the isolated individual, including a kind of biological group intelligence. Curiously simple rules of engagement can lead to these complex collective forms.

Complex systems occur throughout nature at various scales. In the physical world they are found at all levels from the subatomic to the clustering of galaxies. One famous example at the molecular level is water, H_2O, which has a low molecular weight and would be expected to be a gas at room temperature based on the properties of an individual molecule. But because of hydrogen bonding between molecules, it interacts with itself in aggregate with unexpected force sufficient to remain liquid at room temperature (this liquidity is an emergent property) which is essential for life. Complex systems are frequently found in the biological world, including the human cultural sphere (as in traffic jams and stock markets). Competitive environments that supply pressure for adaptation tend to contribute to the formation of complex systems as their emergent properties often lead to selective advantage over less-complex systems. For a broad overview of the range of this kind of phenomena, see Harold Morowitz's *The Emergence of Everything*; a good general introduction to the subject for the lay reader can be found in Steven Johnson's *Emergence*.[5]

In contemporary philosophy as well as neuroscience, the best formulation of the mind is as an emergent phenomenon. The perspective taken is that the mind is a higher-level property arising from the competitive interactions of the full range of somatic processes, body and brain, embedded in a surrounding environment (including the human and cultural fields we are always immersed in). This view of mind is in contradistinction to the mind either being an epiphenomenon (a positivist reading) or an entity wholly separate from the body (such as in the classical Cartesian split). An emergentist perspective is informed by the study of complex adaptive systems as discussed below. This perspective is in accord with what Corbett notes: that maturational processes of the mind continue throughout life and tend to manifest through increasing complexity of affect, reasoning, and our capacity for spirituality, even while the body may be slowing down with the infirmities of aging. Though the body may become more fragile, the mind does not necessarily follow but can continue to develop richness in complexity. The range of experiences a person has had and is able to draw upon potentially increases with age, permitting an agile mind to imagine, form, and synthesize experiences into new combinations in creative ways. For example, seniors who have had years of leadership experience are often able to tolerate and metabolize a range of distressing affects in stressful situations, a trait that allows more balanced solutions to pressing problems than those offered by younger people who may react more impulsively out of emotional pressure to reduce the internal tensions. The creativity in wisdom does seem to require a synthetic capacity that can come only with the ability to hold increasing levels of tension in conflictual situations, an emotional development that usually takes considerable life experience to obtain.

Mental complexity cannot be reduced to genetic programs, though it likely is grounded in changes in the body-brain system arising out of experience—alterations in what is now being called our connectome, "the totality of connections between the neurons in a nervous system," which similarly can continue to develop across the life span.[6] From an analytic perspective, enhanced complexity of personality, with greater capacity for nuance in cognition, affect, and imagination, is probably one of the few agreed upon outcomes of long-term psychodynamic treatment across the various schools of depth psychology in their attempts to define the well-lived life, enriched by the analytic experience.

Enhanced Complexity and Later-Life Development

Formulating maturation in terms of enhanced complexity provides a natural opportunity to build a bridge between later-life development and general systems theory, and in particular complexity theory. Since the 1980s complexity has become increasingly important in scientific studies as the development of high-speed computers has allowed simulations of complex systems that had previously been beyond any quantitative approach. One of the most important outcomes of these studies has been the ability to model emergent behavior.

As previously noted, investigations of systems with multiple components capable of interacting with one another while open to the environment have been shown to produce behaviors or properties in aggregate that are of a higher order than the components themselves. These features involve the whole of a system and thus are identified as "holistic" and cannot be reduced to components. Further, these holistic features are not predictable in terms of the known behaviors of the components and, as noted, are thus thought of as *complex* rather than just complicated. These systems also tend to dissipate energy while simultaneously generating increased levels of internal order and thereby exhibit self-organization (the spontaneous formation of enhanced order, such as the evolution of a storm into a hurricane). The high-order phenomena associated with these self-organizing features are what has been identified here as emergent—something more than the sum of the parts—and these phenomena tend to appear at the edge of order and chaos. The origins of life can be formulated in terms of emergence resulting from the self-organization of molecular systems, just as at a higher level the human mind is acknowledged to be an emergent property of the body-brain interacting with the environment, thus transcending older models of the mind seen as either an epiphenomenon or a wholly separate agency. There is also a general, established coevolutionary link between longevity and species brain size and intelligence: "because the returns to a large brain lie in the future, ecological conditions favoring large brains also favor greater expenditure on survival."[7] From an economic stance, nature is investing more resources in brain capital and so there should be corresponding dividends.

Based on these ideas (of emergence and longevity), I am extrapolating to envision the potential for lifelong development of the psyche occuring in an interactive sociocultural matrix, being capable of producing levels of emergence beyond those obtainable in early adulthood, that is, at the pinnacle of physical development. The argument is that there are new, high-order phenomena that can only manifest with longevity in a culturally rich environment, a likely parallel to the unique spiritual developments mentioned by Corbett that can come in old age. These phenomena as a class offer evidence of some of the more important possibilities and implications of Jung's pioneering efforts to discuss adult development. More research into the range of psychological phenomena made accessible to an individual through increased longevity would be helpful.

Returning to Jung's notion of individuation, becoming oneself as fully as possible, this could be reformulated as seeking to explore the meanings, values, purposes, and activities that come through evolving levels of emergence appearing over a lifetime.[8] This is a never-ending task, mirrored in the way dreams can continue to challenge us toward new levels of psychic awareness into old age. Wholeness then is not a concrete, achievable goal; rather it becomes a way of living, a process toward greater being. Longevity's "purpose" or telos in this model is not primarily for biological advantage (though having elders survive long enough to guide and teach younger members of a community surely has adaptive value), but for psychological maturation.[9]

Wisdom and Folly

The potential for increasing degrees of wholeness to emerge in an individual, who *may* (though not necessarily) benefit the community, generally requires ample opportunities to process a broad range of experiences, positive and negative, with successes and failures to be assimilated and learned from. Folly then may be linked with wisdom, not so much in opposition as stereotypical portrayals of the elderly found in popular culture (with age you become one or the other), but as modes of digesting experiences. Bits of wisdom or folly are potential in any encounter with the world; we need them both for wholeness. The ability to tolerate the irresolvable tensions both within the self and in our interactions with the world creates the conditions necessary for the transcendent function, composed of interacting conscious and unconscious components as in the production of a symbol, to appear as an emergent property of the maturing psyche. Such tensions and the affects that accompany them are often not easy to bear psychologically, so that aging in the psyche requires genuine courage, for example, tolerating an increasingly complex range of emotions rather than taking refuge in safe but rigidifying certainties. We cannot avoid biological aging, though as Corbett rightly points out we may gain tremendous opportunities from slowing it down. On the other hand, psychological aging toward increasing levels of individuation is not automatic and requires ongoing efforts across the life span.

After a lifetime of achievements some people need to be able to loosen up, to allow the seeming purposelessness in events to be felt, risking the folly of not knowing. (This is something often rather difficult for the young; for example, intelligent, newly trained psychotherapists who wish to learn about psychodynamic treatments often experience anxiety when confronting the levels of uncertainty met in practice, and this is frequently a dilemma to be faced when supervising them.) The challenge often remains even with aging, as a clinical vignette may help illustrate.

An elderly academic in long-term analysis dreamed of finding a rock with hieroglyphics on it and thought "how pointless." This serendipitous discovery made in a dream was first dismissed by the dreamer in a manner congruent with his conscious position. In time, however, the discovery proved to be something of an alchemical philosopher's stone, that is, the one the ordinary mind rejects as of no value yet which becomes the foundation upon which the edifice of the psyche can be constructed, a psychological rosetta stone for understanding the communications from the deeper, unconscious layers of the personality.

For this person, retirement had felt like the carved stone, "pointless," a slow waiting for death, thoughts of which were to be avoided by filling in time with social activities despite decreasing pleasure in such encounters. The dream instead offers the potential to reimagine a seemingly valueless, cryptic object and, in the process, examine the mental attitude of facile dismissal; the image holds a symbolic challenge. The "pointless" time in life, retirement, may be in need of re-visioning. When the mysteries and enigmas of a life have been ignored, discarded, or put on hold, they might now be entered into and explored with profit for the spiritual life rather than for personal achievement. In the present case, this was not about "solving" the riddles of unlived life but instead entering into experiences of what had been overlooked. In doing so, the challenge was not only to mourn the losses from paths not taken but also to look more deeply into what the avoidances had been about. This in turn reactivated feelings that seemed intolerable and had in the past resulted in dismissal of what did not fit in with conscious plans. The unacknowledged cost of this avoidance was a diminishment of the personality and a loss of curiosity, especially about aspects of the self that did not fit into a well-groomed persona.

By reversing this path, exemplified by cultivating interest in the dream stone, aspects of the mind that were not aimed at better adaptation to the world began to stir the imagination, stimulating a search for more profound engagement with inner, psychological realities. The explorations were not to fill in what was missed but to appreciate the missing pieces symbolically, as "hieroglyphics." The etymological roots of *hieroglyphics* mean sacred engravings or writing, which take us into the mysteries of being, what is etched upon the soul. Here, the challenge was to open the mind to include seeming pointlessness, to allow a touch of Dionysian chaos to enter, which, for an Apollonic person with high levels of achievement, at just the right moment engendered an experience of the mystery of the emergent, irrational, living edge of his own psyche. Longevity of life span and/or in psychotherapy is often crucial to such psychological transformation.

The Concept of "Useless" in Taoism

This interplay of wisdom and folly is, of course, not solely the product of the contemporary, post-postmodern world. Sages, most often associated with nature mysticism as in ancient Taoism, reached similar conclusions millennia ago. However, symposia like the one on Jung and aging at the Library of Congress suggest that we as an entire culture, not only as rare individuals, are also moving toward these views. For an ancient perspective, consider the fourth century BCE story of the carpenter Shi and a large, majestic oak tree near a village shrine, from the Taoist Chuang Tzu. Shi disparaged the tree to his apprentice for having wood that is of no use, but subsequently he had a dream in which it spoke to him:

> "What are you comparing me with? Are you comparing me with those useful trees? The cherry apple, the pear, the orange, the citron, the rest of those fructiferous trees and shrubs—as soon as their fruit is ripe, they are torn apart and subjected to abuse. Their big limbs are broken off, their little limbs are yanked around. Their utility makes life miserable for them, and so they don't get to finish out the years Heaven gave them, but are cut off in mid-journey. They bring it on themselves—the pulling and tearing of the common mob. And it is the same way with all other things.
>
> As for me, I've been trying a long time to be of no use, and though I almost died, I've finally got it. This is of great use to me. If I had been of some use would I ever have grown this large? Moreover, you and I are both of us things. What's the point of this—things condemning things? You, a worthless man about to die—how do you know I'm a worthless tree?"
>
> When Carpenter Shi woke up, he reported his dream. His apprentice said, "If it's so intent on being of no use, what's it doing there at the village shrine?"
>
> "Shhh! Say no more! It is only *resting* there. If we carp and criticize, it will only conclude that we don't understand it. Even if it weren't at the shrine, do you suppose it would be cut down? It protects itself in a different way from ordinary people. If you try to judge it by conventional standards, you'll be way off!"[10]

This is a biting commentary on judging the aged by utilitarian criteria that is 2,500 years old. The sage suggests, however, that aging has its own purpose. But to discover this requires a kind of uselessness to ordinary intentions, in effect, retirement as a means of pursuing Tao, coming to know ourselves more profoundly at the level of Being. Will the graying of America help us discover how to become more meaningfully useless? That there is life after achievements, and that a lack of employment after retirement can be a potential fount of creative being? Can we as a culture value the emergent properties which may arise out of apparent uselessness? This is a profound challenge for the generation of those now entering their senority.

Our Spiritual Ancestry

With aging often comes an enhanced appreciation of history, be it personal or cultural, perhaps because we feel closer to entering into it at least as a part of an era. Seeing how one's life fits into larger, emergent patterns in the world can offer an important source of psychological orientation. One way to deepen this is to locate the historical background to one's most cherished ideas, exploring who has considered such ideas or their precursors in the past. This could be considered a search for the spiritual ancestors of those ideas, thoughts, feelings, and imaginings that have been at the core of one's life, beginning with an inquiry into just what those core elements are.

Discussions of aging are often, almost inevitably, linked with reflections on death, questions of the reality of an afterlife, the realm of the spirit, immortality, and the fate of the soul. The very notion of the human soul or "psyche" derives from cults of the dead, which archaeologists have located at the dawn of culture in the Paleolithic period. Even Neanderthals are thought by some anthropologists to have ritually buried their dead.[11] While the Egyptians created elaborate rituals and myths about the afterlife, the cult of souls in ancient Greece is the most direct predecessor to our modern notions of unconscious mental life. The late Jungian analyst James Hillman explored these links in numerous publications, for example, in *Dream and the Underworld* he writes: "Heraclitus first brings together *psyche, logos,* and *bathun* ("depth"): 'You could not find the ends of the soul though you travelled every way, so deep is its logos.'"[12] This depth dimension is also associated with that which is hidden and so belongs to Hades, the invisible lord of the underworld, and thus to the chthonic realm. Hence, by implication, the psyche in our psychology is rooted in the imagination of Hades or the realm of the dead. Becoming psychologically minded from a depth perspective is a preparation of the soul for death. This is not to be taken literally, or as a metaphysical statement, but as an attitude which consciousness can cultivate as it seeks to emerge into a condition beyond its grasp, seemingly pointless to quotidian consciousness.

There are various ways in which we might pursue the cultivation of depth psychological awareness. Hillman's preferred mode is through working with images, especially from dreams. However, I would like to end by suggesting a path along the lines mentioned by Corbett in chapter 1, that through an affinity with past and future generations and a longer view of history, we develop an increasingly broad understanding of ourselves and the universe. For me, this has at times taken the form of a study of spiritual ancestry, by which I mean exploring the ancestral roots of the thoughts, feelings, and imaginings that are most compelling to me, often arising out of life experiences. Thus it was a set of clinical experiences with some remarkable coincidences that led me to reexamine Jung's notion of synchronicity (acausal but meaningful coincidences), and through that work doors opened to the various sources he used in formulating the concept.

Jung himself employed a similar method in his synchronicity essay under the heading "Forerunners of the Idea of Synchronicity."[13] Key sources from Eastern and Western philosophy and esoteric traditions are cited. In this way, the concept does not appear out of thin air but rather as the history of the struggle to articulate the phenomena involved is captured. It is like seeing the lines of a magnetic field as they are rendered visible by a medium (for example, iron filing scattered on a transparent surface over a magnet) allowed to distribute itself in response to the field. As metaphor, this analogizes the making conscious through historical reflection what had been unseen in old outmoded ideas. In the present case, by following Jung's sources back into history, while at the same time reformulating the thinking about synchronicity forward with the aid of complexity theory, some rather curious new coincidences emerged.

A brief example of this is Gottfried Wilhelm Leibniz (most known as Newton's rival to the founding of calculus), one of Jung's primary sources for synchronicity with his philosophical ideas of preestablished harmony among monads. This idea arose out of his attempt to define the mind-body relationship. Without belaboring the philosophical fine points, Leibniz argued that the origins of mind and body are of one divine substance but each manifests wholly within its own realm. Once established as separate entities, monads, they remain in conformity with one another though without true interaction, bound together by a divine preestablished harmony. The noncausal yet coordinated appearance of linking proposed by this idea is what drew Jung to the idea as a forerunner of synchronicity.

Leibniz also was the first major Western intellect to study the *I Ching* (the Chinese *Book of Changes*) through the auspices of a Jesuit, Father Bouvet, at the Manchu Emperor's court. Bouvet recognized that the hexagrams of the *I Ching* he sent to Leibniz were arranged in base two, the numbering system that Leibniz had recently discovered and which Bouvet knew about (see figure 2). Leibniz also developed one of the first mechanical calculators using this base; in the modern world, base two is the foundation of digital computing. In 1949, Jung wrote a foreword to Richard Wilhelm's translation of the *I Ching*, discussing his newly minted notion of synchronicity, though probably without knowledge of Leibniz's interest in the *I Ching* at the time—itself a curious coincidence in this story. Although the historical evidence of the Bouvet/Leibniz exchange was first published in 1943, Jung probably did not learn of it until 1951 when Helmut Wilhelm (Richard Wilhelm's son) presented it at an Eranos conference, yet another twist in this tale of coincidence upon coincidence.[14]

There is one further fold yet in this story about my own pathway through the material that may give a feeling of how discovery of spiritual ancestors can emerge. Following a separate strand of inquiry stemming from the origins of ideas about complexity, I discovered that Leibniz was the first person to use the Latinate term *supervenience* in philosophy in a manner that is very closely akin to modern notions of emergence, especially as it is currently employed in the philosophy of mind. As Brown University philosopher Jaegwon Kim points out, Leibniz formulated this idea in isolation, and it was several hundred years before it was picked up again.[15] One of the people who did develop this early in the twentieth century was British philosopher Conwy Lloyd Morgan. To come full circle, Jung derived his ideas on the biological aspects of archetypes from Morgan's work, although without explicit reference to supervenience! He likely did not know of this aspect of Leibniz's philosophy as he makes no reference to it. The conjunction of multiple threads coalescing in nodal points, such

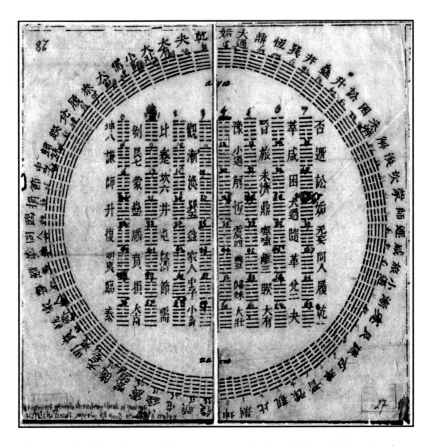

Figure 3.2: The Natural Hexagramm Order (*Hsien-T'ien Tzu-hsu*)
enclosed with Bouvet's letter to Liebniz of 4 November 1701.
(Liebniz Briefwechsel 105, sheets 27–28, plate 20). Courtesy of
the Leibniz Archiv, Niedersachsische Landesbibliothek, Hanover.

as the Jung-Leibniz connection, gives the feeling of increased symbolic
density, enhancing the felt sense of meaning associated with the various
strands, as George Hogenson has been discussing with regard to
synchronicity and activation of archetypal patterns.[16]

The act of constructing a network of connections between figures
of importance to oneself helps to solidify the intuition of spiritual
ancestry that may be unconsciously guiding one's work. These networks
often operate outside awareness but can be glimpsed through the search

for the provenance of thoughts and images. By engaging in such exploration, we may locate ourselves within much larger historical narratives. In discovering and locating our spiritual ancestors we introduce ourselves into the deep background that forms the essence of our minds and psyches. Curiously these pathways often hold keys to future developments both individually and in culture. Exploring the trajectories that form the background to our psychological lives also can provide hints to the unfolding experiences of our later years. As we age we may discover how our ideas are embedded in the unfolding of the psyche, which in turn makes them agents of complexity in the larger human community, bringing us to a deeply interconnected universe. Perhaps longevity's purpose then is to allow us to explore the limits of our cosmologies and find larger visions.

NOTES

[1] T. R. Cole, "The Prophecy of *Senescence*: G. Stanley Hall and the Reconstruction of Old Age in America," *Gerontologist* 24 (1984): 360–366.

[2] Sigmund Freud, *Totem and Taboo,* trans. James Strachey (New York: W. W Norton, 1950); Sigmund Freud, *The Future of an Illusion,* ed. James Strachey, trans. W. D. Robson-Scott (New York: Anchor Books, 1964); Sigmund Freud, *A Phylogenetic Fantasy: Overview of the Transference Neuroses,* ed. Ilse Grubrich-Simitis, trans. Axel Hoffer and Peter Hoffer (Cambridge, MA: Belknap Press, 1987).

[3] Stephen Jay Gould, *Ontogeny and Phylogeny* (Cambridge, MA: Harvard University Press, 1977).

[4] Ludwig von Bertalanffy, *General System Theory: Foundations, Development, Applications,* Revised Edition (New York: George Braziller, 1968).

[5] Harold J. Morowitz, *The Emergence of Everything* (New York: Oxford University Press, 2002); Steven Johnson, *Emergence: The Connected Lives of Ants, Brains, Cities, and Software* (New York: Scribners, 2001).

[6] Sebastian Seung, *Connectome: How the Brain's Wiring Makes Us Who We Are* (Boston: Houghton, Mifflin, Harcourt, 2012).

[7] Hillard S. Kaplan and Arthur J. Robson, "The Emergence of Humans: The Coevolution of Intelligence and Longevity with Intergenerational Transfers," *PNAS* 99, no. 15 (July 23, 2002): 10222.

[8] Stuart A. Kauffman, *Reinventing the Sacred: A New View of Science, Reason, and Religion* (New York: Basic Books, 2008).

[9] James Hillman, *The Force of Character and the Lasting Life* (New York: Random House, 1999).

[10] Burton Watson, *Chuang Tzu: Basic Writings* (New York: Columbia University Press, 1964/1996), pp. 60–61.

[11] Ralph S. Solecki, Rose L. Solecki, and Anagnostis P. Agelarakis, *The Proto-Neolithic Cemetery in Shanidar Cave* (College Station, TX: Texas A&M University Press, 2004).

[12] James Hillman, *The Dream and the Underworld* (New York: Harper and Row Publishers, 1979).

[13] C. G. Jung, "Synchronicity: An Acausal Connecting Principle," in *The Collected Works of C. G. Jung*, vol. 8, ed. and trans. Gerhard Adler and R. F. C. Hull (Princeton, NJ: Princeton University Press, 1960).

[14] J. Cambray, "The Place of the 17th Century in Jung's Encounter with China," *Journal of Analytical Psychology* 50, no. 2 (2005): 195–207.

[15] Jaegwon Kim, *Supervenience and Mind* (Cambridge, England: Cambridge University Press, 1993).

[16] George Hogenson, "The Self, the Symbolic and Synchronicity: Virtual Realities and the Emergence of the Psyche," *Journal of Analytical Psychology* 50, no. 3 (2005): 271–284.

CHAPTER FOUR

Intimations in the Night
The Journey toward
New Meaning in Aging

MICHAEL CONFORTI, PH.D.

For some of us, the calling to the second half of life comes quietly and the transition toward development of a new internal meaning is a gentle process. For others, it may be a more troubled and turbulent time. A first intimation of this process often happens when we are alone at night. Is the night a reminder that the days have now grown shorter and there is less time to accomplish all that we have hoped to do in this life? There is also a beauty and solitude that one finds in the dark. Often we find a sense of peace in the silence, when the traffic and commerce of the day have ended and homes and lives are illuminated by the glow of a gentle light. Then, too, there is the silence that allows internal voices which we may have drowned out during the day to now be heard. What questions might they be asking? What are we now called to do? Is it to reflect on our past experiences? Consider and work through missed opportunities? Or are we now being called to develop a sense of wonder and a spiritual approach to life?

In this silence, we find an intimation of another way of life, where we face our innermost thoughts, hopes, fears, and desires without illusion or distractions. We can then ask our heart and soul if this has been a good life and what we can do to deepen our relationship to psyche and Self. Our questions about this life may now be different from before, asking, for instance, if we cultivated a great love, great friends, and found a passion for life? Have we made a contribution to the human condition? Have we done what we needed to do? And, in these nocturnal moments, the time of *veritas*, we have to ask if we have the courage to live into our destiny. Facing these questions and answers, we are prepared to embark on a journey of transcendence that may lead us to new meaning and a new direction for our autumn and winter years.

Awakening to the Transcendent

A core concept in the Jungian perspective on the second half of life is *transcendence*. This is a sense of wonder, an intimation of a grand design to our life, and an awareness of and striving to embrace what is truly spiritual. Throughout his writings, Jung speaks of transcendence as a relationship to the sacred and to that which is beyond ego and consciousness. It is this reaching beyond our self, into the domain of the ineffable, that allows for a relationship to the transcendent. This point is captured by Jung when he writes that "I do not for a moment deny that the deep emotion of a true prayer may reach transcendence."[1] Prayer, as an intentional alignment with the archetypal, is a direct call for a relationship to the transpersonal and speaks directly to this domain of the transcendent.

To live only amid the daily busyness of life is to miss an important aspect of spiritual life. While there is a beauty to finding those delicious tomatoes for the evening's meal, it is the awareness that, in the preparation and partaking of this meal, we have entered what Rabbi Heschel refers to as a sense of the sacred in time. He writes that "the highest goal of spiritual living is . . . to face sacred moments . . . a grandeur of what is eternal in time."[2] He then adds that "God is not in things in space, but in time" and continues this theme of time and sacredness by saying that "Shabbat comes with its own holiness, we enter not simply a day but an atmosphere . . . we are within the Sabbath, rather than the Sabbath being within us."[3]

In this sacred time, this experience of transcendence, we enter a domain where we are beyond space and time and have now entered a liminal world. This is the world of archetypes, of archetypal fields where, beyond space-time constraints and behind the limitations of material form, we sense the formless and experience the world of the archaic soul. Be it the midlife journey so often beautifully written about by James Hollis or the harvest of the older years, we enter a preformed realm of the psyche, whose rites of passage and initiatives suddenly grip us and shape our life.[4]

As we age, we are compelled to learn profound lessons about life, one of which is to understand what is within our reach while having the courage to accept what is no longer graspable. Hemingway's novel *The Old Man and the Sea* poignantly captures the pull on the aging man (and woman) to linger in the glow of past accomplishments. Here, to linger means to lose the transcendence, because rather than facing the necessary surrender to this greater domain, one desperately clings to the past, to the known. Experiences of transcendence come to us through experiences of wonder, of awe, and allow us to see and feel parts of life and psyche that are excluded when we are tied to the Procrustean bed of conventionality

For Jungians, aging means approaching a threshold. This threshold is perhaps even more meaningful than others we have traversed earlier in life because we now come face to face with the reality of life as we know it. This sense of finality may be the wake-up call needed to rouse us from the slumber of ambivalence, of complacency, and from a weddedness to outdated and nongenerative complexes. What is needed more than anything else is a turning toward interiority and toward the Self which, for many of us, has been excluded and minimized in our lives.

Now that we are coupled with a greater sense of the meaning and significance of our own life and destiny, we can more fully meet the challenges of time and potential disability with a new, internal spirituality and an enhanced sense of purpose and meaning that rests on that spiritual understanding. No longer are there external standards to meet, but only the values, morality, and ethics of the Self which now beckon. Questions about a new direction for personal meaning, of our values for the second half of life, of spirituality and its meaning for us now, are the focus of our thoughts, and so much of this hangs on the understanding and coming to terms with the lived life and the options for moving forward. The task is to shift from the perspective of society (the first half of life) to a more internal orientation toward life and toward one's deepest Self.

We tend to enter our later years still responsive to those mandates that carried us to this point. There is always the need for more money, more opportunities, and more days to do more things. How do we begin to work with these interior voices and begin to silence those attitudes that linger on in outdated discussions about career, finances, success, and status? So, too, we have to acknowledge that our tendency is to brush aside any irritant slowing us down from these consciously derived, desired goals. A dramatic change is called for, and here we begin to turn toward the Self.

The Union of Opposites

Life and death may be the ultimate image of the union of opposites. An example of this union is Philemon and Baucis, whose deepest prayer was an expression of their love and desire to never be separated, even in death. With inspiration and expiration comes a profound understanding of an underlying order of life that no one escapes. Marie-Louise von Franz, echoing the words of the great sages and dreamers who came before us, reminds us that to truly know life, we must know death.[5] It may seem a bit counterintuitive, but it portends a life which, if embraced, is truly spiritual.

Consider those moments of greatest trust and love in one's own life. When my wife and I brought our newborn child home for the first time and placed him in the bassinet next to our bed, I would watch with awe, fascination, and terror the rapid beating of his little heart. This was my child, and with each beat of his heart emerged yet another dream of our life together. So, too, with each of these rapid heartbeats, I dreaded what could be his final heartbeat, fearing that this tiny heart, which was now preparing for the life it would provide, would just eventually beat so fast that it would either fly out of his body or stop from exhaustion. I was terrified; he whom I loved with all my heart, who entered my life ever so quickly, could just as quickly vanish. This was the terror I lived with until a friend and colleague, Dr. Manisha Roy, explained that these fears expressed a profound archetypal reality which spoke to the fact that now I was experiencing a love unlike any other; that it was this hunger for life, for love, for my son, that was inexorably connected to dread and losing what I most loved. Hers was a wisdom of the ages, an understanding about the psyche and soul. These eternal twins of life and death remain united, forever. Each demands their price and their due and will not be denied. The imperative to understand and live with these twins of life and death is especially demanding as we age. Here, the cost of denial, of stagnation, will at some point exact its toll from the individual.

To fully enter the realm of the harvest of life, we need to become a time traveler and make the daily journey between past, present, and future with the clarity brought on by the new morning. When the air is clear, we can only hope that our ability to reckon with what has been while making plans for a rich and meaningful current and future life may occur. Here, the twins of past and future find a third, an archetypal triptych, which offers the promise of a wonderfully rich life. So how do we make the best of a life, become who we are meant to be, and develop that new spiritual direction and meaning for the second half of life? This is a perennial, archetypal question. And when we deal with spiritual questions, we need spiritual insights to inform us about what humanity has learned of this life process.

Speaking of this shift in awareness from the temporal to the eternal, Jung at age eighty-two wrote that

> old age is only half as funny as one is inclined to think. It is at all events the gradual breaking down of the bodily machine, with which foolishness identifies as ourselves. It is indeed a major effort—the magnum opus in fact—to escape in time from the narrowness of its embrace and to liberate our mind to the vision of the immensity of the world, of which we form an infinitesimal part. In spite of the enormity of our scientific cognition we are yet hardly at the bottom of the ladder, but we are at least so far that we are able to recognize the smallness of our knowledge. The older I grow the more impressed I am by the frailty and uncertainty of our understanding, and all the more I take recourse to the simplicity of immediate experience so as not to lose contact

with the essentials, namely the dominants which rule human
existence throughout the millenniums.[6]

With aging comes the implicit need to see our life for what it is,
for what it could have been, and for what we have done with the gifts
and challenges we have been given. Now we must seek an honest and
meaningful reflection on these questions from the waters of eternity.
With reflections come the memories of this life and, so too, from
memories of what has been, begins the shaping of a future. Our hope
is that this future will be shaped by all that has come before, and yet
will take us to a new vista, to a new opportunity, to a way of life that
brings us into contact with Self and soul.

As we age, memories become more frequent guests in our home.
We may see these guests showing up as the aging man and woman
sitting by the window looking at family pictures. It is this absence of
what once was, of the people, of the family dinners, of a future that is
now but a shadow, that is comforted even just a bit by these memories.
But the images and pictures which often accompany these memories
are never of the future. Perhaps the absence of precedents allows for
this future, allows us the freedom to create and to engage in life in
new ways. Our hope is that this future is never a static iteration of
what had come before, but a creative response to what is still possible.

Clearly there is so much more to this world of memories than we
have ever considered. More than a system of storage and retrieval, they
have the ability to transport us to another domain, where the emotions
are as fresh and stirring as the original event. And from these memories
we often see the contours of a future. Memories and experiences of
childhood influence our choice of career, marriage partner, and our
way of being in the world. Memory works by collapsing the space-
time continuum, showing us that past, present, and future are all
embedded within a moment, a singular moment, perhaps of a life that
is seeking to move toward a destined goal.

From the worlds of biology and physics, we find proof of a future
shaping the current life. In biology we have only to think of the concept
and experience of entelechy, where the future shape of a plant is already
present in the beginning stages of growth. That delicate little seed
which turns into a slender seedling is guided by the form it will

eventually assume. So, too, in physics we find examples of a preformed state shaping current behavior in the direction of what is to come. Whitmont address this when speaking about the chemical element cobalt (Co), which is often used for pigmentation in jewelry. He explains that

> cobalt is aware of a future different from its past and it uses this fact in making a spatial distinction between its right and left. It is capable of making a choice between the two directions . . . . In preferring left to right, the cobalt is proving that there exists a . . . well-defined future state. The physicists do not like to admit in forming their description of nature such a "wave of the future" in the direction of the present, for this would amount to saying that a future state can in some way intervene to guide phenomena situated in the present . . . . But nevertheless, in spite of this independence, each element coordinates its activities perfectly with those of others, in such a way that the overall effect is harmonious and permits convergence toward an advanced state.[7]

Jung also sees the future as a dynamic shaper of current life and adds that

> the symbols of wholeness frequently occur at the beginning of the individuation process . . . . This observation says much for the *a priori* existence of potential wholeness . . . it looks, paradoxically enough, as if something already existent were being put together.[8]

Adolf Portmann, the Swiss zoologist and a longtime collaborator of Jung, brought the concept of self-representation into the field of biology when stressing that each and every organism has the essential mandate to express what is unique about it. Diverging from the current biological thinking of his time, which viewed form, design, and ornamentation as strengthening one's survival advantage, Portmann spoke of these as allowing the soul and innate nature of the flower or animal to be expressed. Realizing that the future state of what was to be was already existing as a preformed potentiality, Portmann also stressed the importance of the future in shaping the current form of a life.[9]

It was Jung who spoke of "the secret workshop of the daemon which shapes our fate" and who encourages us to look toward this future as potentiality waiting in abeyance for us to move into it.[10]

Memory Weaves Our Past, Present, and Future into the Tapestry of a Life

Memories can feed our illusions as well as provide a meaningful and truthful commentary on the life we are living. It is our task, perhaps one of the greatest existential and archetypal challenges of our life, to navigate the waters between Scylla and Charybdis while not being lured by the songs of the sirens into an illusion about our life. And then there are moments of utter clarity when we may finally be able to respond to what may be the most profound and vexing question of our life, namely, have we made this a good life? Can we say that the old immigrant couple who raised eleven children and was loved by family and friends lived a good life? And what of the men or women who leave their spouses and children to pursue what they believe is their greatest dream? Ultimately, the final arbiter of truth is one's own psyche and soul, and it is this profound reflection which quiets all of our opinions and beliefs about the life we have lived.

A ninety-seven-year-old relative is struggling with near crippling pain yet wants to go on living. Each day, he religiously does his prescribed exercises, undergoes many painful medical procedures, and despite it all his hope allows him to endure and move into an uncertain, yet desired future. It is his desire for life that protects that oh-so-fragile flicker of light coming from that one remaining candle that maintains a vigilance against the breath of extinction, protecting this life, this light against the wind, against anything that will bring this final darkness. There is something he still lives for. Is it a hope, a dream of redemption, wanting to make up for all the earlier transgressions? Perhaps a giant resounding yes to all of these and, most important, a yes to life itself. There must be some life force, some reason for him to endure, some gossamer dream that provides this strength to go on amid all the pain, memories, doubts, and hopes. This is all part of this grand mystery of life.

The Old Man and the Sea

Self Will Not Tread Where Ego Presides

Clearly there are many wonderful things about the aging process, one of which is the allowing for a life held in abeyance for far too long to now be freed and allowed expression. With aging come concessions, reminding us of those activities that were once part of our life and now are slowly drifting into the realm of memories. To these we can accede gracefully or cling to outdated memories of prior strengths. This issue is poignantly described in Hemingway's novel *The Old Man and the Sea*, which represents humanity's quintessential journey into the world of aging and is a stirring telling of our relationship to those contents of the depths which we can and cannot bring to fruition.

The story focuses on Santiago, an old fisherman, who for the past eighty-four days has not been able to catch fish. The symbol of the fisherman is well-known from the Bible, myths, and fairytales. It represents one whose work is to access contents from the depths. We too become fisherman as we seek to make contact with those contents of the Self and psyche residing in the deep unconscious. We drop our lines into the sea, hoping to make connection with that which will move us even further into the life we are meant to live. Our hope is to find where these fish are and then bring them to the table. It is here that the *coniunctio* between the conscious and the deep unconscious occurs, reminding us of the meal humanity has sought and participated in since the beginning of time, involving the assimilation of these archetypal spiritual aspects of life.

The villagers believe that Santiago is too old to fish. His nets are bare and Manolin, the young boy who had often accompanied Santiago, is now forbidden by his parents to fish with this old man. It was Hemingway's genius to name this boy Manolin, the diminutive of Manuel and Spanish for the Redeemer, to reflect that even though the boy (the redeemer) could no longer physically journey with the old man, he continued to love and care for him despite his challenges as an aging fisherman.

While Santiago's body is ravaged by age and his heart aches over these disappointments, he is not ready to give up and he decides to journey even farther out to sea in search of the great fish. Fishing alone in these remote areas, he feels a tug unlike any other on his line. This fish is different from all the others, and it refuses his attempts to pull it to the surface. Santiago realizes that he has hooked something great.

For days and nights, this great fish pulls Santiago and his little boat even farther out into the sea. This time, it was the fisherman who was at the whim of this magnificent fish, which, if it chose to, could end this battle in a moment. Santiago holds fast to this fish, to the dream, to his pride, and to the promise of regaining his acclaim as a great man, worthy of being called a fisherman. However, the sheer size and power of this fish pushes the old man's hopes and illusions to their limits.

Through hours of struggle and feeling the toll of working such a great fish, Santiago grows to deeply respect and, perhaps, even to love this fish. Despite the cuts on his hands from the fishing rope and the pressure of the line ripping into his back, he holds on. Neither opponent will give up. In this battle to the death, somehow each knows that there can be only one victor, and neither wants to concede. This was the ego's struggle with and relationship to content from the depth which may have just been beyond the old man's capacity to comprehend or "reel in." Perhaps this fish, this aspect of Self, needs to be set free, as its sheer size and strength requires more of the fisherman than he is able to handle at this point in his life.

After days of struggle, the fish gives up its epic battle. When the fish comes to the surface, the old man marvels at not only the size, but also the utter beauty of this great creature. Realizing that while catching this fish was a tremendous achievement, his work as a fisherman is only half completed, as he still has to bring this great fish to port. Now tied to the side of the boat, the fish, this aspect of Self, begins to pour its blood into the sea. A carpet of brilliant crimson, which once served as the life force for this fish, is now its final insult as it becomes an invitation to all the denizens of the depths to feed.

Santiago is indeed a wise old fisherman and knows what is to come. Knowing that he would have only to await the arrival of the great predators of the sea, Santiago grows reflective, and his once victorious mood quickly changes to a sad lament. We now hear his soul, that voice of evening truth, forcing him to admit that "you did not kill the fish only to keep alive and to sell for food . . . . You killed him for pride and because you are a fisherman. You loved him when he was alive and you loved him after."[11] Santiago then concedes that he cannot talk to the fish anymore because the fish has been ruined, and in this touching story, we hear him say, "Fish that you were. I am sorry that I went too far out. I ruined us both."[12]

The sharks, those aspects of the psyche that strive to keep unconscious contents within the domain of the unconscious, found an easy path to their prey. The once and magnificent fish, and this once and great fisherman, were now coupled in an embrace of helpless resignation, knowing that there was nothing they could do to protect and preserve what was most precious. This was a painful moment of truth.

Santiago and the fish, or the fish and Santiago, finally return to port. While his hope had been to sell the meat from this treasured catch, the sharks left him with only the skeletal remains of this fish. No fish to sell, no food to eat, he is left with the reality that while he had successfully fought and landed this great fish, there is now nothing for him or the villagers to do but admire the remains. His work as a great fisherman, as an individual who worked in the depths, was yet again frustrated. But this has been different from all the other days and other experiences. Like so many of us in the aging process, he now has to admit that there are aspects of life and psyche that we know of, can see and even touch, but cannot bring to fruition. Perhaps this is one of our greatest challenges. To walk in the brilliantly clear light of these autumn days knowing what could have been, and what exists as potential, while realizing that there is a piece of life, an aspect of psyche, that will not be ours. Kaufmann speaks to this when writing that "the Greeks . . . knew that the essence of being human is living with limitations. Which only the Gods and sometimes not even they, could overcome. We have to bow to certain inevitability."[13]

Santiago now realizes this only too well. He returns to his home, feeling an exhaustion he has never before known so fully and takes a much needed rest. However, his young friend Manolin, who had been terribly worried about the old man since he left the village days before, now sees his tiny boat in the port and runs to see him. He loves Santiago and allows him to rest and prepares a meal to nurture his body and soul once he awakes. Manolin, the young boy, the redeemer, never stopped loving the old man and never cared if he brought this great fish to the village. His is a love reserved for those sacred moments and relationships. It is the love of a parent for his or her child, for a spouse, for a god, for a redeemer who never fails to reach out a hand to us, reminding us that despite it all, we are loved and that redemption remains more than a possibility. Perhaps if Hemingway had understood this aspect of aging and redemption, he would not have taken his own life and could have continued to see himself as a great man, even with the limitations of aging and recognizing that certain aspects of life would not be brought to fruition. Perhaps it was this challenge facing Santiago that proved too much for Hemingway, and for many of us going through this process, to accept.

Aged Wine or Simply a Wine That Is Old?

While we may want to see aging men and women as wise, this is often far from the truth. As in the case with wine, some age gracefully and deliciously like a robust and full-bodied Barolo, while others simply become foul tasting. How has this old man of the sea fared in the process? Contrast his actions with the appearance of the wise old man or wise old woman in myths and fairy tales. Jung addresses this issue:

> The old man always appears when the hero is in a hopeless and desperate situation from which only profound reflection or a lucky idea—in other words, a spiritual function . . . of some kind can extricate him . . . . Often the old man induces self-reflection and mobilizing the moral forces.[14]

Jung then adds that "the intervention of the old man—the spontaneous objectivation of the archetype—would seem to be equally indispensable, since the conscious will by itself is hardly ever capable of uniting the personality to the point where it acquires the extraordinary power to succeed."[15]

With the publication of *The Old Man and the Sea* in 1951, Hemingway's brilliance as a writer was once again recognized, and he received the Nobel Prize in Literature in 1954. However, amid this success, something deeply troubling remained in his heart and soul. This book was his last piece of fiction to be published; in 1961, Hemingway took his own life. His battle with greatness, with fatigue, with obscurity, and with life came to an end. Santiago, like Hemingway, returned home from his epic battle depleted and with the awareness of having participated in the loss of something truly magnificent.

Even before knowing the timing of Hemingway's death, I sensed that this story was a foreshadowing of his eventual suicide. Through this story, he tells what it must be like to connect to such powerful content within the depths and the consequences of not being able to know one's limitations. Santiago/Hemingway needed to set this creature free, to allow it to live once again as a vital and dynamic aspect of Self and psyche. But he could not let go and admit that this process was bigger than him and that he was unable to bring these contents to fruition as a conscious aspect of his life and destiny. Some aspect of potential magnificence was now wasted and, in some intrinsic way, he knew it.

This is as much humanity's story as it is Hemingway's, because it speaks to our individual and collective struggles with aging, letting go, and sacrificing breadth for depth. The call to be Santiago is present at every corner and experienced as we desperately cling to outdated behaviors and attitudes. As sanctity and spirituality are eclipsed by the promise of temporal gains, we share in Santiago's long and fruitless journey home.

No one wants to see the decline in his or her ability to function in the world. However, this too is a universal reality and inevitability. So what is to be done to make life as meaningful and rich as possible as we age? Perhaps we can ask the seventy-three-year-old woman what it was like to dream of finding so many dried up and ruined tomatoes still on the vine. Or we can ask the newly retired professional what he now sees as the life unfolding within and around him when he dreams of having found a cache of wood that has been curing for more than fifty years underwater and is now ready to be brought to the surface.

This gift of a life may be likened to a richly grained piece of wood. Left untreated and unattended, the beauty of its grains and depth of color remains *in potentia,* unseen by all around it. However, it is the working with the wood, of sanding it with ever finer grades of material and then using the finest of oils, that allows for its innate nature and beauty to emerge. What was existing as potential has now burst forth with a vibrancy of texture and depth. So, too, does a life well lived bring out the richness of one's nature and soul, and this vibrancy and twinkle in the eye is an expression of a life lived in accord with one's destiny.

Somehow this journey of life and aging all boils down to a relationship to Eros and destiny. The creative muse and daemon allows us to cultivate a rich and deeply satisfying career. Here, our talents find a place to flourish and contribute to our personal development and to the collective. With Eros, we come to know something of love and tenderness, and one hopes and prays that as the sun sets ever earlier in the evening sky, we have truly known love. In its absence, one struggles, as did Tantalus, seeing that which is most desired remaining just out of reach. So, too, without the kiss of Eros, one joins in Orpheus's lamentation over the loss of his beloved Eurydice.

With a meaningful relationship to psyche, Eros, and the muses, one approaches the aging process with a sense of purpose, peace, hope, and acceptance. With an awareness that life is more than good enough, we can begin to accept all that comes with aging. While not inviting infirmity or death to the table, we understand that one day, and hopefully many days from now, this journey will come to an end.

We all falter, yet there is a benevolence within the psyche that continues to welcome home its prodigal sons and daughters. There is an honesty and compassion for a life that has gone astray, and often we are given yet another opportunity to do some of what we were meant to do and have some of what we were meant to have in this life. Then, if there is grace, we will return home to welcoming arms and embraces. There is a sense of urgency and permanence to this homecoming, because this time, we are facing the final act of going home. We nod to the elders, those wise ones who came before us, who realized something profound not just about life but also how one could live a spiritual life. If we put our ear to the ground and listen carefully, we may just hear Rabbi Heschel's gentle homage to spirit when he wrote: "Never once in my life did I ask God for success or wisdom of power or fame. I asked for wonder and he gave it to me."[16]

Perhaps this is the spiritual attitude we need in order to make this journey into the later stages of life and, ultimately, an attitude that is needed to take us home.

NOTES

[1] C. G. Jung, "Letter to Pere Lachat, in *The Collected Works of C. G. Jung*, vol. 18, ed. and trans. Gerhard Adler and R. F. C. Hull (Princeton, NJ: Princeton University Press, 1950), § 1536.

[2] Abraham Joshua Heschel, *The Sabbath* (New York: Farrar, Straus and Giroux, 1951), p. 4.

[3] *Ibid.*, pp. xiv-xv.

[4] James Hollis, *The Middle Passage From Misery to Meaning in Midlife* (Toronto: Inner City Books, 1993); James Hollis, *Finding Meaning in the Second Half of Life* (New York: Gotham Books, 2005); James Hollis, *What Matters Most* (New York: Gotham Books, 2009).

[5] M.-L. von Franz, *The Puer Aeternus* (Salem, MA: Sigo Press, 1970), p. 161.

[6] C. G. Jung, *Letters, Vol. 2, 1951–1961* (Princeton, NJ: Princeton University Press, 1976), p. 580.

[7] E. C. Whitmont, "The Destiny Concept in Psychotherapy," *Journal of Jungian Theory and Practice* 9, no. 1 (2007): 8–9.

[8] C. G. Jung, "The Psychology of the Child Archetype," in *The Collected Works of C. G. Jung*, vol. 9i, ed. and trans. Gerhard Adler and R. F. C. Hull (Princeton, NJ: Princeton University Press, 1959), § 278.

[9] Adolf Portmann, *New Paths in Biology* (New York: Harper and Row, 1964); and A. Portmann, "Metamorphosis in Animals: The Transformation of the Individual and the Type, " in *Man and Transformation: Papers from the Eranos Yearbooks* (Princeton, NJ: Princeton University Press, 1972).

[10] Jung, "The Psychology of the Child Archetype," CW 9i, § 278.

[11] Ernest Hemingway, *The Old Man and the Sea* (New York: Scribner, 1952), p. 13.

[12] Hemingway, *The Old Man and the Sea*, p. 115.

[13] Yoram Kaufmann, *The Way of the Image: The Orientational Approach to the Psyche* (New York: Zahav Books, 2009), p. 21.

[14] Jung, "The Psychology of the Child Archetype," CW 9i, § 404.

[15] *Ibid.*

[16] Abraham Joshua Heschel, *I Asked for Wonder*, ed. Samuel Dresner (New York: Crossroad, 2001), p. ii.

CHAPTER FIVE

An Adaptive Perspective on Aging

ROBERT LANGS, M.D.

F acing the prospect of growing older and old age is a challenge we all must accept. How we respond to that universal challenge and what resources and/or impediments we have to bring to this process is the subject of this chapter. As will be described in detail in other chapters, Jung developed a theory of how individuals can adapt to the process of growing older as a natural process. He called this period of adaptation the second half of life. My contribution here is to talk about how Freudian thought addresses the challenges of aging.

Freud did not specifically address the psychological problems of the later years of life. Nevertheless, as a neo-Freudian or Freudian revisionist who has forged an adaptation-centered view of the mind, I have given the subject of our senior years considerable thought.

Freud and Aging

Indications are that Freud avoided discussing growing old and its culmination in death for compelling psychological reasons. It is well known that Freud looked only to the past in his writings and avoided looking to the future in any significant way. He openly dreaded getting old and had a pervasive, chronic fear of dying.[1] He also was a hypochondriac who suffered from migraine headaches, a cardiac neurosis, and other imagined ailments. His anxieties about dying also are reflected in the fact that he twice tried to predict the year of his death and got it wrong both times.

As for the question of why Freud was so anxious about aging and dying, my research into his personal life as presented by historians and encoded in his written narratives indicate that a major early life trauma played a significant role in this regard: Freud was never certain of the identity of his biological father.[2] There are indications that, on some level of awareness, he was convinced that his half brother Philipp, who was his mother's age, fathered him rather than Jacob, who was twenty years older than his wife. While several historians have unearthed convincing evidence that Freud's mother, Amalia, had an affair with Philipp, Marianne Krull is the only writer who has conjectured that this liaison resulted in the conception and birth of Sigmund, and she did not pursue this possibility further.[3] This evident conviction, which has multiple unconsciously mediated effects, involved an unbearable reality and seemed to have raised questions in Freud's mind about his very existence—an issue of life and death in which the threat of non-existence was a key and intolerable feature.

The encoded messages in Freud's writings strongly point to his uncertainty as to his origins. When Jacob Freud died, Sigmund dreamed what he called a double dream, that is, two simultaneous versions of the same dream, in which he is twice told to close his eye(s). Implied here is the idea that on the occasion of the death of one of his fathers, he actually had the loss of two fathers to mourn. On the occasion of the first anniversary of Jacob's death, Freud suddenly and without substantial reason abandoned his reality-centered trauma theory of neuroses and quickly replaced it with the fantasy-centered theory of the Oedipus conflict, thereby distancing himself from reality and its traumas because the implications of the reality of his origins was unbearable to him. Thus the shift in his view of the cause of neuroses was to what we wish for in our imaginations from what we do not wish to happen in a reality over which we have little or no control—including the reality of our personal mortality. Even so, the exciting incident of the myth takes place when Oedipus is told that his caretaking parents, the king and queen of Corinth, are not his biological parents. Thus Oedipus's primary quest is to discover the identity of his biological parents. Furthermore, the central theme in Freud's last major contribution, which has been viewed as his deathbed confession, is that Moses, the father of the Jews, was not a Jew.

The nature and development of psychoanalytic theory also reinforces the Freudian focus on one's past. Historically Freudian psychoanalytic theory was concentrated on the needs of each patient. The psychoanalytic model is also centered on early life events. As M. Ralph Kaufman explains,

> Historically, the psychoanalysis of Freud grew out of the therapeutic needs of patients and, before it became a psychology of the total individual, it was a therapeutic discipline whose main object was to aid and understand the individual who came in as a patient . . . . The fundamental psychoanalytic hypotheses concerning the structure of the human personality were firmly based on factors of unconscious motivations and particularly the tremendous importance of the earliest period of life. [4]

Thus, as a discipline, psychoanalysis is rooted in examining early life and working with the unconscious to understand these early experiences. The challenges of growing older were not a strong focus of this model of the individual due to the importance of the events of childhood. One does find in psychoanalytic literature a consensus that old age reduces the intensity of drives and lessens the tendency to conflict; the tension between the ego and the superego is reduced.

It appears then that from the very moment of his origins Freud's life hung on the thin thread of a potential incestuous affair. Traumas of that proportion promote a turning away from the realities of life and yet, because the effects of these untoward events are inextinguishable, they influence everything of major significance that we do during our lives, including our last years on earth.

Ancients Views on Aging

I would like to go back (even further) to Greek mythology and the Bible to get a sense of the views of the classical age on understanding and coping with our later years. For the Greeks, Geras was the spirit (daimon) of old age. His father is unknown but his mother was Nyx (night). His siblings included such spirits as those of doom, violent death, death itself, blame, and misery, and also sleep and dreams. One version of this story has it that winning over Geras brings virtue and wisdom, but that element pales in the face of his family ties. It seems that, like Freud, the Greeks dreaded old age, and while they saw it as a possible opportunity to gain fresh wisdom, they mostly viewed it as some kind of emotional plague.

As for the Bible, death and aging do not exist in the original paradise of Eden. But then comes the most fateful moment in the history of humankind: Eve's partaking of the fruit of the tree of divine knowledge. This is in a sense the beginning of human life on earth, and in this context, she and Adam immediately become aware of their vulnerabilities, chief among them their mortality. They quickly seek out the tree of eternal life which stands in the middle of the garden and which they previously had disregarded. But God blocks the path to the tree, and they are expelled from the garden forevermore. Awareness of death is thus the price paid for divine wisdom and quite soon, as when Cain kills his brother Abel, murder and violence are very much in evidence.

The Bible also introduces the problems of the later years of life by telling the story of Abraham when he is about hundred years old and his wife, Sarah, who is about ninety. The main challenge for these barren seniors is to have a child, that is, to extend the chain of life into the future. They succeed, thereby showing that elder years can be fulfilling and creative. This is a most promising and reassuring message.

Not so with the next tale of the aged. This story is about Abraham and Sarah's son and descendant, Isaac. He is well on in years and close to death when the time comes for him to bless his eldest son, Esau, and pass on to him his birthright and the future of his tribe. But Isaac, who is half blind and confused, allows himself to be duped by his younger son, Jacob, and passes his heritage to him. We may take this as the first allusion to Alzheimer's disease in the history of humankind, and it reflects the frailties of growing old and the mistakes that are made because of them.

Trauma and the Senior Years

An individual's trauma history plays a largely silent but compelling role in the quality of his or her later years. The resolution of the lingering effects of past, current, and anticipated traumas, and of the death anxieties they inevitably evoke, is one of the requisites for rendering these years as fulfilling as possible. This necessitates dealing with painful realities over which we have had little or no say, and it requires that we become cognizant of and make peace with the ever-present shadow that death casts over our existence.

T. S. Eliot put our dilemma beautifully in these lines from "Burnt Norton":

> Go, go, go, said the bird: human kind
> Cannot bear very much reality.
> Time past and time future
> What might have been and what has been
> Point to one end, which is always present.[5]

As humans, we have evolved a language-based mental module—a collection of mental faculties—called the *emotion-processing mind*.[6] Its primary function is to enable us to cope mentally with physical and psychological traumas. It is a companion resource to the immune system, and together the two systems serve as our bastions against predatory threat. This pair of adaptive entities shares many archetypal features: a two-system design (T and B cell systems for one, and conscious and unconscious systems for the other); the ability to destroy or neutralize attempts to harm us (microscopic threats for one and macroscopic threats for the other); and knowledge acquisition, memory, the ability to distinguish self from not-self, operations guided by selectionist principles, and much more.

The emotion-processing mind perceives and responds consciously to many types of dangers and deals with them accordingly. This knowing level of adaptation tends to be highly individualized. But many disturbing threats are unbearable to awareness and therefore are perceived unconsciously (subliminally) and processed without conscious awareness interceding. These latter coping efforts, which are far superior to those we muster consciously, can be ascertained solely through a process called *trigger decoding*.[7] This effort is carried out by

remembering a dream or making up a story and then associating the
elements of the narrative with incidents from real life. The resultant
pool of themes is then decoded in light of the implications of the
traumatic triggering event that stimulated these images in the first
place. The configuration for this decoded level of insight is *not* that
this is what a trigger caused us to *imagine,* but what it *actually compelled
us to experience.* Notably, this hidden effort to cope with reality is
strongly guided by trauma- and death-related archetypes, that is, they
are programmed in our genes. Thus death anxiety, our conscious and
unconscious fears of annihilation and nonexistence, is a basic
psychobiological phenomenon. I turn now to the psychological issues
raised by these concerns.

The Nature and Role of Death Anxiety

There are three types of traumas and each evokes a particular type
of death anxiety.[8] Both the incident and the anxiety may be
experienced consciously, but the more critical level of experience
takes place outside of awareness. The three types of death anxiety
are: (1) *predatory:* the threat of harm from others, usually other
humans, and from natural disasters; (2) *predator:* the threat of self-
punishing harm to the point of self-annihilation caused by the guilt
experienced when we harm others; and (3) *existential:* the result of the
awareness of human mortality.

The unconscious experience of these threats involves their most
terrible and terrifying aspects. Each type of resultant anxiety is dealt
with by means of a series of archetypal responses.

Predatory death anxiety prompts a mobilization of resources,
physical and psychological, in an effort to survive the threat. In later
years there is a need, then, to discover who our enemies were and are
and the nature of the harm they did to us. On that basis we must
then find the means to forgive them their ill intentions and to make
peace with the residuals of helplessness and rage that they evoked.

Existential death anxiety stimulates a turn to a wide variety of
obliterating mechanisms through which we try to deny our mortality.
These may be innocuous, as when we engage in trivial distractions.
But they often endanger others and ourselves; this happens when, for
example, we deny the implications of evident symptoms of a serious

illness or try to exercise excessive power though financial exploitation or actually harming others. The unconscious delusion is that if you can harm or kill others, in reality or symbolically, you yourself will become immortal. Denial of death also is served unconsciously when we violate rules and boundaries. In this case, the unconscious belief is that if you are an exception to an unconsciously wrought ideal ground rule, you thereby become an exception to the existential rule of life, namely, that it is always followed by death. In this regard, the elderly need to discover the sources of their existential death anxieties and find ways not only to make peace with them, but also to discover how to use these anxieties creatively.

Last, there is the unconscious archetypal response to having harmed others, to acts whose damaging effects are often missed consciously but clearly detected unconsciously. By evolved design, the unconscious mind possesses a pristine, uncompromising system of morality and ethics. Acting beyond awareness, this system sees to it that we unwittingly pay a severe price for our immoral deeds by prompting us to engage in self-punishing behaviors. Many seemingly absurd self-destructive lapses and efforts to unnecessarily provoke others to harm us stem from the very real demands of this system. Death anxiety comes into play because in the unconscious mind, all acts of harm and violence are seen as attempts at murder. As a result, the *talion* punishment (the Babylonian term for punishment equal to the magnitude of the crime) for these behaviors is suicide or its equivalent. Getting in touch with this derailing guilt in later years enables us to be alert to the dangers of engaging in self-defeating acts and also can be the basis for healing acts of contrition, reparation, and atonement.

The Bible and Coping with Death Anxiety

I return now to the wisdom of the Bible to offer an adaptive view of what Yahweh and Jesus have to offer humankind when it comes to effectively dealing with the three forms of death anxiety as they emerge in later years.[9] For those who believe in the Old Testament and Yahweh, the situation is uncertain. Yahweh protected the Jews from some of their predators, like the Egyptians, but enslaved them to others, like the Assyrians and Romans. He punished some of those who were evil or harmed others, as he did with the flood and the destruction of

Sodom and Gomorrah, and thus offered a moral compass. But he also protected Cain from those who would avenge his murder of Abel and rewarded Jacob, who stole his brother's birthright, by seeing to it that he became the father of the twelve tribes of Israel. In addition, existentially Yahweh does not offer humans immortality but only a good death. There is not much succor there.

Matters are very different with Jesus. He had an adaptive solution for each of the three types of death anxiety: for predatory, turn the other cheek (and keep the peace); for predator, his dying on the cross for the sins of all believers who thereby are relieved of their predator death anxieties and needs for punishment; and for existential, his invitation at the end life on earth to sit with him in heaven beside God's throne for all eternity.

These are remarkable feats and promises, and evidently they have enabled many elderly believers to find and sustain inner peace. But these acts and words of wisdom have not brought peace to many others nor to the world at large. Jung has spoken of the need for religion to evolve, and so it must. The future path religion takes may benefit greatly from a deeper knowledge of the nature of human death anxieties and how they are best dealt with. The fresh wisdom so derived should serve everyone, believers and nonbelievers, as they enter and go through their final years of life.

Some Practical Advice

I conclude with a few simple words of advice that can help ensure a happy end phase to one's life.

First, have a partner whom you love and who makes you want to live.

Second, heed the words of William Osler (1849–1919), physician and father of modern American medicine, who wisely said that if one has a chronic disease, one will live forever.

And finally, take on a pressing, intractable problem and endure the struggle and frustration of trying to solve it. This will create a resolve to not die until you find the answer to the problem. And if, by chance, you do solve the problem, you need not fear. The resolution of a serious challenge always brings with it a new unsolved puzzle.

Think of this as turning the impossibilities of life into living life to the fullest.

NOTES

[1] Max Schur, *Freud, Living and Dying* (New York: International Universities Press, 1972).

[2] R. Langs, *Freud on a Precipice: How Freud's Fate Pushed Psychoanalysis over the Edge* (Latham, MD: Jason Aronson, 2009).

[3] Marianne Krull, *Freud and His Father*, trans. Arnold Pomerans (New York: Norton, 1986).

[4] M. Ralph Kaufman, "Old Age and Aging: The Psychoanalytic Point of View," *American Journal of Orthopsychiatry* 10, no. 1 (1940): 73. Accessed at Wiley Online Library, July 22, 2012.

[5] T. S. Eliot, *Four Quartets*, in *Collected Poems 1909–1962* (New York: Harcourt, Brace and Co., 1963), p. 176.

[6] R. Langs, *The Evolution of the Emotion-Processing Mind: With an Introduction to Mental Darwinism* (London: Karnac Books, 1996).

[7] R. Langs, *Fundamentals of Adaptive Psychotherapy and Counseling* (London: Palgrave-Macmillan, 2004).

[8] R. Langs, *Death Anxiety and Clinical Practice* (London: Karnac Books, 1997); R. Langs, *Love and Death in Psychotherapy* (London: Palgrave-Macmillan, 2006).

[9] R. Langs, *Beyond Yahweh and Jesus: Bringing Death's Wisdom to Faith, Spirituality, and Psychoanalysis* (Latham, MD: Jason Aronson, 2008).

~ PART III ~

Gerontological Perspectives on Successful Aging

Chapter Six

Opportunities for Ongoing Jungian-Gerontological Partnership

Michael E. Carbine, M.A.

The biggest surprise in a man's life is old age.
—Leo Tolstoy

Introduction

C G. Jung pointed out that while modern society prepares its youth for navigating the first half of life, it provides little if any guidance to help people prepare for and navigate the second half. Until recently, the most prominent markers for the second half of life have been the midlife crisis, retirement, grandparenthood, Medicare and Social Security eligibility, and the transition into a retirement or assisted living community. These markers often imply a life of leisure, freedom from work, and in some cases physical and mental decline and a disengagement from society.

Recent social and economic developments are shifting our thinking about these markers. Many adults must, for economic reasons, remain in the workforce past retirement age (65 to 67). And a growing number of aging services professionals are envisioning aging as a time of continuing exploration, growth, and involvement in society rather than decline and disengagement. This view is in harmony with Jung's belief that psychological and spiritual growth are independent of age and that the second half of life can be a time of robust psychological growth and development as well as spiritual enrichment.

While programs and services for older adults originally were created by the federal government to ensure their financial well-being in retirement, the advent of the field of gerontology led to the creation of programs designed to help older adults take advantage of opportunities for self-expression and engagement. Rather than focusing on aging as a time of disease, disability, and relentless decline, gerontologists are more often concerned with the possibilities and opportunities of aging, leading to the development of programs that address quality of life issues. More recently, the creative aging movement has focused on helping adults reconnect with their creative powers and reap the physical and mental health benefits of increased social connections. These benefits include improved health outcomes and higher levels of life satisfaction.

Despite the synergy between many programs for adults and Jung's ideas about late-life growth, few of his ideas have made their way into the aging community (adults in the second half of life as well as professionals and others working with and for the aging); they remain a well-kept secret despite their potential value.

This chapter identifies four areas where I believe the Jungian community possesses unique program opportunities that could be of significant benefit to gerontologists, social workers, health-care professionals, and others who work with adults—four areas in which aging services professionals and the Jungian community might work to enhance and deepen their shared interests. To this end, I encourage social service and health-care professionals to reach out to the Jungian community to explore opportunities for bringing Jungian ideas about vibrant aging into their work, and especially into academic programs that are training future aging services professionals. Gerontologists, social workers, and other aging services staff, including caregivers and volunteers, would benefit from such linkages by bringing what they learn from the Jungian community into their direct client work. The health-care delivery system, meanwhile, is dealing with a growing number of older patients, and there are several areas in which Jungian ideas could be integrated into health care and wellness services.

Aging services professionals may not be aware of or necessarily interested in such clinical Jungian concepts as individuation, the collective unconscious, or archetypes. But they are deeply interested in enhancing the emotional as well as the physical health and well-being of those with whom they are working. Many of them are now following the whole-person model discussed by Kelley Macmillan in chapter 7, so they are looking for ways to help their clients (and their client's families and loved ones) thrive spiritually and psychologically. They are interested in helping their clients understand and successfully navigate the difficult and often bewildering transitions that are a natural part of the aging process. They want to help their clients find meaning in aging-related losses, illness, and suffering so they can learn from these experiences and incorporate the lessons they have learned into their lives. And they want to help their clients approach death and dying as a natural part of life. Jungian-based ideas address all of these issues and, in most cases, can bring new, deeply enriching and practical insights and perspectives to their work, potentially broadening not just their clients' horizons but their own.

Aging of the Population: Programs, Services, and Opportunities

The oldest of the baby boomer generation (those born between 1946 and 1964) began turning 65 in 2011. When the trend peaks in 2030, the number of Americans age 65 and older will reach about 72 million—representing one in every five Americans. By 2050, for the first time in the nation's history, the number of people age 60 and older will be greater than the number of children from birth to 14 years.[1]

A host of public and private sector agencies and groups—ranging from county-administered agencies on aging to churches, schools, senior and community centers, and local and regional nonprofit service organizations—currently sponsor a variety of programs and services for aging adults. Many of these programs focus on quality of life issues that disproportionately impact older adults, including marginalization, isolation, and lack of family, social, and community engagement. Community-based programs also offer lifeline services designed to address senior hunger (Meals on Wheels, congregate meals, and other nutrition and food security programs), lack of transportation (Dial-a-Ride, volunteer drivers, taxi vouchers, and other services), and barriers to medical and health-care services. Research points to strong causal links between these problems and poor physical and mental health, depression, late-onset alcohol and prescription drug abuse, and suicide. Many local and national programs offer opportunities for continuing education (such as Osher Lifelong Learning Institutes based at colleges and universities), travel, civic engagement, computer literacy, adapting to and experimenting with new social roles (including mentoring), and a range of leisure activities, many designed to promote health and well-being.

Some programs and services for the aging are sponsored or supported by local Area Agencies on Aging (called Triple As), for the most part county-based agencies funded by the Older Americans Act with augmented funding from state and county sources. But the vast number of programs are sponsored by small local and regional nonprofit organizations, civic groups (some with national ties), and faith-based entities that work on the local level to ensure that older adults have access to the resources they need to remain as independent as possible and thrive as they age. The focus of many of these programs is to help prevent institutionalization and enable adults to age in their homes and communities to the extent possible.

The recent economic downturn, shifting government priorities, and subsequent budgetary constraints are impacting programs and services for the aging at a time when the aging of the population is creating more demand for them. Many program and service providers are seeking new program ideas and resources and are actively partnering with community-based organizations in an effort to strengthen and enrich their programs and, in some cases, survive. In this regard, the Jungian community would be a source of new ideas and expertise. Incorporating Jung's unique perspectives on and approaches to psychological and spiritual growth in the second half of life could help those working with older adults bring added depth and richness to their work with aging adults.

By Jungian community I am referring to Jungian analysts and the people who work for and with the Jungian institutes, centers, societies, and Friends of Jung groups that operate across the country. In most cases, an institute's mission includes training future analysts, providing continuing education opportunities and resources for practicing analysts and other helping professionals, and sponsoring education programs for the lay public. Centers typically offer continuing clinical education programs for analysts and education programs for the lay public. In some cases, they are affiliated with universities or graduate institutes through which they offer graduate degrees in psychology. Societies and Friends of Jung groups, meanwhile, usually have been formed by groups of lay people interested in Jungian psychology, and their primary mission is to offer Jungian-based education programs for the lay public. But it should be noted that the mission and goals of these organizations can differ from community to community. Jung encouraged diversity and an individual approach to bringing to life his vision of growth and development in the second half of life, and the Jungian community reflects and honors this approach.

I would suggest that those working in the aging services field look primarily (but not exclusively) to the Jungian societies and Friends of Jung groups when considering potential linkages, since these entities are grassroots organizations with predominantly lay memberships that have deep roots in their local communities. Many already have ties to local organizations and groups through their members and offer Jungian-based programs that could be used as a resource for aging adults and those who work with them. Participation in these programs could help aging services professionals expand and deepen the work they do with their clients by bringing new tools and perspectives to their work. And they could also form the base for new programs that could be presented in senior living, assisted living, continuing care, home health care, long-term care, community-based health and social service programs, and other settings in which they work.

As Lionel Corbett writes in chapter 1, many Jungian-based ideas can be used to promote a more holistic and positive view of "successful" aging. I would propose that the Jungian community also possesses unique insights and perspectives in four areas: (1) revitalizing curiosity and openness to exploration and discovery, including inner exploration toward deeper self-awareness and acceptance; (2) reenergizing the capacity for creativity; (3) exploring the spiritual questions that often arise because of the losses, illnesses, disabilities, and other traumas associated with aging; and (4) acceptance of death as a natural part of life. Social service professionals could use these insights and perspectives to help adults more effectively and productively navigate the often difficult and bewildering transitions that are a natural part of the aging process. Health-care professionals, meanwhile, could use them to bring a rich, whole-person orientation to their work, benefiting not just patients, their loved ones, and their caregivers but also professionals, volunteers, and others working with older adults in health care and home-based settings.

Addressing Aging-Related Transitions: A Jungian Perspective

The absence of Jung's ideas about growth and development in the second half of life from the aging services field, and especially from schools of social work, nursing, and gerontology, represents a tragic—and ironic—loss for society. Tragic because of the contributions these ideas could make to current efforts to meet the psychosocial needs of our rapidly aging population. And ironic because gerontologists and social workers in the trenches tend to be concerned with quality of life issues. The gerontology community especially is interested in "reinventing aging" and making the whole-person model central to its work with aging adults. As a result, there is tremendous dedication to ensuring that adults have the opportunity to explore their inner and outer worlds, fully engage their creative powers, give full rein to self-expression, and thrive up to the time of their death—very much the same goals that Jungian analysts and Jungian-oriented psychologists strive for in their work with clients.

Using Jungian-based ideas, gerontologists and others working with aging adults could become trusted guides in helping adults recharge their curiosity and openness to the new, revitalize their creative powers, deepen their spirituality, and open themselves to an understanding and acceptance of death. Sondra Geller, a Jungian analyst, describes the use of the expressive arts in creating a safe place in which residents of a nursing home could explore their feelings.[2] Michael Conforti, a Jungian analyst and director of the Assisi Institute, sees a parallel role for those using Jungian-based ideas with aging adults, in effect becoming sympathetic, resourceful, and trusted guides who could help adults as they make their way into and through the transformations that lead to new ways of experiencing and living one's life (personal communication, April 20, 2012).

Curiosity, Openness, and the Search for Meaning

Interest in the use of adult play and humor to bring forward into adulthood the abilities and psychological vitality of our youth and reconnect with the forces of growth are gaining interest among programs for the aging. This interest dovetails with Jung's efforts to reconnect with his "lost child" to unlock his curiosity and creativity and his belief that everyone can realize the potential of the child archetype at any age because the soul is always young. Jung himself turned to a form of childhood play to facilitate the journey into his own unconscious, a journey that led to the formation of his theory of individuation (the full development of one's potential) and to the use of active imagination as a tool for inner exploration and discovery.

Play has long been used in limited therapeutic settings and is now being extended into other venues as an approach to helping adults rediscover the giftedness that exists in all of us. Researchers, including Stuart Brown, M.D., at the National Institute for Play, are studying the impact of social play on adults. Humor also is gaining attention as an important factor in promoting health and well-being among adults. A study of the elderly in Zürich, Switzerland, illuminated the role humor plays as a coping mechanism in helping adults maintain a state of well-being in the face of age-related adversity.[3]

Gerontologists and social workers could work with the Jungian community to bring this approach to their direct client work with aging adults, as well as to community-based programs for the aging. These could include programs that offer adults the opportunity to explore humor, play, and playfulness as ways to reconnect with and regenerate their curiosity and creativity and enhance their ability to transcend the adversities that come with aging.

Story making and storytelling, meanwhile, have proven to be excellent vehicles for helping adults find meaning in and make sense of their lives. For Jung, understanding one's personal myth, "the myth in which you live," was a core task in life.[4] Looking back as adults to

discover and understand the myths and stories upon which we have
built our lives is an invaluable tool for deepening self-awareness and
understanding not just of oneself but of others. Especially important
is understanding how our stories have changed over time and are
continuing to change. Programs for adults featuring life story writing
(often called memoir writing) have become immensely popular. But
too often these programs focus on producing a chronological and linear
record of one's life rather than identifying the threads and themes that
have contributed to the direction one's life has taken and the
possibilities that still exist in a new story yet to emerge. Notable among
the exceptions to this are the Birren Center's approach to guided
autobiography and programs using maieutics (such as those developed
by the Educational Center in Charlotte, North Carolina) to help adults
find elements of their personal story in the stories of others, including
sacred texts, mythology, novels, short stories, poetry, and film.

Jungian-based educational programs for adults addressing story
making and storytelling would bring a deep and rich perspective to
this popular field. They would provide opportunities for adults to
reframe and rework their personal myths so they can understand that,
as James Hollis writes, we are not what has happened to us but what
we choose to become.[5] Such programs could be of value in various adult
services settings, especially senior living, assisted living, continuing care,
and other venues where gerontologists, social workers, life enrichment
directors, program specialists, and other professionals work directly
with aging adults.

Using Creativity To Promote Self-Discovery and Potential

As Corbett writes in chapter 2, Jung believed creativity to be one
of the most powerful of human instincts, and he predicted that the
person who does not build will demolish and destroy. Increasingly,
creativity is being used to help older adults achieve a renewed sense of
usefulness and self-esteem and reestablish and/or strengthen their
connectedness to friends and community. Gay Hanna, in chapter 8,
discusses how creativity becomes the vehicle for facilitating inner
awareness and reawakening human potential in the second half of life.
Citing psychiatrist Gene Cohen, she notes that creativity helps us use
our life experiences to invent new ways of living, enabling us to continue
to be generative and contribute to society.

Jung developed methods and techniques—notably active imagination and dream work—to help his clients use the power of their creativity to explore and bring to life their unused potential and live in ways that validated their existence. He also believed that we could unlock our creative powers by revisiting and reworking the traumas we experience in life. Cohen describes creativity as an innate capacity for growth. "It enables us to view life as an opportunity for exploration, discovery, and an expanding sense of self." And, Cohen adds, "it knows no age."[6] He and others also have addressed the strong links between creativity and positive health indicators such as fewer doctor visits, fewer falls, and a more positive outlook on life.[7] In chapter 8, Hanna cites a growing body of research suggesting that helping older adults connect with and give voice to their creativity is a valuable tool for preventing isolation and loneliness among older adults and the depression, late-onset substance abuse (including prescription drug abuse), and suicide that often results from isolation and loneliness.

A growing number of artists, artistic groups, and organizations are engaged in the use of the expressive arts with adults as part of the creative aging movement. More recently, some Jungian analysts and Jungian-oriented psychotherapists are working with older adults in nonclinical settings using tissue paper collage, scribble drawing, sand trays, work with clay, music, and guided imagery to facilitate self-discovery and unlock potential. As noted above, Geller cites the example of the use of the expressive arts with residents of a nursing home to provide a "safe" place in which they could explore their feelings about being in a nursing home and could freely and without criticism engage in exercises that helped them tap into their sense of usefulness, creativity, and self-esteem.

Gerontologists, social workers, and others in the field of aging should consider reaching out to and bringing together aging services professionals with the Jungian community and the creative aging movement in order to deepen their work and bring it to new audiences in retirement communities, assisted-living communities, neighborhood-based aging in place communities, senior centers, public libraries, churches, and other venues. The National Center for Creative Aging (NCCA, of which Gay Hanna is executive director) serves as an organizing and funding resource for the growing creative aging movement and is always looking for ways to strengthen its resources and expand its reach. Closer ties between the Jungian community, the creative aging movement, and the field of aging would help achieve this goal. The NCCA's website includes a searchable Directory of Creative Aging Programs featuring arts programs serving older adults. The database is designed to help artists and arts organizations find partners. The directory can be accessed at www.creativeaging.org/programs-people/cad.

Aging, Spirituality, and Health

Another area to which Jungian-based ideas and programs could make an invaluable contribution is aging and spirituality, a subject that has become immensely popular among adults. Jungian psychology stands alone in valuing the role of spirituality not just in the aging process but in life itself. As Jerome Bernstein writes, Jung's psychology remains the only one that unqualifiedly embraces transpersonal experience and spirituality as an integral part of normal human experience and an essential consideration in clinical practice.[8]

Over the past two decades, numerous churches and faith-based organizations have been offering workshops and discussion groups focused on issues relating to aging and spirituality, typically within the context of traditional belief systems. What is missing to a large extent is the opportunity for older adults outside of traditional belief systems to cultivate a spiritual practice that is relevant to their specific needs and circumstances. Jungian-based ideas about the importance of spirituality in the health of society and individuals and its key role in later-life growth and development would provide an invaluable resource for the large (and growing) number of adults who are seeking a personal spiritual grounding that can help them navigate the aging process. This is a key area in which gerontologists, social workers, and others working with older adults could link with the Jungian community to strengthen their work with clients.

Heightened awareness of the important ways in which spiritual beliefs come into play in health and medical care settings is also an area where gerontologists, social workers, and health-care professionals could come together with the Jungian community to benefit both older adults and the delivery of health and medical care. This is becoming an especially critical issue given the aging of the population and the subsequent dramatic increase in older adults who are being treated in the health-care delivery system, especially hospitals. Our spiritual beliefs impact how we cope with an illness or disability and influence our decisions about treatments and options. They are also the wellsprings for the development of personal creativity and the redefinition of meaning in the second half of life that have been shown to enhance health and longevity.

Local hospitals and the medical community would be prime venues for programs addressing this dynamic, including how the ability to find meaning in illness and suffering among older adults impacts their health-care choices and their ability to cope. Several hospitals have affiliated centers that address spirituality (the Institute for Spirituality and Health at the Texas Medical Center in Houston is one example). A growing number of hospitals include spirituality in their support and wellness programs for patients, caregivers, and medical staff, thanks in many cases to work being done by the George Washington Institute for Spirituality and Health (GWISH) in Washington, D.C., to integrate spirituality into the delivery of health-care services (www.gwumc.edu/gwish/index.cfm). Bringing a Jungian perspective to these programs would deepen these and other efforts and make spirituality an integral part of patient care.

Finding Meaning in Illness, Suffering, and Death

One area in which the inclusion of Jungian-based ideas could make an especially important contribution is helping adults find meaning in their aging-related illnesses, losses, and suffering. Jungian psychology stands apart from other psychological systems in that it addresses the *why* of living and not just the *how*, which is the sole focus of most other psychological systems. This is important because, as Nietzsche observed, "He who has a why to live for can bear with almost any how."[9]

Corbett points out that each transition during the second half of life becomes a rite of passage, during which we enter a liminal stage wherein we lose our sense of who we are and where we are going, a "betwixt and between" period before we are "reintegrated" into our new role and status. This is an archetypal process, Corbett suggests, because it is a transpersonal process and critical to the development of psychological and emotional maturity. Helping adults discover and work with the meaning to be found in these liminal periods will enhance their ability to reframe the various crises that arise during the aging process as important changes in their sense of self and assumptions about life and not as something that reflects the collapse of their essential self, so that they can work toward new and deeper levels of awareness and maturity.

Corbett also reminds us that Jung saw death as an essential part of life and encouraged us to envision death not as a meaningless cessation but as a goal and a fulfillment of life's meaning. Yet society for the most part still views death as the enemy rather than as a companion accompanying us to the completion of our life. Ira Byock, M.D., a palliative care physician and advocate for greater societal acceptance of death as a natural part of life, observes that most people still have a cultural aversion to talking about mortality and acknowledging the fact of their own mortality. The result, Byock suggests, is a lack of preparation for dying and death resulting in unnecessary psychological as well as physical suffering, anxiety, and burden. He calls it "the sorry state of dying in America."[10] He identifies certain "developmental landmarks" and "task work" that, he says, can provide a pathway for this journey and open opportunities for growth right up to the time of death, including an enhanced sense of meaning and connectedness and a sense of contact with the transcendent.[11] Addressing such landmarks and task work has always been a core focus for Jungian psychology.

Elizabeth Cook and Tina Picchi write about the role of palliative care in preparing individuals to participate consciously in their final journey home. Living consciously into one's death helps the dying individual, as well as his or her loved ones, family, and friends, bring completion to his or her relationships. They note that Jung believed that psychological health, with which physical and spiritual well-being are interwoven, is contingent upon a conscious relationship with and preparation for death.[12]

Programs using Jungian-based ideas about illness and suffering would bring this unique perspective to the work being done by hospitals, medical groups, cancer centers, hospices, wellness centers, visiting nurses associations, disease-specific support groups, and support groups and other resources for caregivers and volunteers. Programs could be designed jointly by gerontologists, social workers, health-care professionals, and the Jungian community not just for patients, their loved ones, and their caregivers but also for the physicians, nurses, health and social service professionals, and lay people (especially volunteers) who are working with adults who are ill, disabled, or dying. One largely overlooked audience for such programs is the Veterans Administration health-care system, which is now paying close attention to ensuring that the psychosocial needs of its patients, their family members and loved ones, and their caregivers are being identified and addressed.

Conclusion

Admittedly not all adults are able or willing to engage in the kind of psychological and spiritual work typically sponsored by Jungian institutes, centers, societies, and Friends of Jung groups. And many Jungian organizations lack sufficient resources to become actively engaged in an effort to bring Jungian-based programs and ideas into the field of aging. But some have found that when offered as nonclinical education programs, and when widely advertised as opportunities for personal discovery and growth, their public programs attract a large number of adults and aging services professionals. A growing number are looking at the aging of the population and asking how they might become involved in helping to meet the needs of this expanding group of citizens.

I encourage aging services professionals and others working with older adults to think about how they might integrate Jungian-based ideas into their work and then approach the Jungian community to discuss their ideas for achieving this integration. At the same time, I would encourage the Jungian community to become proactively involved in this effort, since it carries multiple benefits.

For the field of aging, the benefits are the inclusion of new, more holistic, and more positive approaches to aging and a rounding out of the whole-person model. For the Jungian community, the benefits include helping society address a critical need and build strong communities and, in doing so, attract a new audience with new ideas, energy, and resources.

For aging adults, the benefits would be significant. Including Jungian-based ideas and approaches in programs and services for the aging would help them reap the benefits of deeper relatedness, creativity, and a sense of meaning that would carry them forward on

their journey. It would open new doors for discovering a "why" to live
and from that a more resilient "how" to live. It would help foster an
openness to and acceptance of the mysteries of life, what Jung called
the unexpected and incredible, the inexplicable mysteries that,
while often perplexing and discomforting, can become a source of
illumination, discovery, and enchantment.[13] And it would make
possible the envisioning and acceptance of death as a journey to
one's final home, the one Jungian analyst John Hill describes as "a
home that outlasts our short life here on earth." Helping someone
view his or her life as an epic journey toward the natural fulfillment
of life's meaning rather than its cessation, Hill writes, can be one of
the greatest gifts we can impart.[14]

NOTES

[1] U.S. Department of Commerce, Bureau of the Census, *The
Next Four Decades: The Older Population in the United States: 2010
to 2050*. Online report, May 2010. Accessed March 2013 at http://
www.census.gov/prod/2010pubs/p25-1138.pdf.

[2] Sondra Geller, "Sparking the Creative in Older Adults,"
Psychological Perspectives 56, no. 2 (July 2013): 200–211.

[3] W. Ruch, R. T. Proyer, and M. Webster, "Humor as a Character
Strength among the Elderly," *Zeitschrift fur Gerontolgie und Geriatrie*
43 (February 2010): 8–12.

[4] C. G. Jung, *Memories, Dreams, Reflections* (New York: Pantheon
Books, 1973), p. 172.

[5] James Hollis, *The Middle Passage: From Misery to Meaning in
Midlife* (Toronto: Inner City Books, 1993), p. 97.

[6] Gene Cohen, *The Mature Mind: The Positive Power of the Aging
Brain* (New York: Basic Books, 2006).

[7] National Endowment for the Humanities, *Framing a National
Research Agenda for the Arts, Lifelong Learning and Individual Well-Being*
(Washington, D.C.: Author, November 2011).

[8] Jerome Bernstein, *Living in the Borderland* (New York: Routledge,
2005), p. 123.

[9] Quoted in Viktor E. Frankl, *Man's Search for Meaning* (Boston:
Beacon Press, 2006), p. 76.

[10] Ira Byock, *The Best Care Possible* (New York: Penguin Group, 2012).

[11] Ira Byock, *Dying Well: Peace and Possibilities at the End of Life* (New York: Berkley Publishing Group, 1997).

[12] Elizabeth Cook and Tina Picchi, "The Temenos of Palliative Care," *Psychological Perspectives* 56, no. 2 (July 2013): 212–220.

[13] Jung, *Memories, Dreams Reflections*, p. 356.

[14] John Hill, *At Home in the World* (New Orleans: Spring Journal Inc., 2010), p. 37.

~ CHAPTER SEVEN ~

The Whole-Person Services Model and the Second Half of Life

KELLEY MACMILLAN, M.S.W., PH.D.

I attended a winter solstice celebration in 2012 that was rich in metaphor and symbolism for me. During the celebration, several stones were passed around and we were instructed to select a stone that held energy and spoke to us. As I scrutinized the stone I had selected, I became aware of the imperfections in the rock surface despite its many weathered years. There were creases and slight pockets on the surface of the rock because the elements of wind and water had not worn it into a smooth and polished gem. I was reminded of my own imperfections as I enter my sixty-second year.

Upon further reflection, I came to understand that the imperfections I perceived did not take away from the strength and beauty of either specimen. Looking ahead to a later stage in life is an unknown, however, and I wondered how I might change and adapt. Would my creases and pockets become liabilities or assets? Whatever the outcome, would I embrace a notion of myself as aging well? Like the stone, how will my internal character and strength hold out, and will my exterior, visible to others who might be my helpers later in life, reflect beauty? More important, will those helpers embrace my personal interpretation of aging well?

As a society, we are returning to a more holistic and positive view of aging, a view that is still held in some cultures and that was once held by most Americans. Our challenge is to view aging as something other than a decline toward death. We all have seen allegorical images of the infant and youth ascending a staircase, reaching the zenith of middle age, and then descending downhill from there to death (figure 1). Ultimately, we don't escape death; yet what I am suggesting is that the staircase depiction is a powerful metaphor that old age—beginning with middle age—equates with death. So how can depicting the stages of life in a different manner reduce the stigma of old age?

Figure 1. *Trap des Ouderdoms* (*The Life Cycle of Man and Woman*), an engraving by Jan Houwens (Rotterdam, seventeenth century). (Atlas Van Stolk, Rotterdam)

First, we can return to older cyclic models of aging that were imbued with spiritual elements. For example, in medieval times, life was depicted as a wheel with a spoke from each stage of life pointing to a hub containing a spiritual image at the center (figure 2). Another example is Thomas Cole's *The Voyage of Life* at the National Gallery of Art in Washington, D.C., which illustrates birth to death in four scenes, yet in a natural, pastoral context that illustrates the changes in life not as a descent but rather as transitions from one stage to the next.

Figure 2. Christ-centered wheel of life, from a Psalter (1339) belonging to Robert de Lisle of Yorkshire. (MS Arundel 83, fol. 126v, British Library, London)

Second, theories about aging well suggest a new paradigm, one that views the process of aging in a broader context and incorporates the physical aspects of aging while adding a focus on the strengths of older adults in physical, psychosocial, and spiritual domains. Research on aging well has focused on the physical and psychological qualities and factors that predict whether individuals will age successfully.[1]

This research has been instrumental in repositioning social theories of aging from a stance of disengagement and decline to a stance that integrates the positive and negative aspects of aging and provides a more balanced view of aging.

We know from demographic data trends that baby boomers may spend as much time in retirement as they did in their work career. The opportunity exists to depict this stage of life as a fulfilling and purposeful stage. This is evident in books and retreats designed to help older adults identify and honor their elder energy. And it is possible for the physical health and well-being of older adults to be better than it was for previous generations because of improvements in health-care delivery systems and health insurance coverage. This is important because as people age, there is an increased likelihood that they will need acute and long-term care, rehabilitation services, and other kinds of support. It is beyond the scope of this chapter to identify all of the factors that are positively influencing geriatric care of older adults. Instead, I will focus on *aging well theory* because it normalizes aging and challenges a historical medical view of aging as a stage of life beset with disease and decline. Aging well theory emphasizes the resilience of older adults and their interest and capacity for actively engaging in meaningful activities, community service, and the pursuit of spiritual and creative interests.

Current theories of aging, specifically successful aging, provide geriatric professionals with a viewpoint that older adults can age well. An aging well paradigm has replaced a view of older adults as dependent and needy and also suggests the need for geriatric professionals to develop effective and innovative practice interventions *with* older adults to enhance their health and psychosocial and spiritual well-being. The development of social theory about aging well has emphasized the role of older adults as a key participant in the process and that the process draws on their life experiences, competencies, and values. For instance, criteria for aging well include quality of life goals defined by the older adult, and they consist of affective states, meaning in life, and maintenance of valued activities and relationships.[2]

Selective Optimization with Compensation

Psychologists Margaret and Paul Baltes have developed a social theory of aging in which selective optimization with compensation (SOC) serves as a meta-theory of human development that is based on a stress model of coping and adaptation.[3] Examples of the SOC process consist of psychological and behavioral coping strategies older adults use when adapting to limits as a result of aging. This model proposes that older adults proactively contribute to their own successful aging by using the strategies of selection, optimization, and compensation.

In addition to including older adults' perspectives, SOC theory acknowledges the capacities of older adults to identify and utilize coping and adaptation behaviors in response to illness, chronic health conditions, and functional disability. Aging well is a process in which older adults adapt both themselves and their environment to compensate for losses due to age, disability, and disease when responding proactively to the challenges of aging. We refer to this as resilience, a theme throughout this book. Specifically, older adults select and focus their effort in areas of high priority, such as walking, and on the maintenance of these high-priority functions as physical and cognitive reserves decrease. Optimization is the continual engagement in behaviors that augment and enrich their physical and mental reserves, especially those selected as high-priority behaviors. Optimization might include exercising to maintain physical strength and endurance or engaging in mental activities to enhance cognitive functioning. Finally, the individual compensates by utilizing psychological and technical strategies. The way eighty-year-old Arthur Rubinstein managed to maintain his excellent piano playing provides an illustration of SOC theory in practice. He played fewer piano pieces (selection), practiced these pieces more often (optimization), and to address his loss of speed he played slow passages more slowly before faster passages in order to make the latter seem faster (compensation).[4]

Selective optimization with compensation has several advantages as a framework for understanding the process of aging for older adults. First, SOC is a life-span development theory that can be applied to all age groups and provides a general understanding of life-span development and growth from birth to old age. A life-span development perspective frames aging as a normal development process with positive and negative aspects instead of only focusing on the negative aspects of aging. Second, SOC is a way to describe the resilience of older adults in response to the physical and cognitive challenges due to aging. Third, at the heart of SOC is a person-centered perspective that views older adults as taking an active role in their life course. This perspective of older adults as self-empowered recognizes their resilience, capacity, and motivation. Meaningful engagement in the life of an older adult is the heart of the person-centered approach.

The Person-Centered Approach Is Central to Understanding Older Adults Values and Preferences

The person-centered approach articulated in aging well theory is also being emphasized at the practitioner level by those working in the fields of health, aging, disability, and long-term services and supports (LTSS).[5] The Institute of Medicine (IOM) report *Crossing the Quality Chasm* specifically includes a person-centered approach as one of several recommendations for improving the health-care system.[6] The components of a person-centered approach include:

1. Respect for patient's values, preferences, and expressed needs
2. Coordination and integration of care
3. Information, communication, and education
4. Physical comfort
5. Emotional support and alleviation of fear and anxiety
6. Involvement of family and friends
7. Transition and continuity

These person-centered components warrant discussion to illustrate how they can contribute to a whole-person approach in the second half of life.

Over the past twenty-five years Margaret Gerteis and her colleagues at the Picker/Commonwealth Program for Patient-Centered Care have studied and written about the needs and concerns of patients and families. Their focus was on hospital care in the United States, but they have pointed out that a person-centered approach also can be applied to primary care and other health and social service settings.[7]

Today federal, state, and local programs providing long-term services and supports to children and those with intellectual, physical, emotional or mental, and chronic disabilities are adopting a person-centered approach. What will be evident in this following discussion is the interrelationship between the components of person-centered care and aspects of the Jungian perspective that emphasize creativity and vitality as precursors to improved psychological and physical health.

Respect for Patient's Values, Preferences, and Expressed Needs

One day I ran into the medical director of the specialty hospital where I worked. I asked him how his day was going, and he responded by saying that he was frustrated. The patient he had been treating in the hospital for several weeks was not responding to his treatment goals. I asked my colleague whether he knew what the patient's goals were, and he replied that he did not. Later that day when I saw him again, he reported that he and the patient had had a conversation. The patient told him what her goals for her recovery were, and he discussed his goals. Between them they came to a mutual agreement about their goals, which he believed were achievable.

It is accurate to say that historically medical treatment was "done to" patients; they were the recipients of medical treatment. This approach positioned the medical team as experts who know what is best for the patient. It ignores the patient's input and perspective. It is true that the medical team has expertise that is valuable in the care of patients. Yet medical and treatment expertise should be combined with knowledge of the patient's values, preferences, and expressed needs when developing a plan of care. This involvement of the patient in treatment is central to a person-centered approach.

In the field of long-term services and supports, a similar view of older adults has been the historical precedent. Older adults were viewed as being dependent and at a stage of life where care needed to be provided to them. This was reinforced in residential long-term-care settings, which were often large and built around an efficiency model of care. In such settings, all the residents are awakened at the same time, share all their meals at the same time in a large dining room, and are bathed in communal bath areas. Now, in some settings, this paradigm has given way to the principles behind the Green House Project model, wherein a more homelike atmosphere is central to the structure and the care provided.[8]

The person-centered approach is a priority for the Administration for Community Living (ACL), a unit within the Department of Health and Human Services that funds aging and disability resource centers (ADRCs) for older adults and individuals with disabilities. ACL-funded centers use a person-centered approach when working with individuals to identify the LTSS needed to help them maintain their independence in the community and to ensure that services are consistent with their preferences, values, and expressed needs.[9]

Coordination and Integration of Care

The issue of care coordination and integration of care has been moved to the forefront with the passage of the Patient Protection and Affordable Care Act of 2010. The focus on coordination and integration of care is already changing how care is provided by primary care physicians and their staff and by hospitals when they discharge patients at risk of readmission. In addition, integration of care now includes the integration of behavioral health (mental health and substance abuse services) with treatment of those with chronic health problems.

Coordination and integration of care is also being promoted as one of seven components of the patient centered medical home (PCMH) model of primary care. PCMH is a concept that emerged in the field of pediatrics in the 1960s, and it emphasized the central location of medical records for children with complex and chronic health conditions receiving medical care from a cadre of specialists. The PCMH concept eventually developed into a primary care model that emphasized coordination of care within and external to the primary care practice, including but not limited to other physicians, hospitals, nursing homes, and home health agencies.

To be sure, the primary care physician is not working alone in the office; a team model of primary care is necessary for coordination, integration, and treatment. Physician assistants, nurse practitioners, social workers, nutritionists, and, in some settings, behavioral health professionals are a few of the primary care team members involved. Each primary care office organizes its functions and teamwork to suit the needs of its patients, building on the strengths of the primary care team. The integration and coordination of primary care has greater relevance because the delivery of inpatient care has also evolved. The IOM recommendation focusing on calling for care coordination and integration is critical because the health-care delivery and LTSS systems are complex and often fragmented. One of the benefits is that the primary care team provides patient-centered, whole-person care in one setting; in addition to medical care, the patient also may receive mental health services, patient education about medications, nutrition counseling, and chronic disease management. These co-located practitioners can be available to offer services without the need for the patient to make additional appointments; and the model enhances the opportunity for team-based care. The patient also benefits from this model following hospital discharge.

Hospitals now employ medical specialists known as hospitalists and intensivists to care for hospitalized patients. As a result, the primary care physician may not attend his or her patient in the hospital and therefore may be unaware of the admission and care trajectory. In addition, patients may require follow-up appointments with other specialists, rehabilitation stays in skilled nursing facilities, and/or home health services after being discharged. Although patients receive excellent care in these settings, they benefit when the primary care physician coordinates and integrates all facets of the care across the settings. Benefits include receiving accurate and timely information from the discharging hospital, rehabilitation center, and/or any medical specialists who treat the patient. To assist the patient with the transition back to the community, care transition teams, made up of nurses, social workers, and pharmacists are being employed by hospitals; they monitor the patient for thirty to forty-five days after the discharge. The care transition team schedules primary care appointments for follow-up within seven to ten days and transmits information regarding the hospital course to the primary care team. Prior to discharge, the care transition team assesses for reconciliation with the discharge medication orders, provides medication education (and medications as needed), and addresses any psychosocial and economic issues that might hamper the patient's ability to follow the care plan following discharge.

After discharge, the care transition team provides patient education regarding nutrition and disease management, monitors medication adherence, makes referrals for community-based LTSS, and follows up with these referrals. In addition to the benefit of care coordination, the efforts of the care transition team can reduce the potential of readmission because the team is monitoring the patient closely along with the primary care team in the clinic. In all situations and no matter how the care is coordinated and integrated, the purpose is to ensure that patients have care plans that they understand, that barriers to following the care plans have been identified, and that they have access to health-care professionals whom they can contact twenty-four hours a day when problems or questions arise. The patient may also have a personal health record developed by the team to take to their physician appointments. The patient can record symptoms and questions for discussion with the physician as well as provide the physician with a summary of medications and current treatments. In addition, coordination and integration of care is also dependent upon information, communication, and education. An ultimate benefit for the patients is a timely recovery so that they can resume their purposeful and gratifying life activities.

Information, Communication, and Education

Information, communication, and education can occur in numerous settings and, depending upon the delivery, can provide patients with a degree of control and responsibility for their own health. Electronic health records and information technology plays an increasingly larger role in sharing information and aiding communication between providers and with the patient, as well as enhancing patient education. Since care coordination and integration rely on information, communication, and education for and about the patient, it must include the patient. In addition, patients experience greater benefits when they learn about their diseases and how to self-manage them through education provided by the medical team in the primary care office, as well as from hospital-based care transition team members. Several information, communication, and education strategies are discussed below.

The Affordable Care Act emphasizes the need for development of electronic health records (EHRs) so that health information can be transmitted in a timely and efficient manner between points of care, such as from the hospital to the primary care office, and from the primary care office to the home health agency. The information transfer improves the transition of care from one setting to the other so that treatment is not interrupted and there are no gaps in care. For example, the Veterans Health Care system uses EHRs so that the medical records of veterans are available to all VA hospitals in the United States. In Maryland, hospitals, laboratories, physicians practices, radiology centers, and other health institutions participate in a private, secure, and statewide health information exchange. This newly emerging health information exchange creates the infrastructure for participating health institutions and services to upload and download patient health information in a timely manner.

Communication in the form of teamwork is another area in which innovative practices are being implemented. The growth of interprofessional teamwork is taking root in professional education, frequently although not limited to universities with professional schools (medicine, nursing, social work, and pharmacy) and at the practice level in hospitals, primary care clinics, long-term services and supports, and in mental health settings. A key component of interprofessional practice is the team assessment and intervention, which is distinguished from an interdisciplinary assessment and intervention. The interprofessional assessment involves a shared and coordinated treatment plan, and leadership of the team is not hierarchical. Interprofessional teamwork is a collaborative approach to assessment and intervention that also includes the patient, family, and community providers as team members.[10] Including the patient and family builds on the person-centered approach, which emphasizes patient goals, preferences, and values in addition to improving communication and, at times, patient education.

Patient education is another of area of growth because of the implementation of chronic disease self-management programs (CDSMPs). Self-management of chronic disease by the patient builds on the belief that the patient can and should take an active role in his or her health and well-being. Health education has traditionally been provided in health-care settings; however, the CDSMP provides education and support over a longer period of time, for example, weekly sessions over six weeks in a community setting. The extended education model provides opportunities for reinforcement of key health-related self-management behaviors, the support of CDSMP staff, and a venue for questions to be asked by patients as they implement new behaviors and integrate new health knowledge. Improved health status and management of chronic disease enables older adults to engage in valued activities and interests.

Physical Comfort

Physical comfort is a standard and essential component of health care. An equally important requirement for providing comfort care is understanding from the patient's perspective "what hurts and where does it hurt." Suffering and discomfort are individual, and there is interplay between physical, psychological, emotional, and spiritual pain and suffering. Although not a new technology, and now a routine method for dispensing medication, intravenous infusion pumps allow patients to control the delivery of narcotic pain medication with the press of a button. This method is used for postoperative patients and for individuals who experience chronic pain. The infusion pump is programmed to provide a set amount of medication and prevent an overdose of medication. This method of self-administering pain medication postoperatively can lead to reductions in medication doses and length of medication use. Other benefits are an increase in patients' self-efficacy because they are managing their pain themselves and the reduction of psychological stress associated with the anticipation of pain. Overall, this can help to dispel older adults' experience of pain and suffering as an expected and unmanageable condition of aging.

Another area where physical comfort has gained greater presence is palliative care. To be sure, palliative care for psychosocial and spiritual issues is also important and necessary. A benchmark of hospice care is physical comfort at the end of life, and palliative care is one way that is achieved. But palliative care is not restricted to persons at the end of life. Any number of medical and chronic conditions involve human suffering, and palliative care teams consult with the patient and health-care team to identify and prescribe treatments to reduce physical as well as psychosocial and spiritual suffering.

Emotional Support—Relieving Fear and Anxiety

Fear and anxiety are natural experiences when people are hospitalized, undergoing diagnostic workups, and being treated by a physician. They also come into play when people are living with chronic conditions that require home- or institutional-based care. Fear and anxiety can be related to the clinical treatment and prognosis, the impact of the condition on the person and the family, and the financial impact of the condition. Everyone regardless of age needs emotional support when they experience a health crisis or are living with a chronic condition. For those in the second half of life, a health crisis or chronic condition brings home the fact that life is finite and that one's independence and autonomy may be compromised. Yet older adults often possess spiritual and psychological resources that can help offset the fear and anxiety associated with the aging process. For some older adults, these spiritual and psychological energies may inspire creativity, as was the case for Elizabeth Layton, who began her drawing career at the age of sixty-eight.

All health and social service professionals play an important role in the provision of emotional support when treating a patient. In addition, the professionals—pastoral counselors, social workers, psychologists—whose primary role is to provide emotional support can also educate, train, and mentor their colleagues regarding supportive approaches with the patient and family. Attention must also be focused on cultural and ethnic differences regarding how illness, disability, and mortality are viewed as well as how to best provide emotional support. Respecting a person's values, preferences, and expressed needs is central to the individual's cultural and ethnic identity and go hand in hand with and are a critical component of providing emotional support.

Involvement of Family and Friends

This element of the person-centered approach recognizes the important role family and friends play in decision making, providing both care and emotional support. Health care and long-term service and support systems professionals must balance a patient's right to privacy and privileged communication with the needs of family and friends who are participating in the patient's care. While the ethical and legal considerations inherent in this issue are beyond the scope of this chapter, professionals must be aware and mindful of them.

The greater risk when the health professional involves family and friends is the degree to which the patient's values, preferences, and expressed needs are ignored or given less weight. This situation often occurs with older adults when the health-care team talks almost exclusively to family members in the presence of the patient or has conversations with family members about the patient's care and treatment without the patient being present. This often occurs when family and/or health professionals believe that the patient will be upset by the content of the conversation or when a patient's cognition is compromised and he or she would not comprehend the content of the conversation.

In the case where the person has some short-term or long-term memory deficits, the family and the health team should not assume that the patient lacks the ability to comprehend the impact of decisions that will change the course of his or her life drastically. Individuals may not recall what they had for breakfast, but they have core beliefs and knowledge about how they want to live their life. Decisions about being placed on life support or entering a nursing home, whether on a short-term or permanent basis, will be grounded in a patient's view of himself or herself and his or her values and preferences. Granted, the intention to not involve the person is well meaning. But adults are entitled to know their health status, prognosis, and the recommended treatment interventions. The involvement of social workers, pastoral counselors, and other support staff is valuable during and after such conversations.

The involvement of family and friends can be valuable when the person has health, long-term care, and personal care decisions to make related to treatment, rehabilitation, and changes in living situations. There are differences in the amount of control over decisions the person wants to maintain, share, or relinquish and the impact on overall satisfaction with decisions. For instance, some older adults report resentment when not involved in decisions regarding discharge plans and rehabilitation care, even after they have returned home.[11] The health-care team, using a person-centered approach, interviews the person and learns what the person wants through active listening to avoid making assumptions or imposing unhelpful interventions. Finally, family and friends are sometimes in a good position to provide emotional support because they have more intimate knowledge of the person. This familiarity can provide support during uncertain and trying times. There are times when the person may want family or friends to provide some aspects of care because they are not strangers and are viewed as trustworthy.

The person-centered components described in this chapter are focused on older adults when they are accessing health and long-term service and support delivery systems because of an acute, chronic or disabling condition that negatively impacts their health and personal life. This shift to a person-centered approach will occur once we have trained health and social service personnel to see older adults as the psychosocial and spiritual beings that they are. The good news is that students in the health and social service professions are being trained in person-centered approaches now, so we can expect to see a greater integration of person-centered practice in health and social service settings. At the same time, current practitioners are also receiving training in person-centered approaches, and primary care practices and social service agencies are integrating a person-centered approach into their models of care.

Aging Well

While any or all of these services are necessary when the need arises, it is important to emphasize the fact that a whole-person model includes numerous additional services, behaviors, attitudes, and pursuits during the second half of life. For instance, older adults may also want to pursue integrative health behavior, incorporating alternative treatments such as acupuncture, tai chi, energy medicine, or herbal medicine, to name a few, into their traditional medical model of care. There was a time not too long ago when the Western-trained health-care providers never took these health behaviors seriously. Today, they are considered complementary and may even be provided within the traditional primary care clinic.[12]

Exercise, nutrition, yoga, spiritual retreats, and meditation are lifelong disciplines that are essential for healthy aging and quality life in old age. In fact, when these behaviors are a routine part of a person's life, regardless of age, there is an increased likelihood of healthy aging and less likelihood of functional impairment in everyday life and living. Ultimately, in a global society, a holistic view of aging recognizes that the second half of life is a period of growth, exploration, creative expression, and engagement with life. And while it is true that poor physical and mental health can interfere with an older adult's ability to age well, bringing the whole-person services model to the delivery of health care and social service can make a positive difference in quality of life for older adults in the second half of life. It is the partnering of health-care providers with older adults that enhances the positive outcomes for older adults and, ultimately, contributes to their ability to age well. Now is the time to push this whole-person services model forward.

NOTES

[1] Margaret M. Baltes and Laura L. Carstensen, "The Process of Successful Aging," *Ageing and Society* 16 (1996): 397–422; Paul B. Baltes and Margaret M. Baltes, "Psychological Perspectives on Successful Aging: The Model of Selective Optimization with Compensation," *Successful Aging: Perspectives from the Behavioral Sciences,* ed. Paul B. Baltes and Margaret M. Baltes (Cambridge, England: Cambridge University Press, 1990), pp. 1–34; Robert Havighurst, "Successful Aging," *The Gerontologist* 1, no. 1 (1961): 8–13; Eva Kahana and Boaz Kahana, "Conceptual and Empirical Advances in Understanding Aging Well through Proactive Adaptation," *Adulthood and Aging: Research on Continuities and Discontinuities,* ed. Vern L. Bengtson (New York: Springer, 1996), pp. 18–40; John W. Rowe and Robert L. Kahn, *Successful Aging* (New York: Random House, 1998); and Carol D. Ryff, "Successful Aging: A Developmental Approach," *The Gerontologist* 22, no. 2 (1982): 209–214.

[2] See also Paul B. Baltes, "On the Incomplete Architecture of Human Ontogeny: Selection, Optimization, and Compensation as Foundation of Developmental Theory," *American Psychologist* 52, no. 4 (1997): 366–380; Eva Kahana and Boaz Kahana, "Evaluating a Model of Successful Aging for Urban African American and White Elderly," *Serving Minority Elders in the 21ˢᵗ Century,* ed. May L. Wykle and Amasa B. Ford (New York: Springer, 1999), pp. 287–322; George E. Vaillant, *Aging Well* (Boston: Little, Brown, 2002); and Gail M. Wagnild, "Resilience and Successful Aging," *Journal of Gerontological Nursing* 29, no. 12 (2003): 42–49.

[3] Baltes and Carstensen, "The Process of Successful Aging"; Baltes and Baltes, "Psychological Perspectives on Successful Aging"; Baltes, "On the Incomplete Architecture of Human Ontogeny"; David L. Featherman, Jacqui Smith, and James G. Peterson, "Successful Aging in a Post-Retired Society," *Successful Aging: Perspectives from the Behavioral Sciences*, ed. Paul B. Baltes and Margaret M. Baltes (Cambridge, England: Cambridge University Press, 1990), pp. 50–93; Jochen Brandstadter and Klaus Rothermund, "Self-Percepts of Control in Middle and Later Adulthood: Buffering Losses by Rescaling Goals," *Psychology and Aging* 9, no. 2 (1994): 265–273; Ryff, "Successful Aging"; Richard S. Lazarus and Susan Folkman, *Stress, Appraisal, and Coping* (New York: Springer, 1984); and David A. Chiriboga, "Comments on Conceptual and Empirical Advances in Understanding Aging Well through Proactive Adaptation," *Adulthood and Aging: Research on Continuities and Discontinuities*, ed. Vern L. Bengtson (New York: Springer, 1996), pp. 41–45.

[4] Baltes, "On the Incomplete Architecture of Human Ontogeny."

[5] The person-centered approach may also be referred to as the patient-centered approach; the phrase is context bound. For consistency, person-centered approach will be used here.

[6] Institute of Medicine, *Crossing the Quality Chasm: A New Health System of the 21st Century* (Washington, DC: National Academy Press, 2001).

[7] Margaret Gerteis, *Through the Patient's Eyes: Understanding and Promoting Patient-Centered Care* (San Francisco: Jossey-Bass, 1993).

[8] For more information, visit thegreenhouseproject.org.

[9] For information on aging and disability resource centers, visit www.acl.gov/Programs/Integrated_Programs/ADRCs/Index.aspx.

[10] E. Pecukonis, O. Doyle, and D. L. Bliss, "Reducing Barriers to Interprofessional Training: Promoting Interprofessional Cultural Competence," *Journal of Interprofessional Care* 22, no. 4 (2008): 417–428.

[11] Mitsuko Nakashima, et al., "Decision Making in Long-Term Care: Approaches Used by Older Adults and Implications for Social Work Practice," *Journal of Gerontological Social Work* 43, no. 4 (2004): 79–102.

[12] See, for example, the Northwestern Memorial Physicians Group's integrative medicine offering at www.nmpg.com/integrative-medicine.

CHAPTER EIGHT

The Central Role of Creativity in Aging

GAY POWELL HANNA, PH.D., M.F.A.

As one grows old, life and art become one and the same.
—Pablo Picasso

Introduction

From the point of view of an artist like Pablo Picasso, living is the vehicle for the making of art—in fact, longer life gives time for the creation of masterful art![1] More time to live gives more time to practice, to understand, and to gain insight, making one better able to create something new of value—and this is true not just for artists, but for everyone. This chapter will explore the creative process and its central role in aging vitally.

Whether the creation is an original Picasso, Jonas Salk's discovery of the polio vaccine, or a successful variation of one's favorite family recipe, it contributes to the individual's self-esteem and society's capacity to move forward.[2] C. G. Jung believed creativity to be one of the most important human instincts. As Corbett writes in the opening chapter of this book, Jung suggests that the person who does not build will demolish and destroy. Corbett further notes that creativity, like psychological and spiritual development, is independent of age but fertile ground for aging well (see chapter 2).

Creativity allows the relativizing of the ego that is so important in Jung's ideas about individuation. The ego participates in a larger reality through creative expression. The creative process demands surrender of oneself so that one can merge with the transpersonal dimension. There is an important connection between one's creativity and one's spirituality. For many people, creativity is a divine gift. It is certainly a process that makes one feel engaged and productive and enables one to learn new things.

The Creative Age

> While problems certainly accompany aging, what has been universally denied is the potential around aging. The ultimate expression of potential is creativity.
> —Gene Cohen, M.D.

Awakening the human potential in the second half of life, Gene Cohen insisted, is about being creative in using life experiences to invent new ways of living, enabling one to continue to be generative and to contribute to one's own life and the lives of those across generations. He described creativity as being "little c creativity" or "big C creativity."[3]

Big C creativity includes contributions to society at large that change its knowledge base and revise structures through discoveries. It includes major works of arts and scientific discoveries that enable society to move forward by, for example, overcoming diseases or social prejudices or developing new technology or belief systems. Big C creativity allows individuals and their communities to decrease suffering and enhances the freedom to live life by producing more time to pursue happiness. From the invention of the printing press to that of the data chip, creativity comes in all shapes and sizes, in which the human experience is amplified to reach new levels of consciousness.[4]

David Galenson, author of *Old Masters and Young Geniuses: The Two Life Cycles of Artistic Creativity*, describes two kinds of creative genius: the youthful burst of prodigies like Mozart and the slow and methodical work of a master like Beethoven. Galenson found that the majority of creations are produced later in life. Through living and experimenting, the artist or scientist gains insights and information that lead to major breakthrough or advances.[5] Charles Darwin, for instance, discovered the animal variations of the Galapagos Islands in his twenties. Yet it took him thirty more years to gain an understanding of these variations and develop the theory of evolution. Big C creativity often takes a lifetime of work to achieve its seminal discoveries, and this makes creativity in later life extremely important.

Little c creativity is accomplished by exploring and finding potential in new ways of carrying out the everyday activities of work and pleasure. New methods of gardening, cooking, and arts and crafts are often developed from family traditions or stimulated by community settings through social engagement. Many cultures hand down methods of creative expression that define their overall society based on customs related to family, faith, and work—such as the totems of the Northwest or the grass baskets of the South. Improvements in skills and individual interpretation result in new creations to be shared and treasured.

Little c creativity can become Big C creativity as the contributions shape the subsequent generations and inspire further exploration. For example, Mrs. Smith enjoyed growing apples late in life, and she happened upon a seed variation that produced the delicious Granny Smith apple that bears her name today and graces many a lunch box. Julia Child discovered French cooking when she was in her late thirties; her TV shows and famous cookbooks appeared when she was in her fifties—and she was writing books and appearing in television productions well into her nineties.

Creative expression compounds and amplifies itself, sparking increased self-knowledge and self-esteem. The potential of creative expression does not diminish with age but can be enhanced by it, through the exploration of personal preferences and environmental opportunities. Like Jung, Cohen describes later life as a time for self-reflection, evaluation, and liberation. The question, "If not now, when?" Cohen says is the impetus for trying something creative. He explains that age brings freedom—an older person asks, "What can anyone do to me in any case, if I try and fail?"[6]

There are three key entry points to the engagement in creative expression or activities. An older person can become engaged in creativity for the first time late in life. Alternatively, some older people become engaged in the arts as children or young adults, have to stop because of other demands on their time and energies, and then later in life begin again. Finally, there are older people who have been able to maintain creative pursuits all their lives.

The Beginning Participant

The person who begins to have a strong interest in creative expression in later life is, according to Corbett, accommodating a rebalancing, usually stemming from an internal revelation (p. 27). In fact, many folk artists and untrained artists (sometimes called "outsider artists") often begin making art late in life using their life skills to express a story or image that they feel compelled to share. In some cases, the older visual artist, for example, transfers skills learned in a job making functional objects to making transcendent ones. Older folk artists often feel driven to share their beliefs about their faith or love of the natural environment or to express the joy of making new things out of useful objects through art making.

The Returning Participant

The person who was once involved in creative activities (such as playing in a school band or singing in a chorus) but discontinued these pursuits as job and family commitments took priority often returns to them in later life. Both Corbett and Cohen describe this return as usually accompanied by a loss or a change in life status—perhaps retirement, the death of a spouse or other family member, or the person's own encounter with illness (p. 26).[7] For this older person, being involved in creativity in later life means returning to an activity that has brought joy and is now bringing comfort and a renewed sense of meaning and purpose.

The Lifelong Participant

The person who has been substantially involved in creative expression throughout his or her life may be a professional artist, a scientist, or some kind of innovator in their field. They found creativity early in life and have kept exploring its paths while obtaining substantial enough support to maintain creativity as a central aspect in their life's work. These individuals have been identified as role models for successful aging because they stay highly engaged in a larger reality where they do not lose their purpose or meaning. Retirement for them may not be an option in that they would not chose another way to live and are satisfied with their life choices.

Above Ground

> "How are you doing today?" the researcher asks.
> The 97-year-old artist responds, "Well, I'm above ground."
> —Joan Jeffri et al., "Above Ground: Information on Artists"

In the research study "Above Ground: Information on Artists III: Special Focus on New York City Aging Artists," Joan Jeffri writes, "Artists who have learned how to adapt their whole lives have a great deal to offer as a model for society, especially as the workforce changes to accommodate multiple careers and as the baby boomers enter the retirement generation."[8] This study interviewed 213 visual artists, 146 of them professionals between the ages of 62 and 97 in all five boroughs of New York City and across cultures, interviewing in English, Spanish, and Chinese. It found remarkable evidence that a life spent making art leads to satisfaction with oneself and one's career choice. Despite a low average income (approximately $30,000 annually) and discrimination because of age, gender, and sometimes an artist's discipline, these older people displayed remarkable resilience. They visited with their artist peers at least weekly and sold works continually. They found ways to adapt their art making when their physical abilities weakened. For instance, if a chosen medium (such as stone carving) became too difficult to continue, the artist might turn to ceramics as a less demanding way to create sculpture. To give up making art was not an option. When asked about retirement, the older visual artists responded that to retire from making art would be for them retiring from life itself.[9]

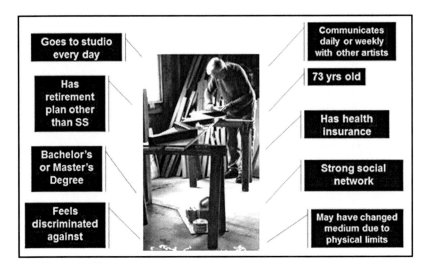

Figure 8.1: Profile of an older artist. Photo courtesy of the Research Center for Arts and Culture.

A Framework for Accessing Creative Potential in Later Life: Policy, Research, and Practice

In March 2011, the National Endowment for the Arts (NEA), in partnership with the U.S. Department of Health and Human Services, convened leaders from the public and private sectors to explore the relationship between the arts, health, and well-being. Rocco Landesman, the NEA chair at the time, opened the summit asking, "How do the arts help build us as a people and as individuals? We share a fundamental mission—how to improve the quality of life. The arts are central to human development."[10] Human development encompasses a complex web of factors affecting the health and well-being of individuals across the life span. Together, these factors yield cognitive and behavioral outcomes that can shape the social and economic circumstances of individuals, their levels of creativity and productivity, and their overall quality of life.[11]

This summit focused on three developmental areas: early childhood, youth, and older adulthood. The section "The Arts and Older Adults" made the case for arts participation because of its optimization of health outcomes through creative expression and cognitive enhancement, imagination and arts processes related to

Alzheimer's disease and neurocognitive disorders, and building community and strong social networks.[12] From the summit, an intergovernmental task force developed and produced a subsequent workshop by the National Academies on the arts and aging, "The Arts and Aging: Building the Science," convened in September 2012.

This workshop focused on research gaps and the opportunities for exploring the relationship of the arts to the health and well-being of older people. Presentations illustrated exciting possibilities for the therapeutic use of the arts as interventions to improve cognitive function and memory, general self-esteem and well-being, as well as to reduce stress and other common symptoms of Alzheimer's disease and other neurocognitive disorders (such as aggression, agitation, and apathy). Some interventions were found to promote psychosocial benefits as well. Interventions reviewed in the five papers presented at the workshop included music, theater, dance, and visual arts, with a strong focus on environmental design, especially the use of universal design to accommodate various physical and cognitive disabilities.[13]

Early studies are being replicated and expanded to further confirm findings that community arts program have a significant positive impact of the health and well-being of older people. A key study focusing on chorales and using a control group of equally active people with a mean age of eighty found that the health of choral group participants significantly improved during a three-year period. The key findings were that, compared to the control group, less medication was used, less depression was recorded, and greater social interaction occurred.[14] Based on these results, possible savings in Medicare expenditures in billions of dollars were projected. A national task force is continuing with the aim of encouraging further research and policy changes that could result in increased funding despite the dire economic environment in the governmental sector.

Creativity in Later Life for Health and Well-being, Lifelong Learning, and Community Engagement

From the grassroots activism of the 1970s, when Robert Butler wrote *Why Survive? Being Old in America*, to the macro governmental systems of the twenty-first century with an asset-based focus on the benefits of creativity in later life, accessibility to the arts and other creative opportunities are evolving into communities of practice.[15] Creativity supports increased health and well-being, lifelong learning, and community engagement. Professionals in arts education have unprecedented opportunities to grow the field through developing support services in lifelong learning, health and wellness, and community engagement. This final section of the paper identifies ways in which creative expression can positively and significantly impact older people, their families, and their communities. Each area of practice is not mutually exclusive but builds and reinforces the others in a structure that resembles Maslow's hierarchy of needs.[16]

Health and Well-being

Health and wellness in later life certainly means staying active by living a robust physical, social, and spiritual life. Later life is a time of reflection that, according to Erik Erikson, should bring the resolution of past failures and a celebration of accomplishments, helping to integrate one's life story.[17] This is crucial to successful aging through, in Jung's term, the arch of life.

Physical health becomes more dependent on nurture in later life. The casual engagement in physical activities by youth give way to the imperative of the body-mind connections of later life. Through creative activities, the mind, body, and spirit can be renewed and refreshed (as shown in the research mentioned above). One can dance, sing, recite poetry, or act in a play, tapping all the senses and engaging the body in movement. The brain processes new information and solves new problems, while the spirit's reflections provide content for meaningful expressions that build self-knowledge and a legacy to share with others.

Community-based programs such as those involved in field-tested studies—including Elders Share the Arts (Brooklyn, New York), Encore Chorale (Greater Washington, DC), and the Center for Elders and Youth in the Arts (San Francisco, California)—are accessible to older adults with differing abilities and economic status and encourage vibrant, healthy living in later life. Programs like these are being developed around the country but are still the exception.

Older adults who have significantly compromised cognitive abilities because of chronic diseases such as Alzheimer's and Parkinson's can access the arts through highly innovative programs such as TimeSlips, Songwriting Works, Alzheimer's Poetry Project, and the MoMA Alzheimer's Project. These programs focus on imagination rather than memory to create common experiences between people with cognitive disability and their families, caregivers, and the community at large, enabling them to retain meaning and purpose in later life as well.

Lifelong Learning

As Corbett writes in the opening chapter, the misconceptions about later-life learning have been part of the view of aging as relentless decline. With the discovery at

Figure 8.2: Creating poems with Alzheimer's Poetry Project. Photo by Elizabeth Thomas.

the end of the twentieth century of late-in-life neurogenesis, what we thought to be true about the inability of older people to learn new things has been scientifically refuted, but these stereotypes still persist in society. As mentioned earlier, artists and scientists who have made creative pursuits their life professions have always defied the aging stereotypes by producing the majority of their best work in later life. Because mind, body, and spiritual connections are involved in creative expression, solving the mysteries of bringing new identities into existence, the brain is fully stimulated to regenerate itself and grow. It does not matter if it is a Big C or a little c creation—the positive benefits are the same.

The major challenge to providing lifelong learning is finding ways for people to access this kind of community programming. While opportunities exist, there is no infrastructure through which one can easily find classes that cater to adults, much less creative programs for older adults in such things as visual arts, music, dance, writing, and drama.[18]

Higher education classes (credit and noncredit) exist but are not uniformly open to helping adults build new skills for new jobs or life enrichment. Osher Lifelong Learning Institutes, which include the arts, are being established across the country through university partnerships, and Oasis programs are offered in retirement or community centers. Classes based in arts organizations such as museums and theaters are finding a new market in lifelong learners. The number of summer camps for older adults, such as Chautauqua, is growing. One of the earliest educational services for older people, Elderhostel, now called Road Scholar, is gaining attention and increased participation. Distance learning opportunities for those with cognitive impairments are being designed by major museums such as the Cleveland Museum, where museum educators can work directly with caregivers to provide innovative programs based on the museum collection. Older distance learning programs such as Dorot use the telephone in a low-tech, high-touch way to bring quality enrichment programs to older people, especially those in underserved areas. Senior Center Without Walls brings many programs to older people in a virtual way as well.

Figure 8.3: Man leading dance class. Photo courtesy of Stagebridge Senior Theatre.

The potential market is huge, but currently business plans mostly target those with economic means. As Corbett observes, successful aging in this country pivots on social status and economic means.

Community Engagement

Health and wellness coupled with lifelong learning enhance more than the individual and his or her family. If successful, these two protocols for aging with integrity produce wisdom, as noted by Corbett, Cohen, and Jung. This wisdom influences neighborhoods, communities, and society at large by creating social capital. The functional work of bringing wisdom into community is creativity.

Social capital has the largely untapped potential of being built through the late-in-life creative age. This involves the mature genius of lifelong innovators such as artists and scientists as well as the contributions of late-in-life community volunteers (as Marc Friedman describes in his books, *Encore* and *The Big Shift*).[19] Late-in-life wisdom can be applied creatively to solve intractable problems such as school delinquency and food insecurity, and it can lead to the renewal of underutilized community resources such as parks, libraries, and other public spaces.

Corbett writes about the Gray Panthers in the 1970s dedicating themselves to changing the paradigm of older people consuming resources into one where the older person produces resources (p. 28). Wisdom and creativity are central to this kind of resource development. As we have thirty more years to live than our

Figure 8.4: Beautiful mind. Photo courtesy of DSM.

ancestors of the twentieth century, the potential to gain from the active engagement of older people in community life is exponential.

In summary, creativity plays a central role in aging well. Creative engagement benefits the individual and society at large. It builds the infrastructure for an individual to gain self-knowledge and wisdom internally, as well as providing ways to tap the potential of the enlightened individual for the benefit of the community. Creativity comes in all forms, from the profound to the whimsical, and can be used at will throughout the life span. It is particularly important in later life—a time of reflection and rebalancing as one moves toward the end of the arch of life. Gaps exist in providing access to creative opportunities because of a lack of arts services for older adults, despite the potential market for programs promoting health and wellness, lifelong learning, and community engagement. The disparities between individuals based on social status and economic means constitute barriers for all successful aging initiatives, including the utilization of creative programs. However, because of the instinctual nature of creative expression, given society's growing attention to the benefits of these activities in later life, with little means but self-direction, time, and a safe, supportive environment, creativity can flourish.

NOTES

[1] David W. Galenson, *Old Masters and Young Geniuses: The Two Life Cycles of Artistic Creativity* (Princeton, NJ: Princeton University Press, 2006).

[2] Kevin F. McCarthy, Elizabeth H. Ondaatje, Laura Zakaras, and Arthur Brooks, *Gifts of the Muse* (Santa Monica, CA: RAND Corporation, 2004).

[3] Gene Cohen, *The Mature Mind* (New York: Basic Books, 2005), p. 146.

[4] Cohen, *The Mature Mind*, p. 11.

[5] Galenson, *Old Masters and Young Geniuses*, pp. 162–187.

[6] Cohen, *The Mature Mind*, p. 52.

[7] Cohen, *The Mature Mind*, p. 59.

[8] Joan Jeffri et al., "Above Ground: Information on Artists III: Special Focus on New York City Aging Artists" (study for Research Center for Arts and Culture, Teachers College, Columbia University, 2007), p. 4.

[9] *Ibid.*

[10] National Endowment for the Arts, "The Arts and Human Development" (white paper, Washington, DC, 2011), p. 3.

[11] *Ibid.*, p. 7.

[12] *Ibid.*, pp. 24–28.

[13] Mary Kent and Rose Li, "The Cuts and Aging: Building the Science" (paper prepared for the National Endowment for the Arts, Office of Research and Analysis, 2013).

[14] Gene Cohen, Susan Perlstein, Jeff Chapline, Jeanne Kelly, Kimberly Firth, and Samuel Simmens, "The Impact of Professionally Conducted Cultural Programs on the Physical Health, Mental Health, and Social Functioning of Older Adults," *The Gerontologist* 46, no. 6: 726–734.

[15] Robert N. Butler, *Why Survive? Being Old in America* (Baltimore: Harper and Row, 1975).

[16] Abraham H. Maslow, Motivation and Personality (New York: Harper and Row, 1954).

[17] E. H. Erickson, J. M. Erickson, and H. Q. Kivnick, *Vital Involvement in Old Age* (New York: Norton, 1966).

[18] Bill Ivey and Steven J. Tepper, *Engaging Art: The Next Great Transformation of America's Cultural Life* (New York: Routledge, 2008).

[19] Marc Freedman, *Encore: Finding Work That Matters in the Second Half of Life* (New York: Public Affairs, 2007); Marc Freedman, *The Big Shift: Navigating the New Stage Beyond Midlife* (New York: Public Affairs, 2011).

~ CHAPTER NINE ~

Some Thoughts on
Aging Well

MARY A. McDONALD, M.D.

I am a physician specializing in geriatrics and palliative/hospice medicine. I also teach medical students, medical residents, and geriatric fellows how to care for older adults. All my comments are filtered through my own personal experiences, moral compass, and life story.

Doctors and patients alike all know what healthy aging means in terms of exercising and eating a well-balanced diet. Patients have long been advised to take their medications, seek out vaccinations, and to adhere to screening recommendations, such as colonoscopies at age fifty and other procedures. The positive health benefits of these approaches have been robustly represented in published literature, and I have nothing further to add on those subjects.

What is more intriguing to me is the healthy aging of the mind and the spirit, the core of what makes us delightfully unique and human. The human body, it would appear, has a predetermined shelf life. Taking all of the aforementioned advice can allow someone to reach their maximal life span, but bodies and organs still wear out despite the most stringent adherence. The senescence of the human spirit, however, takes a much less predictable course, and the preservation of a person's individuality and their "oneness" is less represented in medical journals. This is my particular area of interest and the topic for this chapter.

I work primarily with frail older adults. My patients typically are over the age of eighty and are managing their lives through the filter of multiple chronic diseases and physical debility. I suggest that those adults who are unhealthy agers have died by this age, and they are not included in my study population. Natural selection has provided me with an opportunity to interview and observe healthy agers as they navigate their way through the last years of their lives. I get to know them as individuals and to understand their roles within their families and their communities. Some of my patients live at home with little or no assistance, while others live in long-term-care facilities and require assistance with all of the activities of daily living.

The Art of Aging

Older adults are wonderfully diverse from a medical standpoint. All humans are born with very similar bodies and physiologies. The typical medical examination of a newborn is very much targeted at trying to identify any abnormalities so as to be able to intervene if possible. The normal newborn is well defined. These similarities carry with us through our toddler years, adolescence, and young adulthood. It isn't until late adulthood that the human body starts to differentiate and take less predictable paths.

Back in my early training, I saw patients of all ages. If I was preparing to walk into the exam room of a six-month-old child, I had a pretty good idea of what to expect before I opened the door. I already knew about what size they would be and their physical and cognitive developmental level, if they were progressing as expected. But there is no one-size-fits-all approach in geriatrics. If I walk into an examination room to meet a new eighty-year-old patient for the first time, I have no idea what I am about to see. I have eighty-year-old patients who are robust, vital, and active, and I have some who are frail, sick, and dependent. I have some older patients who have maintained their cognitive level, their sense of humor, and their intellectual vitality, and I have others who have been ravaged by dementia, depression, and introversion. Each encounter that I have with an older adult demands that I avoid preconceptions, and that I approach each individual as a wonderfully unique person. There is no such thing as a predetermined treatment algorithm for an eighty-year-old patient, and I am professionally thankful for that. The true art of medicine does not involve following a prefab treatment protocol. Rather, the art is in getting to know each individual patient and individualizing each treatment plan to best suit the needs and wishes of the patient.

Of all the things I do in my practice day, using treatment algorithms and protocols is very mundane. Knowing how to use medications correctly and safely to lower blood pressure to some acceptable level is not the real challenge of medicine. Neither is lowering blood sugars in a diabetic or prescribing the appropriate salve to heal a wound. The art of medicine involves seeing each patient as a unique individual and not just the sum of chronic disease states. The role of the physician is much more than the keeper of the prescription pad. The roles of physician that I most enjoy are those of the negotiator, the tour guide, the cheerleader, the drill sergeant, and the advocate. Which role I choose to portray depends on what a particular patient needs at a particular time.

As negotiators, physicians work out treatment recommendations and desired outcomes based on what the patients value and what they want for themselves. When patients are unable to communicate for themselves, I communicate with a patient's surrogate decision maker or power of attorney. In these cases, I find myself reminding the surrogate that I want to know what the patient wants, not what the surrogate wants. I work as a tour guide, helping patients navigate the health-care delivery system to get to where they want to be and get what they need. I also work as a cheerleader or a drill sergeant at times. And I often adopt the role of patient advocate, especially when patients can't advocate for themselves.

I had been caring for Mrs. T, a seventy-two-year-old outpatient in my geriatrics clinic, for a few years. She was certainly not one to just follow my advice without asking questions and negotiating for a plan of care that made sense to her. I had been encouraging her to get a bone mineral density test to check for osteoporosis. She balked at my recommendation repeatedly, and I finally asked her why she didn't think she needed to know how strong her bones were. She politely explained to me that she lived on a horse ranch and owned four horses. She rode these horses every day and took in other peoples' horses to get them saddle-ready. She had been thrown off four horses in the past three years and had never broken a bone. The way that she saw it, her test of bone strength was more meaningful than mine. I had to agree and I dropped the subject from that point on.

Key Ingredients in the Recipe for Healthy Aging

Over the years, I have tried to come up with a recipe for healthy aging based on my observations and interviews with my study population. I have yet to perfect the recipe, but I have come to know some of the main ingredients. There are several consistent similarities that I have noted in my patients who have been able to maintain a healthy spirit, an appreciation for the beauty around them, and a love of life. Four of these ingredients are engagement, resilience, hope, and a sense of humor.

Engagement

Several years ago, I directed a required course called Medicine across the Life Span for third-year medical students at the University of Kansas School of Medicine. It was a four-week course that covered development, physiology, disease states, and screening recommendations from birth to death. One of the assignments for the course was for each student to sit and interview an older adult who was not related to them about any topic of interest and then write a short paper summarizing their findings. Each year, 175 medical students were assigned this task, and each year up to a third of them approached me for help because they were unable to identify an older adult to interview. My patients were delightfully accommodating and willing to help these students, but it really got me thinking about the topic of engagement in society. Medical students are, for the most part, well-intentioned, bright, and leaders among their peers. What was happening in our community that these young people had no interaction at all with older adults in their daily lives?

Some older adults withdraw and abandon their roles in their communities and even in their families. They retire and then disappear. Perhaps there is a societal expectation that older people remove themselves from active engagement. This perceived lack of contribution to the community is very detrimental to the overall well-being of older adults. I see daily examples of the peril of disengagement as well as the benefits of staying involved with the world around you.

Many families are committed to keeping their loved ones at home as they age, and they go to great expense and great sacrifice to do so. Multigenerational families are the norm in much of the world and within some cultures in the United States, but they are becoming less and less common here. I am, among other things, a house call physician. I visit the homes of patients who are sick and frail and unable to leave home. Many of these patients live with their adult children. For some, the vibrancy of family life draws them in, and they maintain a role in the family. They are engaged in the goings on of all members of the family and participate in group decision making. These older adults are the lucky ones. When I visit them, they walk or are transported to the common areas of the house for my visit. If they are bedridden, it is most common to see a living room or dining room that has been converted into a bedroom, thus allowing the senior to be surrounded by family and friends. It is my experience that, in these situations, it is more common for the entire family unit to be involved in providing the physical care that frail older adults need. I have met countless grandsons who are proud that they are strong enough lift Grandma onto the bedside commode.

Mrs. R is a seventy-two-year-old female living in a two-bedroom apartment with her adult daughter. She is unable to walk or get in and out of her wheelchair by herself due to severe rheumatoid arthritis. Her daughter has one of the bedrooms and the other is a guest bedroom for any of Mrs. R's other four adult children if they wish to stay over. Mrs. R sleeps in a hospital bed in the common area. The only other furniture here is a very large formal dining room table, a large television on a stand, and a reclining chair. It struck me as odd on my first visit that so much space in this large apartment would be occupied by this large table until I spoke to Mrs. R. She maintained a very close and loving relationship with all of her children. Her apartment had become the gathering place for them and all of her grandchildren. Her building was next door to a subway station. Two of her sons came by every morning to eat breakfast before going to work, and they would get her out of bed to the wheelchair. Another son stopped by every night on his way home from work, ate dinner at the apartment, and then put his mother back to bed. "You should see this place on Sundays," she told me. Every Sunday, all five of her children along with many grandchildren came to the apartment and ate a feast. They would sit around the large dining room table and watch football or whichever sport was in season. One or more of her grandchildren often spent Sunday night in the guest bedroom, and they would argue over whose turn it was. Mrs. R was frail and disabled but she was still one hundred percent engaged in her chosen community: her family. She was happy.

Being in a home full of family is no guarantee that one will stay engaged with community. I have encountered countless families who are committed to keeping their older members at home, but who then isolate them in some back bedroom, disengaged from the rest of the family and the rest of society. No amount of impeccable physical care of an older, frail adult can make up for the damage done by social isolation. Television sets and radios are not effective replacements for real human interactions. The need to engage socially with others is best documented in old medical literature that investigated failure to thrive in baby monkeys. From this data, the importance of socializing with our developing children is well understood. Nobody would think it acceptable to keep a baby in the bedroom, spending much of its time alone. Regardless of how clean and well-fed that baby was, he or she would be damaged psychologically. All human beings thrive with engagement. Engagement, in fact, is necessary for survival.

Ms. P was a seventy-seven-year-old female who lived alone in a senior housing apartment complex. She was cognitively intact but had severe arthritis that made getting around painful and slow. I routinely ask my patients what they are doing for fun, and I will never forget her reply. "I ride the bus," she replied. I asked her what she meant, and she responded. "Ooooh, Dr. McDonald . . . two dollars and unlimited transfers . . . and there are some FINE-looking men in this city." Ms. P and some of her friends from the apartment complex would ride the bus around the city for hours just taking in the sights. She was maintaining her engagement in her community. She was happy and well adjusted, despite her frailty.

In cases where I have encountered socially marginalized patients who lived in their own homes, I work with the family to develop techniques and lifestyle changes that will promote increased engagement with the patient. My work is based on the premise that families have the best intentions when committing to caring for older adults in the home. I do not shy away from pointing out that adult day-care centers and even long-term-care facilities actually do have the advantage of increased socialization for their loved ones. Having to place one's mom or dad in a nursing home does not have to be a sign of lack of commitment or lack of love or willingness to sacrifice for them. It may simply allow them to blossom in a more socially rich environment. *Blossom* is the perfect word to describe what I have observed when a socially disengaged older adult reengages. They literally start to look different. Their skin tone improves. Their eyes brighten. They look younger.

Resilience

I love the word *resilience*, but I'm not sure how best to define it. There are many published definitions of the word, but none of them are quite right. I certainly know resilience when I see it in my patients. I have encountered many patients who have been through personal trauma, physical illness, and loss of loved ones, but they're still happy and engaged in society. They have adjusted their expectations for their future but have avoided collapsing inward into their grief and disappointment. They may have been hurt by others, but they haven't lost their ability to trust. They may have been betrayed by their bodies, but they don't just lay down and cease attempting to help themselves, although they may have become dependent on others. I have been trying to put my finger on just what makes some people resilient while others just fold.

> *Ms. N was only fifty-seven years old when she had a stroke due to untreated high blood pressure. She went from being a fiercely independent woman who lived by herself to living in a nursing home. She is paralyzed on one side of her body and must be assisted in and out of a wheelchair. She is unable to dress, groom, or bathe herself without help. Her stroke affected the language center of her brain, and she is unable to speak anything but gibberish and can no longer read or write. She does, however, understand everything that is said to her, and her cognitive ability is intact. The only two-word phrase that she says that is comprehendible is "Ta da," like a magician says after a great magic trick. I look forward to visiting Ms. N because she is always smiling and welcoming and a joy to be with. She lost nearly everything with her stroke—her job, her independence, and her ability to communicate with her adult children who live out of state. What she has not lost is her ability to make an impact on her community. She didn't lose her spirit or whatever it is that makes her a wonderfully unique individual. Her community now is the nursing home. She is very active in the facility and takes part in most of the activities provided. She looked beautiful when she attended the spring formal recently and appeared to be genuinely enjoying herself. Ms. N is the type of patient who appears to possess a never ending supply of resilience. Many people faced with the same physical and emotional challenges would have turned inward and would have disengaged, spending the rest of their life just waiting for the release that death will someday provide.*

My patients who lack resilience most often exhibit bitterness and despair. I so wish that I could bottle resilience like any other medication and prescribe it to these patients. Although some of them may respond positively to antidepressant medications, these are no substitute for resilience. I have encountered patients who seem to be completely devoid of resilience, and the slightest physical or emotional challenge appears so difficult that they are led to the point of despair. They live their lives bracing themselves for the next obstacle to present itself. Turning inward with dissatisfaction in one's life tends to make people acutely aware of every single ache and pain that comes with an aging body. They are unable to find distractions from their suffering. It is akin to the toothache that you hardly notice during the day, but which becomes excruciating at night as you lie in bed. People who are resilient have the ability to work through their physical symptoms by distracting themselves with rich, satisfying lives. People without resilience are consumed by their physical symptoms and experience much misery.

Hope and Spirituality

Many of my patients over the years have pointed to their spirituality as the source of their hope for things to come. They lean on their spiritual core during times of trouble, sadness, and illness. But I have come to learn that spirituality or belief in a deity is not a prerequisite for hope. Having hope and an inner belief system that brings comfort are not necessarily spiritually based. I routinely talk with patients about their spiritual beliefs or their inner belief systems. I have to know a patient's belief system in order to care for the patient. I talk about core belief systems every day with my patients. One benefit of this is that I have been having an ongoing conversation with myself about my own core beliefs for years now. My own beliefs have been molded by my experiences and by the beliefs of others. They have changed over time, and they are fluid.

Mrs. V was a seventy-four-year-old woman who was dying of ovarian cancer. She was a deaconess of her church and was very spiritually grounded in her faith. She came to the inpatient hospice unit in a lot of physical pain and distress. Over the next several days, we were able to manage her pain and other symptoms, and she was looking forward to going home to die. The fear that I had seen in her eyes when she was in pain was gone, and she looked peaceful and comfortable. On the day of her scheduled transfer home, I went to her room to say goodbye and wish her well. She thanked me for helping her transition to the "other side." She assured me that when my time comes, she will be waiting for me on the other side and will help me with my own transition. I found a quiet place to reflect on those words. I'm not sure if they are

*consistent with my own belief system about death and dying, but
I was so very moved by her conviction and the intention of her
words. I learned from this experience, as I always do.*

I have cared for people with a wide variety of spiritual and religious
belief systems as well as agnostics, atheists, and those who are unsure
of an actual name for their core beliefs. I have yet, however, to meet
anyone who claims that they don't have any core beliefs. In an
unthreatening and nonjudgmental environment, I have found that
most people relish exploring these beliefs, which can hold the key to
facing their fears about dying. These are often the same fears that have
left people unable to truly live life to its fullest. These are the fears
that have interfered with finding resolution with dysfunctional
relationships, and they interfere with the ability to honestly
communicate with loved ones. Without exploring core beliefs in life,
people are unable to complete tasks that are necessary to reach a place
where they are at peace with death.

Sense of Humor

I suspect that I will have to stop being a doctor when I stop seeing
humor and having fun doing what I do. The response from my
colleagues as I was finishing residency training baffled me. I announced
to them that I was applying for geriatrics fellowship training, and the
overwhelming response was, "Oh my God. Why?" I have subsequently
trained as a hospice physician, and I work with patients and their
families as they approach the end of their lives. Many of my well-
meaning friends, neighbors, and colleagues over the years have pointed
out that my chosen career must be depressing. Being surrounded by
so much sickness and death, in their eyes, sounds horrible. I couldn't
disagree more. I have always been one who values honest, unmasked
interactions with others. I value conversations that are real, deep,
and meaningful and not confined by social niceties. I dare you to
find a group of people who are more real than people who are dying
or people who have lost everything due to illness and have had to
redefine themselves. I defy you to find a group of people more
honest than those with dementia who have lost their inner filter for
polite conversation. I have learned more about living life well from
dying people than I ever have from others. I have learned more about

being human to the core from my dementia patients than from any of my friends and colleagues.

> *Mr. R is an eighty-four-year-old nursing home patient who is wheelchair bound. He is able to maneuver his wheelchair with his feet, and he spends his day visiting people throughout the facility. When I pass Mr. R in the hall, he always says, "Hi, beautiful," and gives me a high five. He stops me most mornings to tell me his joke of the day. I have to remind him to keep it clean, and he laughs. Mr. R is widowed and rarely gets to see his family. We have become his surrogate family, and he is able to find joy and laughter even after everything that he has endured.*

I have observed that many of my hospice patients find humor in the absurdity of the position in which they find themselves. I laughed out loud when I asked one patient who was dying of cancer how he was feeling, and he responded, "Well, I'm not dead yet, so I have that going for me." I suspect that humor is not only of social benefit in that it brings us together and strengthens our bonds, but that it also serves as a coping mechanism. I encourage family members to sit and talk about their loved ones' impact on their lives. This frequently turns into shared laughter as they recall funny stories from the past. They laugh a little, and then they cry a little. It is a beautiful thing to watch.

Dementia is an illness that affects not only cognitive abilities but also functional level and personality. The humor that dementia patients enjoy is typically akin to what makes a toddler squeal. They have developmentally regressed, and mature humor or sarcasm is often lost on them. Silliness or the element of surprise, however, are often maintained even late in the disease process. I have come to learn this the hard way, as I gravitate toward sarcastic humor, and I have been taken aback at responses to some of my feeble attempts at humor in the dementia unit. Because my dementia patients often don't remember me from visit to visit, I always reintroduce myself when I see them. I might say, "Hello, Mrs. T, I'm Dr. McDonald, and it is so nice to see you again." One patient looked at me with confusion and said, "I don't remember seeing you before," to which I sarcastically replied, "Well, I get better looking each day, so it doesn't surprise me if you don't remember me." Without missing a beat, she looked at me with all seriousness and said, "I don't think you are that good looking." I had to leave the room because I was laughing so hard at her honest remark.

I have watched so many of my dementia patients laugh with their whole being about something that struck them as funny. One day I was sitting at a table in a nursing home with a group of patients from the dementia unit for the annual Thanksgiving dinner. The woman sitting beside me very purposefully picked up a slice of bread, placed a slice of pumpkin pie on the bread, and then placed another slice of bread on top. I pointed out to her that she had made herself a pumpkin pie sandwich. She took a big bite of the sandwich and then looked at me with delight. She and I both broke out in laughter at the situation, and I will never forget the look on her face. She was truly, unabashedly happy for just that moment.

Conclusion

My advice to anyone seeking healthy aging is to strive always to maintain fun in your life. I routinely ask patients what they do for fun, and it often surprises them the first few times. I contend that if you don't have a ready response for that very simple question, then it does not bode well for your ability to age well. No one should reach a point in life where they no longer expect to have fun. Children are not taught to look for fun. College students don't have to be encouraged to go out and have fun. For some, the natural tendency to look for fun and the drive to seek out fun in their lives is lost. There is an old saying by an anonymous source that sums this up well: "You don't stop having fun when you get old, but you get old when you stop having fun."

PART IV

Finding Meaning
Spirituality in the Second Half of Life

~ CHAPTER TEN ~

Conscious Aging as a Spiritual Path

MELANIE STARR COSTELLO, PH.D.

The decisive question for man is: Is he related to something infinite or not? That is the telling question of his life. Only if we know that the thing which truly matters is the infinite can we avoid fixing our interests upon futilities, and upon all kinds of goals which are not of real importance. Thus we demand that the world grant us recognition for qualities which we regard as personal possessions: our talent or our beauty. The more a man lays stress on false possessions, and the less sensitivity he has for what is essential, the less satisfying is his life . . . If we understand and feel that here in this life we already have a link with the infinite, desires and attitudes change. In the final analysis, we count for something only because of the essential we embody, and if we do not embody that, life is wasted.
— C. G. Jung, *Memories, Dreams, Reflections*

C onscious aging pulls us into conversation with an underlying stream of life that informs and shapes our experience over time. Our inquiry reflects psycho-spiritual development in later life back to corresponding processes of decay and renewal as found in nature. We set the stage in this chapter by attributing resilience in the face of change to symbolic modes of perceiving. We then discuss literary and mythological formulations that illumine the relation of the principle of death to Eros as a force of renewal, presenting life and death as a unity. Next, the link between the diminishments of aging and corresponding processes of spiritual maturation is explored. The chapter concludes with biographical sketches that portray those qualities found in individuals who realize the spiritual potentials of aging in depth and suggests ways in which the fruits of conscious aging pass from the individual to the community.

The Symbolic Life

The epigraph for this chapter, drawn from Jung's memoirs, puts spirituality at the center of the human developmental process. We have inherited from Jung the conviction that psychological well-being hinges upon our engagement with the essential—that is, with ultimate sources of meaning. It seems our relation to the essential influences our health overall and, consequently, our life span. In fact, religious affiliation, a sense of purpose, and proximity to family are major cross-cultural determinants of longevity. These three features are found among nine habits shared by communities with the highest life expectancies. According to explorer and National Geographic writer Dan Buettner, knowing one's *Ikigai*—the term Okinawans use for sense of purpose— can add seven years to life expectancy. Attending faith-based services four times a month will add four to fourteen years to life expectancy.[1]

Of the five communities that met Buettner's criteria for exceptional longevity, only one is found in North America: the Seventh-day Adventists living near Loma Linda, California. Sadly, the structures of belonging and purpose observed by Buettner's team are no longer central characteristics of North American life. Before World War II, about a quarter of the U.S. population lived in multigenerational households; today about 16 percent do so.[2] More than 27 percent of people sixty-five and older live alone, and according to a Pew Research

Center survey, these adults are not in as good health and are more likely to feel sad, depressed, or lonely than are older adults who live with another person.[3]

In regard to religious affiliation, traditional community and belief structures are in sharp decline. Attitudes toward traditional forms of belief have become sharply polarized. Two axial principles—relativism and absolutism—clash at every point. On the one hand we witness an unprecedented surge in religious and political fundamentalism, while on the other hand moderate ideologies and moderate faith perspectives are losing ground. The quest for definitive spiritual knowledge, historically the motive force of philosophy and theology, is overshadowed by doubt and suspicion. Many hold that religion itself is to blame for the major crises of our time.

Given the link between healthy longevity, spirituality, and purposeful affiliation, these currents present significant challenges to us as we age. Identity forms out of the matrix of family, community, and cultural heritage; thus, religious affiliation is a powerful medium for fostering meaningful connections with contemporaries and with ancestors. Shared symbolic forms—beliefs, rites, and ritual practice—give people a sense of belonging to one and the same world and to one transcendent reality. Many do still benefit from affiliation with their family's faith tradition. At the same time, we see a growing number of people seeking alternative routes to meaning and connection. For some, the loss of religious community and spiritual certainty is a cause of profound suffering.

As individuals and as a society, we are vulnerable to psychological imbalances that accompany the breakdown of community and socially shared formulations of meaning. By its negative example, religious extremism demonstrates the need for psychological resilience in this era of rapid change. A modern psychological phenomenon, extremist communities coalesce around a refusal to adapt to shifting social, economic, and ideological structures. Religious extremism's core features—intolerance of moral ambiguities, rigid adherence to doctrine, demonization of those with conflicting viewpoints—characterize psychological regression to primal states of human consciousness.[4] So too will these primal, maladaptive responses be found in individuals who lack resilience. At best, the failure of an individual to adapt to environmental and physiological change shows ego fragility; at worst, it signals the presence of serious mental illness.

In the absence of the kind of certainty provided by traditional structures of belief and community, how do we approach our basic needs for meaning and purpose, for a sense of belonging to self, others, and the world as we age? From the perspective of Jungian theory, spiritual vitality and resilience in the face of changing life circumstances may be found through the symbolic life—a meaningful, investigative engagement with ideas, objects, dreams, and spiritual practice. As a distinctive feature of our humanity, the symbolic function connects us with a source of biological and spiritual vitality that transcends understanding, a larger reality that may or may not be described in explicitly religious terms. Representations of human experience—by word, image, or practice—are considered symbolic where they foster our participation in this transcendent source of vitality and meaning.

In essence, the symbolic function lies behind every form of creativity. Observing how representations (images, ideas, practices) of the transcendent element are central to all human cultures, Jung spoke of the religious impulse as an instinct in its own right. He considered the symbolic function an essential property of human consciousness. As a major determinant in individual and group psychologies, it remains the primary focus of Jungian studies.

Given this emphasis, Jungian theory has made its imprint upon contemporary spirituality. These days we enjoy a vibrant cross-fertilization of psychology and spirituality generally and witness an interweaving of Jungian perspectives with Buddhist teachings and with Christian and Jewish revitalization efforts. Outside of spiritual communities, many people look to psychology rather than religious teachings for perspective on their lives; thus the boundary between psychotherapeutic and spiritual approaches to healing and wholeness cannot always be deciphered. At one time, the word *spirituality* denoted practices and accountings of religious experiences as formed *within* the respective faith traditions. But the term has come to be applied to the general cultivation of life meaning, to practices found outside as well as within the bounds of religious tradition. Indeed, it is common to hear the word *spirituality* used to denote something altogether dissociated from religion, as in the expression, "spiritual but not religious."

Despite a growing collective ambivalence toward traditional religious belief and practice, more people than not report themselves to be spiritual, and spirituality remains a formal subject of study.[5] Spirituality most often involves a relationship to an ultimate reality—sometimes conceived as an immaterial source of being and sometimes conceived as the universe itself. The term denotes our deepest values, our pursuit of meaning, and the means by which we enliven our inner world. Spiritual practices such as prayer, meditation, and contemplation promote a relationship between the conscious personality and more subtle mental, emotional, and imaginative reaches of one's inner world. Inner work aims toward building awareness of a more-comprehensive self.

Jungian psychology's contribution to evolving perspectives on aging lies in its extensive researches into the importance of spirituality in human development during the second half of life. The particular features of that spirituality will vary from person to person, from tradition to tradition. What is essential is that we stay in proximity to a living stream of life, no matter how elusive. This proximity conveys a *felt sense of meaning*; it is the foundation of wisdom. As described in Jung's memoirs:

> It is important to have a secret, a premonition of things unknown. It fills life with something impersonal, a *numinosum*. A man who has never experienced that has missed something important. He must sense that he lives in a world in which in some respects is mysterious; that things happen and can be experienced which remain inexplicable; that not everything which happens can be anticipated. The unexpected and the incredible belong in this world. Only then is life whole. For me the world has from the beginning been infinite and ungraspable.[6]

As will be shown below, a wise elder, *through her or his being*, gives us access to these subtle underlying life currents.

Our spirituality defines our relation to mystery. It is the means by which we engage the transcendent element, however symbolized. The symbolic function, a uniquely human capacity, makes this engagement possible. In what follows I take my cue from Jung and view the symbolic function as the cornerstone of later-life development. Our inquiry revolves around the question: Are there spiritual potentials specific to aging? If taken up with spiritual intention, might the aging process bear fruits such that aging may reveal itself as not just inevitable but purposeful, something to strive toward?

Death and Eros as Cooperative Forces of Spiritual Renewal

Pondering these questions, I consulted the *I Ching* or *Book of Changes,* a wisdom source used by the Chinese since ancient times. I was led to a hexagram entitled *Ta Kuo* ("The Preponderance of the Great").[7] It speaks of a transitional period that must be approached with special regard to its meaning. Two parallel images are offered:

> A withered poplar puts forth flowers.
> An older woman takes a husband.
> No blame. No praise.

These images portray actions that do not accord with one's natural place in the life cycle. The commentary says that, while there may be no harm in responding to later-life callings with acts belonging to a more youthful age, little would be gained. Jung put it a bit more severely: "We cannot live the afternoon of life according to the program of life's morning, for what was great in the morning will be little at evening, and what in the morning was true will at evening have become a lie."[8]

At play are the images of the great round of life, the cycle of the seasons, the cycle of the day—these images portray the irrepressible laws of the natural world. The human personality, like any living thing, moves through times of growth and times of decay, periods of ascent and descent. Our passages from one stage of development to another will be marked by some degree of sacrifice. These transitional points— what poet David Whyte calls "periods of molting"—dissolve our established orientation to make way for new growth.[9] Refusing this, we become something other than who we were meant to be.

Making a transition from adulthood into midlife and beyond is particularly challenging for Westerners. Imbalances in our collective value system place us at odds with the natural course of aging, as the phrase "midlife crisis" makes clear. Favoring youth over wisdom, progress over cooperation, doing over being—imagining ourselves on a continuous upward trajectory over time—our course runs out of sync with the way things truly are in nature. Poised to conquer rather than envisaging ourselves as residing within the natural world, we are at odds with the fundamental laws of human development. Ecological crises and midlife crises stem from the same root: in a progress-driven culture, we suffer an overextension of the heroic impulse toward mastery over nature and over resources; we keep building, producing, consuming. Our bias toward progress places us at odds with the demands of aging, which naturally involves a great deal of letting go of things rather than building them up.

The consciously aging person assumes a path that is discordant with commonly held assumptions and values. It is a path of least resistance, building on one simple observation: nature demands cultural and biological productivity in early adulthood, but *the principle of transformation holds sway in mid- and later life.* In conscious aging, we reflect upon change as life's insignia. We cultivate psycho-spiritual growth through our assent to the ways of nature. A consciously aging person assents to the developmental changes manifesting in his or her body and psyche, no matter how discordant with mainstream values. Conversely, *unconscious aging*— marked by the absence of reflection—makes us vulnerable to consumption-driven, youth-obsessed cultural stereotypes that envisage aging in terms of loss. From this perspective, we are victims of time and death, shadows of our former selves and, as time passes, something to be cast aside, hidden from public view: outsiders.

Psycho-spiritual transformations place us at a threshold between the known and the unknown, between loss and new discoveries. A period of spiritual transition announces the midlife journey. It is a time of reassessment, a time of rebalancing. The motive force of early adulthood—the drive to build structures of security and family, to exercise one's powers and make one's mark on the world—must give way to a reformulation of values and identity.

Early intimations of this transition can be quite disturbing. Even when we have brought a wealth of creativity to building our profession, to raising children, and to making meaningful social contributions, the time may come when these responsibilities no longer energize or lend meaning but rather start to feel burdensome. Grave doubts about oneself and one's life choices are common at these transition points.

One may suffer internal feelings of isolation or flatness. Even established spiritual or religious practices may no longer prove enriching.

In Christian tradition, the painful experiences associated with transitions to mature spirituality are called the "dark night of the soul," referring to a sixteenth-century poem and treatise written by Saint John of the Cross. Here, the seeker, having lost his connection with divine grace, suffers feelings of despondency, humiliation, and worthlessness—the kinds of feelings we associate with clinical depression. Such intimations of psycho-spiritual transition can be very frightening. In fact, the pharmaceutical industry has profited greatly from our collective ignorance of later-life developmental needs, for when we do not meet these intimations as meaningful communications from within oneself—when we carry on as usual—prolonged anxiety and depression is a likely outcome.

Our collective resistance to aging betrays our refusal to accept death as part of the life cycle. At the same time, we are instinctively repelled by those who covet youth excessively. A recurring theme in myth and literature, refusing death always leads to tragedy. Consider, for example, the Greek myth of Tithonus, the mortal lover of Eos, goddess of the dawn. In the Homeric hymn to Aphrodite, Eos asks Zeus to make Tithonus immortal, but she forgets to ask for his eternal youth. Tithonus is thus subjected to a horrific fate: with the passage of time he loses his physical and mental powers with no hope of death's release. He is an abomination in the sight of the immortals. Eos, too, abandons him and shuts him away in a golden chamber where, having lost his human community long ago, his isolation is complete.[10] The myth warns us that if a goddess can't outwit the laws of nature, so much worse the moral agony of hubristic men who try the same.

A version of this story is found in Alfred Tennyson's poem "Tithonus." Here Tithonus himself makes the fateful request, not to Zeus, but to the goddess. In time his unnatural longevity torments him not just because he is deprived of eternal youthfulness but because his unnatural condition separates him from his mortal community. His former wish becomes his eternal prison, and the isolation that accompanies immortality robs him of his true self, in essence, kills him:

Me only cruel immortality
Consumes[11]

Tennyson sets the torments of immortality against the common lot of Tithonus's long gone fellows resting peacefully under the ground. Tithonus wishes only to be released, restored to the ground like the "happier dead." We sense that the true object of this longed-for restoration is his former humanity with all that this implies. Resistance to nature's true course distorts our humanity. Death, aging's endpoint, is life's bedfellow.

The distortions of humanity that accompany the quest for eternal youth are also featured in Oscar Wilde's *The Picture of Dorian Grey*. The story follows the incremental corruption of a soul whose insecurity and vanity lead him into an unholy pact in defiance of aging. Unlike Tennyson's Tithonus, who endures excruciating moral suffering as a result of his bargain, Dorian Gray never attains true penitence after embarking on the life of soul-destroying debauchery mirrored by disfigurement in his portrait. Wilde's attitude toward his protagonist's dilemma is much more ambiguous than Tennyson's. Sneers and distortions do mar Grey's image each time he sins; but the portrait also registers his perversions through physical signs of aging as though diminishments of the body and corruption of the soul were one and the same thing.

This motif may reveal something of Wilde's personal moral and aesthetic biases, but the association of aging with moral decay is not uncommon. Consider the often-used expression "dirty old man." This cruel pairing stems from biblical tradition. In Genesis aging, death, and toil are the consequence of humanity's first sin (Genesis 3:16–24 RSV). Scriptural tradition thus attributes aging to an original act of defiance and a consequent fall from grace; it weaves together, inextricably, the fall from innocence and the loss of youthful immortality. Accordingly, agedness can be indiscriminately associated with ugliness in terms both aesthetic and moral.

It is likely that such an association lay behind prevailing attitudes toward sexuality and the aged. Indeed, one of the last pervasive sexual taboos is that placed on old age. The topic is aptly treated in Ronald Blythe's classic work, *The View in Winter*. Blythe notes that the old conceal their eroticism not because they themselves believe it to be

shameful or unnatural at their time of life but rather "to protect
something which has in the past brought them so much love and
delight from contempt."[12]

> The hope that sexuality itself would wither away and not add
> its desperate frustrations to agedness has long since been turned
> into the quite unfounded assurance that with age we naturally
> become asexual. What evidence we have to the contrary we
> manipulate to prove the social desirability of a sexless old age
> and to advocate the controls needed to achieve it. We tell the
> old, if you do not conform to this negative ideal you will be
> either ludicrous or indecent, that people will be frightened of
> you and think of you as pitiful or as a nuisance, for you are
> engaging in what is next to impossible or unthinkable.[13]

Our desexualization of old people betrays the degree to which we
have lost touch with the symbolic affiliation of erotic love with the
principle of death. In ancient Greek mythology Eros (love) and
Thanatos (death) are brothers. They work in tandem: death breaks
things down and parses out the residual elements; Eros, the principle
of relationship and bonding, is the force that pulls these elements
together and gives things form. In Greek mythology, Eros is the
embodiment of love, a powerful god known to the Romans as Cupid.
Doing his work by means of emotion and sexual passion, he wields
love as a force more powerful than the human faculty of the will. The
most ancient sources describe him not as the son of Aphrodite but as
a primordial god, fashioner of the cosmos.[14] In both personages, his
binding powers make him a force of generativity. As life principles,
creativity and erotic longing both reenact Eros's binding actions. Eros
is the force that brings disparate elements into relationship. Binding
is the means by which we re-form or give form to something as we
engage in acts of creation. Thus the need to create and be creative
continues throughout the life span. Creativity revitalizes us as we go.
The creative person appropriates the binding powers of love.

As with our relation to death, we remain collectively unconscious
of the symbolic depths underlying the erotic dimensions of experience.
We relegate the erotic to youth and youthful beauty, not just because
procreation is a biological imperative, but because we hold the spiritual
and the physical as distinct categories and cannot envision them as

aspects stemming from a common root. This split accounts for an epidemic of voyeurism in our time: our obsession with bodies, body parts, body image. Media-driven views of sexuality make us consumers of sex, outside observers more than participants in a mystery.

An alternative perspective emerges, however, when we consider the mythic interdependence of death in its work of breaking down old forms and Eros as a creative, animating principle of nature. The proximity of death to the erotic is celebrated as a sacred mystery in nature-based religions. Viewing the human developmental process and the seasonal cycles as spiritually correspondent, agricultural societies envision nature and spirit as one unitary reality. Transitions from season to season rest upon vegetative cycles of death and rebirth; these are sacred times, times of ritual observance and celebration. Divinities personify animating forces behind the natural process; as symbolic formulations, myths and rituals transmit to celebrants a felt experience of the spiritual mysteries embedded in the great round of life.

One of the earliest known pairings of the principles of Eros and Thanatos is found in the Greek myth of Persephone, queen of the underworld. Here the lord of the dead, Hades, abducts the daughter of the agricultural goddess, Demeter. Once she is in his kingdom, the virgin is tricked into eating the fruit of the dead and so is bound to Hades as wife and queen of the underworld. Consequently, the abundant vegetation of the topside world falls into decay as the mother goddess grieves her daughter. Eventually a bargain is struck: the ascent of the daughter ushers in spring and the earth grows green; but she must return to the underworld, and with her descent, vegetation too retreats to a secretly generative underground existence, a cycle of seasons. Life and death principles form a union in Persephone's work, marriage, and godhood. Like the queen of the underworld, we are subject to the erotic pairing of death and life.

Mythological personifications of the decay and withdrawal of vegetation into the earth transmits realities that include but also exceed the facts of winter. Like all myths, the story of the virgin's abduction by the god of death conveys truths that cannot be captured through any other medium. Initiates into Persephone's cult felt themselves in possession of the highest order of spiritual knowledge. These mysteries were celebrated under the full moon in autumn. Exclusive to women,

the Eleusinian feast of Thesmophoria ritually linked marriage and
fertility with the theme of decay. Archaeological sites at Eleusis contain
rich organic matter, buried residues of seed mixed with the sacrificial
remains of pigs: a ritual commemoration to the swine swallowed up
by the earth along with the virgin.

The archetypal affiliation of death with marriage aligns psycho-
spiritual development with the natural process. It is implicit in
marriage rites as they bring about the passing of the old self into new
life and new identity. Death itself is often cloaked in marriage
symbolism. For example, ancient Greek funeral rites treat death as a
form of marriage, often calling the grave *thalamos*, the bridal
chamber—an architectural reflection of the relation of death to the
principle of union. In Artemidoros's *Interpretation of Dreams*—a work
from the second century A.D.—we read that wedding dreams may
portend death because marriage and death are regarded as turning
points in human life and "the one always points to the other."[15] In
fact, modern dreams of erotic encounters or of marriage often do
presage an approaching death. It would appear that, from the
standpoint of the unconscious psyche producing such dreams, death
is a passage rather than the end of the developmental process.

Drawing on Neoplatonic perspectives, Jung suggests that in death
the individual soul conjoins with the *anima mundi*, the soul of the
universe. As the animating force of the universe, the *anima mundi* greets
us as a bride or bridegroom or as a mother, the womb of nature. Jung's
interest in the marriage motif in relation to death sprang largely out
of his own near-death experience in 1944. He reports that, while lying
unconscious after a nearly fatal heart attack, he experienced several
visions of the mystic marriage—the marital union of ancient divinities.
He witnessed, among others, the marriage of Tifereth and Malchuth
(the mystic marriage as it appears in kabbalistic tradition), as well as
the consummation of the marriage of Zeus and Hera. Of these divine
marriages, he relates that he experienced himself as the wedding.[16]

This extraordinary visionary account illumines the spiritual center
of a consciously lived life: our souls are the locus of the mystical
marriage. For Jung the experience introduced the last chapter of his
life's journey. The period following his recovery was perhaps the most
creative period of his life, when he produced the work entitled *Mysterium
Coniunctionis: An Inquiry into the Separation and Synthesis of Psychic*

Opposites in Alchemy.[17] He considered this study of the mystical marriage theme the culmination of his life's work and his most important contribution to the field of psychology.

Spiritual Maturation and the Diminishments of Aging

Whatever awaits us beyond our literal passage, a symbolic relation to the death principle is the heart of spiritual growth and maturation. Death and dissolution are naturally woven into any form of transformation as old forms give way and new forms are fashioned. The death principle releases us from old structures and outworn roles. Accepting its work opens the possibility that our perspectives, our relationships, our sense of self will be in some way reformed and renewed. As Jung puts it,

> From the middle of life onward, only he remains vitally alive who is ready to die with life. For in the secret hour of life's midday the parabola is reversed, death is born. The second half of life does not signify ascent, unfolding, increase, exuberance, but death, since the end is its goal.[18]

A friend speaks of this process of later-life transformation as "throwing oneself on the compost heap." It is no easy matter to allow an old passion to fade or to let go of work in which one invested so much of one's youth. People who had been highly productive contributors to political, artistic, or scientific movements in their youth are especially vulnerable to disorientation as retirement approaches or as they watch their work be subsumed by subsequent generations. As Blythe observes:

> It is a strange thing to be left behind by later generations whose moral or material advance is due to the heart and soul battles of one's own youth. And stranger still to be battling on when the cause has been won and forgotten. Worse, to find that although the cause was a correct one, and of benefit to oneself and to the world, it is now slotted into the general orthodoxy with no very great addition to the sum of human happiness.[19]

Facing the dissolution of intellectual and ethical structures central to our youth, we must traverse a narrow passage lest we fall into a trivial existence or, worse, resort to self-impersonation. It seems that later-

life transitions may require us to return to life's schoolroom, to learn
new pathways to significance. In Blythe's harsh formulation:

> with full-span lives having become the norm, people may need
> to learn how to be aged as they once had to learn how to be
> adult. It may soon be necessary and legitimate to criticize the
> long years of vapidity in which a well, elderly person does little
> more than eat and play Bingo, or consumes excessive amounts
> of drugs . . . just as the old should be convinced that, whatever
> happens during senescence, they will never suffer exclusion,
> so they should understand that age does not exempt them
> from being despicable. To fall into purposelessness is to fall out
> of all real consideration.[20]

Without renewal of purpose, the diminishments of aging place
us in a position of senseless waiting for the end. A culture that
attributes the height of human development to the biological functions
of early life may envisage retirement as a voluntary descent into futility,
cast the elderly into obsolescence, and rob us of the spiritual potentials
of conscious aging. If the death principle is severed from its connection
to spiritual processes of renewal, the aged will bear the brunt of our
collective fear of death and dying.

We readily relate the challenges of aging to the diminishments of
the body. But we forget that the aging person also faces the difficulties
of finding meaningful activity in our youth-oriented culture. It is
helpful to hear from those who have embraced their diminishments
with intention and come into renewed meaning and purpose as their
path unfolds. Those who have written of their own passage often use
nature-based metaphors to describe three phases of psycho-spiritual
transformation: decay, stasis, and renewal. For example, George
Congreve, while an aged member of the Society of St. John the
Evangelist at Oxford, writes of the sense of personal littleness that comes
with the diminishments of aging. He describes how, in time, his horror
of shriveling up as "inconsequentially as a leaf" passed and how "the
small faculty of love, our personality itself" begins to grow as it
contemplates "the infinite Love."[21]

Father Congreve's words resound with those of others who have
passed into a spiritually vibrant old age. The consciously aging person
appears to embrace a paradoxical surrender to diminishment while

concurrently discovering in himself or herself some reflection of a greater mystery, just as Congreve now identifies himself as a small faculty of love contemplating the infinite Love as its source.

In the narratives of the spirituality of aging, the soul is the stage for an ongoing collaboration: with our assent, old forms dissolve; in time residual elements, fashioned by the binding force of Eros, form into a new unity. It may present through subtle changes in perspective; a softening of the personality; an attitude of acceptance or a greater capacity to love. Whatever the outcome, this collaboration between the principles of love and death is behind any form of transformation. Acceptance of this mystery is the hallmark of mature spirituality.

As noted earlier, Jungian psychology anticipates a call to spiritual deepening at the midlife point. Not surprisingly, dissolution and dismemberment are recurring themes in the dreams of people as they enter midlife and pass through successive stages of aging. In the following example, a dream announces the inception of a midlife passage and, at the same time, helps the dreamer cope with uncertainty following the diagnosis of a serious medical condition.

> *I have the sense it is time to die. I am close to the sea (I'm no big fan of the sea). I feel a sense of dread as I walk up the beach. I climb up some rocks leading into a sheltered cove. The tide is coming in. I slowly walk into the tide, knowing if I continue my head will go under the water. When I am under the water I hold my breath, knowing I'll choke if I don't. But finally I decide to take a breath. As I do, water fills my lungs, but I do not cough. The water just flows through me. Slowly I dissolve and my body turns into seawater . . . . The first sensation is that everywhere the water is, I am. I am where I'd been and everywhere all at once, and every place that has ever been throughout time. My body spreads out into ocean, earth, the universe. I am in no particular place; rather, I am everywhere. I have no sense of time, space, or causality.*

The experience of dissolution by water helps the dreamer envisage the possibility of surrendering his identification with athletic endurance and ability. Experiencing himself as an integral part of a totality, the dreamer's fear of death is eased by the dream, and he is encouraged to reformulate his religious perspective. His discomfort with changing life circumstances gives water a special potency as the instrument of this symbolic death. Raised in the desert, the dreamer is not a swimmer. Indeed, the dream suggests that it is important he be aware of the degree to which changes in his body will take him "out of his element"; at the same time, the narrative's dense imagery helps him imaginatively elaborate the situation he now faces. He dreams himself capable of mustering the courage to face his fear of water's power to undo him. Succumbing to his destiny, he is released not just from fear, but from the assumption that this dissolution is final. His consciousness remains intact as he watches his body—and the form of his previous identity—dissolve and be transfigured: he assumes the qualities of the water, of the earth, and the cosmos. This dissolution of his old form releases him to a vastly larger unity. The experience transmitted by the dream sets the stage for the challenges of the next phase of his life journey and images his potential to discover a more comprehensive vision of self and world.

An abundance of water symbolism conveys the dynamic relation of death to processes of reformation and revitalization: the baptismal font, the alchemical *vas*, the bath, the pool, the vast ocean, a drenching rain—our dissolutions are passages to new meanings, revisions of identity, reconciliations with the ways of nature. As such, the consciousness that grows out of our assent to death as a spiritual principle may be seen as nature's own product. Jungian psychology conceives human consciousness and spirituality as continuous with the human body, as extensions of the web of nature and not to be set apart in essence from the physical properties of the natural world. This is a recurring theme in Jung's writing: the human psyche belongs to nature.

This is to say that we have inherited from Jung a psychology that is cosmological in scope, one that refers to spirit as something embedded in nature just as nature is embedded in spirit. Jung is speaking cosmologically when he interprets religious narratives about life after death as nature's way of orienting *itself* to death through symbolic expressions of its meaning. Afterlife narratives are found in most religions; they signify spontaneous productions rising from the unconscious depths of the human psyche. Nature, Jung observes, prepares itself for death by the anticipation of death.

And while these symbolic formulations may console us in the face of death, much more is intended: afterlife narratives view the end of life as a culmination of life's meaning; the truths they embody stem from the human heart.[22]

In one essay Jung offers a radical solution to our struggles against death and dying: accept death as a goal toward which one can strive.

> I am convinced that it is hygienic—if I may use the word—to discover in death a goal towards which one can strive, and that shrinking away from it is something unhealthy and abnormal which robs the second half of life of its purpose. I therefore consider that all religions with a supramundane goal are eminently reasonable from the point of view of psychic hygiene.[23]

Of course, religious constructs may be used in unhealthy ways and the religious crises of our time require us to qualify Jung's appreciation for afterlife doctrines. Afterlife narratives are a powerful weapon in the hands of those who would kill on the promise of heavenly rewards. As history has repeatedly shown, when appropriated for the sake of power, afterlife doctrines can be tools of oppression. But such abuses of doctrine are typically found where beliefs have lost their symbolic valence through literal, authoritarian methods of interpretation. Jung himself frequently warns against the disasters that ensue when literalism squelches the vitalizing spirit out of a symbol. By comparison, we can sense where a doctrinal narrative serves life: a living symbol transmits energy, conveys deep meaning, and activates a sense of mystery.

In this light, I recall a dialogue between two contemplative Christians, a wise elder and a scholar. Both were survivors of breast cancer. Recovering from a radical mastectomy, the younger woman turned to the elder and asked, "At the resurrection of the dead, will I have one breast or two?" The elder responded, "Darling, you will be beautiful."

We cannot know whether or not these two highly educated, rational women hold the doctrine of the resurrection of the dead as objective truth. But the exchange was life affirming, transmitting their acceptance of life and death as part of one vibrant mystery. Mutual participation in this mystery was made possible by means of the symbol.

Conscious aging calls us into relationship with spirit in nature and nature in spirit. Starting at midlife, the archetype of transformation moves to the center. In successive stages we will be called to lay down our lives as constructed, to sacrifice an established self-image and make way for the truer, less socially scripted self that is trying to emerge. In this metaphoric death, one's known self is sacrificed in exchange for what the poet Derek Walcott calls "the stranger who has loved you all your life . . . who knows you by heart."[24]

A soul-filled life is one spent in conversation with this stranger, this ever-emerging self. Conscious aging promotes this dialogue through dream work, writing, or reflection; through relating to the natural world as a subject rather than an object; through creative works; through attending to our emotions and the images that spring up out of the depths; through meaningful conversation, storytelling, prayer, and ritual practices within or outside of a faith community.

Like the seasonal cycles and the planetary courses, the symbolic function belongs to nature. The symbolic life thus represents life lived in a way that is naturally human. Our receptivity to symbolic expressions of meaning "illumines the self" in Jung's sense by connecting us with the web of life. We attain a more comprehensive self by surrendering the illusion that self and world can be fully known or understood in a purely rational way. Nature—through uniquely human forms of expression—transmits the appropriate response to the challenges of aging.

The Elder as a Conduit to Life's Web

Longevity is a modern phenomenon, and we are still working on its meaning and management. In the twentieth century, the average life expectancy in the United States increased by more than thirty years. The number of people living to age ninety and beyond has tripled in the past three decades and is likely to quadruple by 2050.[25] Increased longevity demands reformulation of the image of the aged. If we want our elders to be better regarded, we must take up the collective work of formulating those social and nature-based tasks that give meaning and purpose to aging and being old. Taking up a symbolic approach, aging becomes a spiritual path, one that envisages us moving toward, and not just away, from something of great significance. In the presence of one who has made the journey with conscious intention, aging seems more than a consequence of the passage of time. In the company of a wise elder, longevity seems purposeful, offering possibilities that cannot be accessed by other means.

Jung attributed a cultural, and perhaps, evolutionary purpose to longevity. He writes:

> A human being would certainly not grow to be seventy or eighty years old if this longevity had no meaning for the species. The afternoon of human life must . . . have a significance of its own.[26]

The developmental goal of aging would be more obvious to us if we actually had daily access to people who have lived to a ripe old age. But our society is organized in such a way that we do not often encounter our longest-lived citizens in public venues, and because many live in retirement enclaves, even family members may not enjoy daily encounters with them.

Nonetheless, we get some glimpse into the psycho-spiritual gifts of elderhood where the generations mix. William H. Thomas, M.D., author of *What Are Old People For?*, speaks of elderhood as a time that, like early childhood, favors the experience of mere being over that of doing.[27] As Thomas sees it, transitioning out of adulthood into elderhood, we become more aligned with children than with adults, who, unlike children and elders, are oriented to productivity:

> Elderhood brings us full circle, to a life that favors being over doing. This is a gift of great value. Watching older and younger people together, you get the sense of a secret (or at least submerged) collusion that excludes adults.[28]

Also taking a relational view of the elder's role in community is Unitarian Universalist minister Jennifer L. Brower. Rev. Brower speaks of later life as a time for transmission of the holy through relationship. Even in the face of physical and emotional hardship, moments of healing and transformation emerge where two or more are engaged in the mutual enterprise of sharing from the deepest self and opening to the other's deepest self.[29]

I think we would all agree that old age is no guarantee of wisdom. But evidence suggests some individuals do realize the fullness of their spiritual potential in entering into a state of sagehood. By their concerns, their breadth of insight, and the form of consciousness they have attained, sages are those precious ones who convey a depth of perspective that is cosmic in scope. One such person is wise woman and Jungian analyst Marion Woodman. Woodman speaks of the "crowning of age" as a time when one is relieved of personal desires; one's ego strivings dissipate and the heart is opened. One tends the world's soul and carries the feeling function to the community by caring for the earth and the young.[30]

The movement away from individuality and into a more comprehensive ground of being is a recurring theme in the literature of spirituality and aging. For Jung that broader ground concerned a release into a deeper identification with the natural world. In his memoirs, Jung speaks of his eighties as a time of freedom from individuality and a growing "kinship with all things." He says,

> there is so much that fills me: plants, animals, clouds, day and night, and the eternal in man. The more uncertain I have felt about myself, the more there has grown up in me a feeling of kinship with all things. In fact it seems to me as if that alienation which so long separated me from the world has become transferred into my own inner world, and has revealed to me an unexpected unfamiliarity with myself.[31]

Jung is describing how, over time, one's center of gravity shifts; the personal identity gives way to a more comprehensive consciousness. One's internal landscape becomes contiguous with the natural world.

Consciously aging persons seem to foster this process of identity expansion through reflectivity, attending to their dreams and to the quality of their relationships; they especially show acceptance in the face of loss. I am continually moved as I witness the support and insight my aging patients receive from their dreams as they anticipate physical disability, loss of a cherished social position, or the death of a spouse. In the following dream, archetypal imagery discloses the universal, spiritual depths underlying a man's later-life transition.

> *I dream that my wife is dying. We stand at a cliff, and I see her image fading as the wind blows against our bodies. I embrace her, trying to hold on to her. Her image recedes, and I find in her place the whole universe—planets, stars, galaxies.*

Jung called such dreams "big dreams"—narratives that reflect us back to ourselves as belonging to nature and humanity. Such dreams place our life transitions in a larger, less personal context and thus help us face areas of estrangement and loss. The dream draws a link between an anticipated loss and the dreamer's potential movement toward a more comprehensive awareness. Note how this dream utilizes the motif of the death marriage: the personal bride makes way for the mystical union between the dreamer and the cosmos.

Such dreams may be nature's way of reflecting upon itself through our faculties of consciousness. At the same time, the dream promotes a particular kind of awareness as its cosmic imagery pushes to the center of our imagining. In this instance the dreamer was not facing his own immanent death. Rather, the dream seeks to awaken the dreamer to his spiritual potential as he makes his transition to elderhood. The sage would be one who has attained this union with the divine ground in nature such that his vision is unitive in the mystical sense. As a form of awareness, unitive consciousness supports the spiritual process of the larger community as well as that of the individual. We are instinctively drawn to persons who possess it. In their presence one feels a sense of belonging to life's web.

One such person was the theologian Thomas Berry, who died just a few years ago. Berry was an early and major contributor to the environmental movement. A theologian and historian of Western and Asian thought, much of our understanding of the philosophical and theological backdrop to our planetary crises draws from his work. Through his life and teaching, Berry embodied those core spiritual potentials that Jung enumerates as the goal of aging.[32] First, he possessed a comprehensive awareness of himself as belonging to a larger reality. Berry dedicated his life to helping others awaken to what he called "the human story," a conscious connection to one's place in the larger story of divine revelation through the evolution of the universe. This connection fosters a sense of wonder and extends to an awareness of humanity as that form of being in which the universe reflects on and celebrates itself. Second, through his teaching and through the institutions he founded, Berry was a culture maker and preserver. He served as a grandfather to the generations that followed him by calling for the healing of the planet through the telling of "the Great Story," the primordial sacred story of the universe. Third, through his expansive vision, his storytelling, and poetry, Berry served the community by opening others to archetypal influences. And last, Berry possessed that quality of wisdom that accepts death as a goal toward which one can strive.

One of Berry's most original insights into our environmental crises was his attribution of the plundering of the earth's resources in the West to a collective fear of death. In his teaching he recalls how the devastations of the Black Death in the fourteenth century instilled in the Western psyche an antagonism and fear of the natural world. Our compulsive extraction of the earth's resources signifies a traumatic response. These excesses betray a desperate attempt to exercise control over nature—to take it apart and reconstruct it into "a Disneyland kind of reality." For the sake of survival we must reconcile ourselves to how things are in nature. Death, Berry reminds us, belongs to the natural process.[33]

In one interview, Berry describes the wise elder as one who represents and embodies "the correspondence of the human process with the natural process." According to Berry, the wise elder's presence promotes the making of a healthy society, which requires that all its members experience themselves "in integral relationship with the surrounding forces of the universe."[34] In other words, the gift the sage brings to the world at this critical juncture is that, by his or her mere presence, she or he fosters our reconnection to our roots in nature.

I was first exposed to such a person when I was a child. Mrs. Gurski, an old Slovakian immigrant who spoke little English, kept a small farm next to our home in rural Maryland. She was hardworking, stern, and lean, the sort of person one would expect a young child to fear more than seek out for comfort. The harsh features of her outer personality notwithstanding, her presence relieved me of an acute anxiety accompanying the diagnosis of a potentially life-threatening medical condition. For several years, recurring nightmares of the world's end disrupted my sleep and regular visits to medical labs instilled in me an unbearable dread. Seeking out this aged woman as often as allowed, I would sit beside her for long hours as she carried on her work in silence. Though we never spoke, she seemed fully aware of my presence. She smelled of the earth, and in the quiet of her company I experienced a suspension of fear and dread and a sense of belonging to this world.

In time, a consciously aging person may seem less a personality and more a culture carrier, mentor, defender of community well-being, and guardian of the bio-sphere. This portrait of an elder is presented by ecopsychologist Bill Plotkin. In Plotkin's formulation the elder is one who surrenders her or his sense of personal agency, strives less toward individual accomplishment and more toward the common good. Individuated elders report the sensation of moving deeper into formlessness in that they are released to a sense that something greater than themselves does their life's work *through* them.[35]

Is the state of elderhood or sagehood a potential that is realized *only* through conscious intention? Apparently not. We frequently find in the literature of aging heartfelt acceptance of the diminishments of the body and an affirmation of the simple blessings of being alive. The spiritual fruits of aging are found in Zen-like portraits of the luminosity of a single moment: "How peaceful it is here," wrote the agnostic E. M. Forster in his mid-seventies, "with the West Hackhurst clock still ticking, the Rooksnest fire irons still warm in the hearth, and [the dog] Little Master, his feet on [the] rug, nodding towards the end of a successful career."[36] And a few years on, as he approaches eighty, he wrote:

> My great extension is not through time to eternity, but
> through space to infinity: here: now: and one of my
> complaints against modern conditions is that they prevent
> one from seeing the stars.[37]

Forster's agnosticism was no barrier to his soul's journey. He had arrived at a transpersonal ground. He grasped infinity through an impassioned participation in the natural world, in the very place he stood.

This phenomenon may relate to a study recently published in the journal *Psychological Medicine*. Contrary to the stereotype of the elderly as frequently depressed in the face of loss and oncoming death, the study shows rates of depression and anxiety in later life to be lower than rates reported for working-age adults.[38] In fact, the fear of aging and death is much more common in early and late midlife.

I witnessed this natural movement into simplicity as I watched my mother in her final years. Uncharacteristic of her younger self, she became a kind of hybrid, a cross between a sage and a comedian. By age eighty, and notwithstanding recurring bouts of illness and multiple hospitalizations, my mother had become a kind of trickster, undermining serious moments with a quip or raucous laughter. She took particular pleasure in her night dreams in those last years. In fact, just a few weeks before she died, she repeatedly dreamed that she was making love with some unknown, beautiful lover. Her jokes about these surprising nocturnal encounters would send us into riotous laughter. The experience made her joyful, and I loved seeing her in that state. But it also made me sad. As a Jungian analyst, I'd had considerable exposure to the death-marriage motif in dreams and myths. I knew these nocturnal communions meant she would die very soon. And so it happened.

We tend to see death as dissolution. But such dreams anticipate death as a unity. Where does the truth lie? Throughout the life cycle death and renewal are inextricable. Releasing themselves into identity with the larger web of life, elders make a passage into death long before dying in the conventional sense. If you've known such a person and had the privilege to be present at his or her death, you may have witnessed an indescribable kind of luminosity at the time of their leaving. One is given a rare glimpse into life and death as a true unity— a parting gift from a spiritually vibrant life.

Conclusion

Conscious aging describes a process, a movement toward something of individual and social significance. At the core of this work lies the principle of transformation, the hallmark of later-life development. The tone of the journey will be set by our acceptance or rejection of an ever-changing self and world.

We have seen how a symbolic approach to the processes of aging shapes our perceptions such that life and death may be embraced as a unity. Envisaging correspondences between psycho-spiritual processes of development and the natural process, we are released by increments from the strivings of early adulthood and opened to a more comprehensive awareness of an underlying life stream. The fullest realization of the spiritual potential of aging is found in unitive forms of awareness carried by our wisest elders. Our collective task lies in repairing those social structures that impede our access to elders, while heeding the call to reformulate our assumptions about retirement and the significance of longevity.

NOTES

[1] Dan Buettner, *Blue Zones: 9 Lessons for Living Longer from the People Who've Lived the Longest*, 2nd ed. (Washington, DC: National Geographic Society, 2012).

[2] This percentage has risen from 12.1 percent in 1980 due to immigration and economic factors. Pew Research, "The Return of the Multi-Generational Family Household," *Social and Demographic Trends*, March 18, 2010. Accessed March 25, 2013, at http://www.pewsocialtrends.org/2010/03/18/the-return-of-the-multi-generational-family-household/.

[3] *Ibid.*

[4] Karen Armstrong, *The Battle for God: A History of Fundamentalism* (New York: Random House, 2000).

[5] Although a substantial minority of the unaffiliated consider themselves neither religious nor spiritual (42%), the majority describe themselves either as a religious person (18%) or as spiritual but not religious (37%). Pew Research, "'Nones' on the Rise," *The Pew Forum on Religion and Public Life*, Oct. 9, 2012. Accessed March 25, 2013, at http://www.pewforum.org/Unaffiliated/nones-on-the-rise.aspx.

[6] C. G. Jung, *Memories, Dreams, Reflections*, ed. Aniela Jaffe, trans. Richard and Clara Winston (New York: Vintage Books, 1965), p. 356.

[7] *I Ching*, trans. Richard Wilhelm and rendered into English by Cary F. Baynes (Princeton, NJ: Princeton University Press, 1967), pp. 111–121.

[8] C. G. Jung, "The Stages of Life," in *The Collected Works of C. G. Jung*, vol. 8, ed. and trans. Gerhard Adler and R. F. C. Hull (Princeton, NJ: Princeton University Press, 1960), § 784.

[9] David Whyte, *Midlife and the Great Unknown: Finding Courage and Clarity through Poetry*, compact disc (Sounds True, 2003).

[10] *Homeric Hymn to Aphrodite*, trans. Gregory Nagy, vs. 215–235. Accessed March 13, 2013, at http://www.uh.edu/~cldue/texts/aphrodite.html#_ftnref16.

[11] Alfred, Lord Tennyson, "Tithonus." Accessed 21 March 21, 2013, at http://www.poetryfoundation.org/poem/174656.

[12] Ronald Blythe, *The View in Winter* (Norwich, England: Canterbury Press, 2005), p. 17.

[13] *Ibid.*, p. 16.

[14] He is first mentioned in Hesiod's *Theogony*, vs. 116 ff. First there was Chaos, then came Ge and Tartarus, and then Eros, the fairest god and the one who rules the minds and the council of gods and men. As the uniting power of love, he brought order and harmony over the conflicting elements in Chaos. Hesiod, *Hesiod and Theoginis*, trans. Dorothea Wender (London: Penguin Books, 1973), p. 27.

[15] Artemidorus, *The Interpretation of Dreams: Oneirocritica*, as quoted in Marie-Louise von Franz, *On Dreams and Death*, trans. Emmanuel Xypolitas-Kennedy and Vernon Brooks (Boston: Shambhala, 1986), p. 52.

[16] Jung, *Memories, Dreams, Reflections*, p. 294.

[17] C. G. Jung, *Mysterium Coniunctionis*, vol. 14, *The Collected Works of C. G. Jung* (Princeton, NJ: Princeton University Press, 1970).

[18] C. G. Jung, "The Soul and Death," in *The Collected Works of C. G. Jung*, vol. 8, ed. and trans. Gerhard Adler and R. F. C. Hull (Princeton, NJ: Princeton University Press, 1960), § 800.

[19] Blythe, *The View in Winter*, p. 42.

[20] *Ibid.*, p. 16.

[21] George Congreve, *Treasures of Hope* (London: Longman, 1918), quoted in Blythe, *The View in Winter*, p. 288.

[22] Jung, "The Soul and Death," § 808.

[23] Jung, "The Stages of Life," § 792.

[24] Derek Walcott, "Love after Love." A beautiful reading of this poem is given by David Whyte on *Midlife and the Great Unknown*.

[25] The Centers for Disease Control and Prevention, "Ten great public health achievements—United States, 1900–1999," *JAMA* 281, no. 16 (1999): 1481.

[26] Jung, "The Stages of Life," § 787.

[27] William H. Thomas, *What Are Old People For? How Elders Will Save the World* (Acton, MA: VanderWyk and Burnham, 2004).

[28] William H. Thomas, "The Search for Being," *AARP Bulletin*, November 2004.

[29] Jennifer L. Brower, "Faith, Spirituality and Aging," *Frontline*, interview posted Nov. 21, 2000. Accessed March 30, 2013, at http://www.pbs.org/wgbh/pages/frontline/livingold/etc/faith.html.

[30] Marion Woodman, *The Crown of Age*, compact disc (Sounds True, 2002).

[31] Jung, *Memories, Dreams, Reflections*, p. 359.

[32] Jung, "The Stages of Life," §§ 785–792.

[33] *Thomas Berry: The Great Story*, directed by Nancy Stetson and Penny Morell (Bullfrog Films, 2002).

[34] Bill Plotkin, *Nature and the Human Soul: Cultivating Wholeness and Community in a Fragmented World* (Novato, CA: New World Library), p. 425.

[35] Plotkin, *Nature and the Human Soul*, p. 385.

[36] E. M. Forster, *Commonplace Book*, ed. Edward Connery Lathem (New York: Holt, Rinehart, Winston, 1969), as quoted in Wayne Booth, *The Art of Growing Older: Writers on Living and Aging* (Chicago: The University of Chicago Press, 1992), p. 174.

[37] *Ibid.*, p. 177.

[38] Dan G. Blazer and Celia F. Hybels, "Origins of Depression in Later Life," *Psychological Medicine* 35, no. 9 (2005): 1241; see also Ken Laidlaw and Nancy A. Pachana, "Aging with Grace," *APA Monitor* 42, no. 10 (2011): 65.

CHAPTER ELEVEN

Spirituality and Relationship in Later Life

JERRY M. RUHL, PH.D., AND ROLAND EVANS, M.A.

Introduction

L ove is our true destiny. We do not find the meaning of life by ourselves alone—we find it with another."[1] This quote from Thomas Merton, the Trappist monk and author, points toward a neglected aspect of relationship in the second half of life: that it can become the container for profound inner growth.

C. G. Jung suggested that later life is a time of introspection and the search for meaning and wholeness.[2] He called this individuation, a central concept in his psychology. Individuation—reaching our fullest potential—is a natural process for every human being and, like a plant, it blossoms and thrives given the right environment. That environment is almost always some form of intimate relationship. After the children are raised, the careers advanced, the mortgage paid, what is our life task? It is to deepen our natural growth through conscious intention, effort, and inner guidance. A powerful container for that process is a supportive relationship.

Jung recognized the importance of relationship: "Individuation has two principal aspects: in the first place it is an internal and subjective process of integration, and in the second it is an equally indispensable process of objective relationship."[3] The main focus of Jung's life work was integration within the individual. He did not emphasize interpsychic relations between or among people, though he did underscore that relationships and intimacy are critical elements for personal development.

From an adult point of view, the most important and influential aspect of our physical and emotional environment is that significant other, the person with whom we share our inner and outer lives. As we age, primary relationship becomes increasingly important, not only for our physical welfare but also our psychological and spiritual well-being. We look for new meaning in the relational aspects of existence as we grapple with physical challenges and losses that naturally accompany the aging process. The ability to be close to another person, to share our changing experiences, takes on new meaning. Eventually, this sharing is curtailed by disability, illness, and death. Yet even then, for the survivor a deep relational bond may continue.

There are different forms of primary relationship, marriage being the most common and obvious. However, the term *primary relationship* extends beyond the social definition of marriage. It includes gay and lesbian relationships (which only recently may take the form of marriage), cohabiting couples, and asexual connections that are self-defined as "more than friendship" (often called soul mates). In this chapter, we will often refer to primary relationships as *marriage*, using that term in its widest meaning: an intimate, exclusive, committed union with another. Marriage is no longer always a prerequisite for child rearing and often not for economic and political security. In the past, farms and small businesses were often run by a husband and wife together, but this is less often the case today.

The political marriage, by which royal houses or powerful families join to ensure a continuing dynasty or resolve conflicts, still exists, but it increasingly seems like a relic of the past.

So why marry in this day and age? In the twenty-first century, a deep intimate relationship has come to be understood in some circles as the archetypal container for individuation, what we will call transformative relationships. Our contention is that primary relationship is fundamental for individuation, spirituality, and meaning in later life.

In the film *The Accidental Tourist*, based on the novel by Anne Tyler, we find: "In turbulent, troubling times, a good marriage can be the one safe place we know we can go. Once we've been to that place, known that peace, we can never forget it."[4] A primary relationship then becomes the training ground for attainment of our highest aspirations: love, compassion, forgiveness, surrender, generosity, selflessness, and gratitude. These are qualities that wisdom traditions describe as the means to and rewards of spiritual progress.

As we age, we hunger for meaning beyond the personal, yet many continue to focus on the past and the private self when it may no longer be the most relevant priority. In the second half of life, instead of the continuing analysis of childhood wounds and self-absorbed ego development, we might look to expand the quality of our relationships and explore how they can become containers for profound spirituality, meaning, and purpose.

Individuation and Relationship

Jung believed that there is a destination, a possible goal for life beyond maximizing pleasure, pursuing power, and obtaining material goods. He conceived of individuation as the process for reaching this goal: the process of becoming more self-aware—finding our wholeness. Just as the acorn contains potentials to become an oak, there is a drive that pushes us to individuate, and it kicks into high gear in the second half of life. When it is blocked, we feel trapped, stagnate, and may become physically ill. Postmodern life forces us to develop one-sided personalities, cut off from our roots in the unconscious. To live a more balanced, meaningful life, we must transcend our ego identity—that aspect of our being molded by family and culture—and become fully developed human beings.

Jung's choice of the word *individuation* is unfortunate; he constantly had to explain he did not mean individualism—a sort of pilgrim's progress without a creed aiming not at heaven but at self-centered development. According to Jung, "as the individual is not just a single, separate being, but by his very existence presupposes a collective relationship, it follows that the process of individuation must lead to more intense and broader collective relationships and not to isolation."[5]

Individuation, indeed all spiritual development, is inherently relational; it requires that we listen to the other, whether in the form of another person or promptings from beyond our ego. Thus our conscious plans and desires are constantly modified by forces hidden beneath awareness. The sage of Zürich referred to this inner interference as an act of the deity: "To this day God is the name by which I designate all things which cross my willful path violently and recklessly, all things which upset my subjective views, plans and intentions and change the course of my life for better or worse."[6]

Wow. Sharing your psychic house with someone who exasperates you, changes your plans, spotlights your shortcomings? That sounds very like our experience of relationships. What better container to have our willful and often misguided intentions thwarted than marriage?

Much of psychotherapy and personal growth is searching within—analyzing emotions, cognitive patterns, dreams, and fantasies that occur outside of our willful intentions. This may be incredibly helpful at certain phases of our life journey. However, as we mature, our awareness must extend beyond the personal. Without intimate connection, even spirituality begins to look like a self-centered activity.

What is required is the other—the reflection of our humanity in the eyes of a separate but connected being. A deep relationship to an analyst or therapist can provide a corrective experience for childhood deficiencies, but ultimately such professional relationships are one-sided. We need a mutual other to know the world and ourselves. The Hasidic scholar and philosopher Martin Buber insisted that the sacred comes to us in encounters with one another, what he termed the I-Thou relationship.[7] Every meeting invites a response from our being; relationship is not a means to some end but the point of being alive. We become fully realized in order to be more available for relationship, not the other way round.

Importance of Relationship in Later Life

Consciously or unconsciously, human beings yearn for enduring, supportive, loving relationships. As we age, this need becomes ever more urgent; personal connections in later life, as in infancy, are essential for well-being. The research on aging shows categorically the physical and psychological benefits of intimate relationship: couples live richer, healthier, longer lives than singles.[8] But it is not just relationship per se that is beneficial. As Cory Bolkan states: "the quality of the relationship is the best predictor of health and well-being."[9] We all know instinctively that love is the force that will keep us alive and engaged with life until the last breath.

This accepted folk wisdom is evidence based: 72 percent of men and 45 percent of women over the age of sixty-five are officially married.[10] This statistic does not include couples in nonconforming primary relationships. And getting married does not lose its attraction with age: as many as 500,000 Americans sixty-five and older marry or remarry each year.[11] Even with the high rate of divorce, 33 percent of married couples reach their silver wedding anniversary and 20 percent survive through their thirty-fifth anniversary.[12] It is obvious that as we age intimate relationships are ubiquitous, highly valued, and beneficial for our lives.

Other statistics show that not only physical health but also mental health is influenced by relationship. Aging brings an inevitable weakening of the body but often coincides with a softening of the heart. As work commitments are scaled back, there is increased time for social activities, and couples spend more time together. Men particularly can take a cue from their partners and begin to value intimacy more than when they were working full time.[13] If we view retirement symbolically, we see that it implies a withdrawal from the demands of the material world; it reflects the increased importance of both social connection and spiritual exploration.

These benefits only happen if the relationship is not compromised by emotional distance and unresolved conflicts. If it is, intimate time can become increasingly painful and problematic. If, however, the couple has a solid and steadfast relationship and has moved beyond petty bickering and resentments, retirement becomes a richly meaningful period with increased loving contact. In that fertile soil, individuation flourishes, and the partners can experience the inner reality of marriage.

The Marriage Archetype

More than two thousand years ago, Plato in his *Symposium* wrote of the separation of humans into two halves.[14] The primeval human was round, back and sides forming a circle; it had four hands and the same number of feet and one head set on a round neck with two faces looking opposite ways and precisely alike. One day the gods took offense at the insolence of the new race of humans, and Zeus cut them in two with a thunderbolt. Ever since, we have been looking for our missing half. This powerful myth points to a numinous inner reality: we are all desperately seeking our soul mates, trying to achieve a deeply instinctive union and become whole.

Ancient Greece was not the only culture with myths and rituals concerning primary relationship. While the forms differ, all cultures have religious rites concerning marriage. These rituals are sacramental, indicating a deep archetypal aspect to the joining of the couple. Marriage ceremonies include powerful symbols of wholeness and unity: the wedding ring, the joining of hands, the ritual kiss. They point toward the inner meaning of the wedding; marriage is an archetype—a powerful template characterized by instinct and images that implicitly shape human perceptions and actions.

Traditionally, marriage was a socially recognized bonding of man and woman. More recently, with gay marriage and the increase in numbers of cohabiting couples, the expression of the marriage archetype is changing. Guggenbühl-Craig, in his book *Marriage Is Dead—Long Live Marriage!*, provocatively argues that the cultural and social aspects of marriage are ever changing, but the urge to merge in a sacred joining of two souls is instinctual and archetypal.[15]

Because it is an archetype, it is hard to fully grasp the meaning and power of marriage. Much of its psychic energy and ubiquitous power as a symbol comes from the unconscious. All cultures have rituals around such coupling. The mythologist Joseph Campbell attempts to conveys its depth and authority: "When you make the sacrifice in marriage, you're sacrificing not to each other but to unity in a relationship . . . . It's the reunion of the separated duad. Originally you were one. You are now two in the world, but the recognition of the spiritual identity is what marriage is."[16]

Archetypal energies of relationship arise like the gods of old, archaic and impersonal. We are gripped by the ecstasy and selflessness of falling in love—a state of being enthralled by unconscious forces. We get lost in the compulsion to fight with our loved one, not even knowing what it is about. Relationships have the power to move us to blind rage and sublime altruism, to wound us terribly and to heal us absolutely. As we mature and become more self-aware, and as we connect more deeply with our instinctual and spiritual natures, the power of relationship increasingly turns toward supporting inner growth. As Campbell puts it so well, marriage is not just a social arrangement: "It's *primarily* a spiritual exercise."[17] The archetype of marriage becomes harnessed in service to enlightenment.

A transformative relationship necessarily encompasses the shadow aspects of human nature as well as the light. The fantasy of a totally easy, "happy" marriage still dominates our culture, even in the face of a divorce rate surpassing 50 percent. Self-help books and marriage counselors seldom present the unvarnished truth: relationships are painful and challenging, hard to comprehend and fraught with danger—because that is the nature of individuals. This truth is nicely illustrated by a dream from a female client:

> *The Holy Spirit appears in the form of a truck mechanic. He tells her, "You know you can have a relationship if you want one." To which she replies, "But I am too difficult to live with." As he walks away the Holy Spirit gives his parting shot, "You know, everyone is difficult to live with!"*[18]

We each must face the fact that we are hard to live with. We even have trouble living with our most cherished loved ones. All primary relationships are filled with conflict and suffering as well as joy and contentment. Zeus and Hera, the archetypal married couple for the ancient Greeks, were constantly quarreling. Zeus had innumerable sexual liaisons, and Hera avenged herself pitilessly against her husband's lovers. The image of a strife-filled marriage is reflected not only among the gods but also in popular stories throughout history: for example, many of Chaucer's *Canterbury Tales* tell of marital discord.[19] Disruption, dysfunction, and differences seem to be natural and even essential in all relationships. Even with all the difficulties, even though the majority of relationships include disappointment, we are still driven by the archetype to seek out primary relationships. We have no choice.

To understand the path toward transformative relationships, we begin not in the cradle (though early experiences clearly shape later relationship issues) but in the stormy, hormone-driven seas of adolescence: the emergence of immature, unconscious relationships.

Immature, Unconscious Relationships

Do you remember an early adolescent love? It was wonderful and terrible, uplifting and disheartening; mostly it was simply unreal. We all start with idealized illusory connections—not relationships in a true sense because we are not coherent enough to see the other person, to know what we are feeling, or to understand why it is happening. These early attempts at relating are mostly unconscious: need, lust, affection, hunger, and attachment all wrapped up in unreal expectations. When it happens in our youth, immature love can be rather sweet and endearing, if tragic. As with Romeo and Juliet, these early love entanglements are doomed—and rightly so. They are learning experiences, flexing of the emotional muscles, and should not be confused with enduring relationships. When these patterns of relating continue into adulthood, they quickly turn monstrous.

In Jungian terms, the immature relationships are driven and dominated by unconscious projections.[20] Like the projected images on the movie screen, everything is larger than life, more intense, ultimately unrealistic yet emotionally compelling. Each of the participants is attempting to heal unconscious wounds and satisfy unmet needs stemming from childhood and beyond, using the other person as a projection screen. What we don't or can't recognize in ourselves is first projected upon the other, someone who carries enough of the qualities we desperately seek. As we get to know that person, we gradually realize, mostly to our chagrin, that they are much more or less than we bargained for.

Our psychological makeup and behavior are profoundly influenced by early experiences, deeply programmed patterns that tend to control our choice of partner and character of our relationships. Projection inevitably leads to disappointment. The person we thought we loved is nowhere near as perfect, faithful, or loving as the image we project onto them. So we try everything we can to remake them into that unrealistic image. The deep anxiety of being attached to someone we do not know or understand yet cannot let go of causes inner turmoil. Affection turns to antagonism and the compulsion to control. In Jung's memorable words, "Where love rules, there is no will to power; and where power predominates, there love is lacking. The one is the shadow of the other."[21]

Such immature couplings, if they do not end in chaos and recriminations, tend to burn out, the pair becoming two dead stars orbiting each other endlessly. Jung writes that antagonism leads to decreased affection and ends up as emotional emptiness: "First it was passion, then it became duty, and finally an intolerable burden, a vampire that battens on the life of its creator."[22]

In the unconscious relationship, sex tends to be self-centered—a physical release but not a full emotional or spiritual connection. Eventually, unresolved emotional patterns—be they withholding, controlling, uncommunicative, or insecure—begin to show in how a couple relates sexually.[23] Couples fight and make love unconsciously as the only means to reconnect. Ironically, as resentments build toward total disconnection, couples stop having sex and thus lose their only path to reestablishing harmony.

Whatever the outcome, however dissonant and unkind, it is important to realize that the original impetus to lose ourselves in a shared connection arises from the spiritual power of the marriage archetype. The act of falling in love, however unrealistic, is an attempt to enter into a spiritual identity with the other. The love-struck teenager glimpses the divine and is filled with a heavenly joy, a feeling that eternity is here and now.

Projection is a useful psychological concept for understanding our inability to truly perceive and engage the other. However, it is based on the assumption that most of what is happening in relationship is "just inside my head." In truth, relationship occurs in an intersubjective field and is an exchange of energy more aptly described in the concept of resonance.[24] Think of two strings on a violin, resonating to one pitch. In tune, their combined sound becomes one pleasing note to our ear. Then imagine one of those strings a fraction of a tone off, creating a dissonance that grates and annoys, that sets our teeth on edge. That is what happens continually in an unconscious relationship: the two people keep missing each other energetically, keep getting on each other's nerves. Our nervous systems are not self-contained, but are positively or negatively attuned to those we love.

The majority of immature unconscious relationships end in failure. But there is always the possibility that projections are withdrawn, losing their compulsive power and allowing realistic love to blossom. Then the relationship stabilizes and settles into something we might term a mature, functional relationship. Conscious love participates in a divine mystery that potentially mixes the mundane and the miraculous. We stir the oatmeal, take out the trash, learn to listen and be considerate, and we grow up and put into practice the qualities of mature relationship.

Mature, Functional Relationships

Mature primary relationships are complex, fluctuating processes that change over time. They exist on a continuum: some stay stuck at a more unconscious level, while others evolve toward a state that is not only stable but also transformative. Much of the extensive relationship literature focuses on those skills that are needed for a couple to progress away from immaturity and misery toward maturity and satisfaction. Foremost of these skills is the ability to communicate honestly and intimately.

Problems and misunderstandings arise in every relationship and have to be worked through in order to maintain and deepen trust and connection. Unresolved resentments fester, "no-go" areas promote emotional distance, and poor communication creates mistakes and misunderstandings. Every couple needs to learn to work together to repair ruptures.

We tend to identify communication with speech but that is the tip of the iceberg. A loving touch, a bouquet of flowers, a shared movie, passionate sex: nonverbal sharing is often more communicative and healing than endless hours spent processing problems. To generalize, mature communication must be truthful, heartfelt, fitted to the needs and personalities of the participants, and effective.

In the realm of nonverbal communication, the giving and receiving of pleasure, comfort, and affection through sexual intercourse is possibly the most powerful. A fulfilling sex life is one of the essential elements of a stable relationship that reinforces a deep sense of intimacy and connection. Sexual pleasure is often more possible in the middle and later years as the couple develops deeper levels of trust and acceptance supported by mature and realistic expectations.

Trust and acceptance in a primary relationship require a shared commitment to staying together. Stable couples are seen as securely attached; they have few anxieties about the enduring nature of the relationship and believe that their partner cares for them.[25] In a securely attached relationship, the couple is faithful sexually and emotionally; they may have more or less conflict but the dissonance does not dangerously impact their commitment. They share positive beliefs about marriage and experience satisfaction with the intimacy, communication, and emotional involvement in the relationship.[26] In essence, they have embraced the idea that their marriage is a life attachment—and it is where they want to be.

The maturity of the relationship mirrors the emotional maturity of the participants. Each person must learn to moderate their emotional reactions, to think before they speak, to consider the effect of their words and actions on the relationship bond. The emotional climate of a stable primary relationship should be like good weather: mostly sunny with occasional showers and infrequent thunderstorms. The couple who shares high levels of affection and low levels of antagonism—more love than fights—experiences greater satisfaction in the relationship.[27]

The ability to understand, to show emotional restraint, to be generous and forgiving, requires that we know ourselves, that we become conscious of our own emotional triggers and overreactions. This happens as we withdraw our projections and unrealistic expectations and accept the other person as they are in reality— not as we hope they will become. This is a gradual process: we get used to the person, tolerate their flaws, and learn to accept and love them anyway. Like rocks in a polishing tumbler, the sharp edges gradually are smoothed out. Mature love is less about passion and more about patience.[28]

Of course, it is easier to be patient with someone who shares our attitudes and values. According to research from the University of Virginia, mutual generosity is a core value that strongly predicts decreased probability of divorce, and generous couples are significantly more likely to report that they are "very happy" in their marriage.[29] Generosity is not just the virtue of giving good things to one's spouse freely and abundantly; it also encompasses small acts of service, expressions of affection, and the willingness to forgive mistakes and failings. Spouses who value a generous open heart are rewarded accordingly. Loving-kindness begets loving-kindness.

In a similar vein, religious or spiritual values are strong indicators of marital success. According to University of Virginia researchers, those who share "the sense that God is present in one's marriage—that marriage has a transcendent meaning" are not only least likely to divorce but also experience the most marital happiness.[30] For these mature couples, the later years of a committed relationship bring the highest level of satisfaction.[31] Older couples are more affectionate with each other, have less conflict, and show more respect to each other compared with their younger counterparts.[32]

Espousing values traditionally viewed as religious or spiritual—generosity, compassion, forgiveness, and selflessness—allow the mature relationship to evolve beyond mere functionality. Viewing marriage as a committed sacred path, becoming more self-aware, communicating clearly, honestly, and intimately—these are spiritual practices that allow the individuals and their relationship to evolve far beyond the ordinary. The primary relationship becomes a numinous container for transformation.

Transformative Relationships

What exactly is a transformative relationship? What does it look like? Marion Woodman, a wise elder in the Jungian community, describes what we call transformative relationship as the *inner marriage*: "The relationship is no longer two people in love, but loving each other through God."[33] This form of connection brings a profound sense of wholeness, a sacred quality to the relationship that reaches above and beyond the personalities of the participants.

Woodman suggests that in the inner marriage, the individuals have realized and integrated, to some extent, the masculine and feminine aspects of their own personalities: "Both these energies are in balance in a mature person."[34] This only happens after years of spiritual and psychological work and is most likely to occur late in a couple's life.

According to Guggenbühl-Craig, individuation in older couples is characterized "less by struggling with each other and the world, and more by serving."[35] That does not mean a transformative relationship is free of conflict or personal difficulties; it remains a human relationship with all that entails. Woodman is eloquent in describing these difficulties: "Marriage has an archetypal dimension where we are working out our flaws, our gifts, what we have inherited, and what is unique to us. So a real soul mate is not the perfect partner, in the sense of being there to give us what we want."[36]

To transcend and work through these difficulties requires an attitude of detachment, a profound recognition of who we are and who the other person is in his or her essence. Detachment does not imply not caring but rather "allows destiny to work through you, so that you are totally involved in life at the same time as allowing something else to be lived through you."[37] Such an attitude, acquired after years of loving, allows the other to unfold to his or her full potential.

Love, to Woodman, is a magical numinous force: "By love I mean an energy that is actually vibrant between people. If that vibration is cut off, the cells of the body change . . . I think this vibration which passes between two people changes them. Love transforms."[38] This is resonance at its most sublime.

In sum, a transformative relationship evolves within a stable long-term relationship in which both members take responsibility for their own inner work and recognize the sacred nature of their connection. It transcends the mature functional relationship by recognizing that love has a spiritual quality, that being together has a transcendent purpose, and that the relationship is a container for individuation.

The Transformative Relationship Interview

To explore and illuminate the nature of transformative relationships, we interviewed three couples whose relationships were self-identified as successful and who had been together for more than two decades. They exhibited qualities of connection, contentment, and engagement that were easy to recognize; each couple was known to us as possible examples of wise elders. The ages of the participants ranged from sixty to eighty-eight, and they had various religious affiliations: Christian, Jewish, and Buddhist. The couples agreed to share their experiences in structured face-to-face interviews that lasted about seventy-five minutes each.

The first part of each interview aimed to discover how the relationship had developed and evolved. As expected, all the participants described extensive change in the relationship over the years:

> "Total transformation—another incarnation!"
> "We feel more naturally intimate with each other and more connected."
> "Now what at first felt a difficulty is not even a bump in the road. There's a sense of comradeship."
> "We have become more relaxed and open around the other person's style and needs."

The overriding theme was that the primary relationship had become an essential part of their being and, though there were still differences, these were not experienced as problematic.

All described how their relationship was challenging in the early years, with more fights and struggles. But as one person commented, "How can you get to truth if there are no difficulties?" Over the years, each of the couples developed a more accepting and supportive attitude toward the other and better skills at resolving problems:

> "I don't want to hurt him anymore. I have total acceptance of things that used to bug me."
> "We're less likely to get triggered now."
> "We often walk away unsettled and come back with a willingness to compromise."
> "When we get into a difficult emotional situation we have some awareness."
> "Letting go of fixation of being right and seeing what the other sees."

When asked how the relationship contributed to individual development, the participants emphasized how they learned from their partner and how the relationship made them face things about themselves:

> "From [my partner] I get equanimity, a relaxed quality, an open view."
>
> "You must move from the ego to the Self in that nakedness that you cannot show to the whole world. Your partner knows you with your foibles, weaknesses, cowardice."
>
> "It's also necessary to know the partner loves you anyway with your foibles and faults and failures. It makes it possible to live through it.
>
> "I have given up trying to measure her with my idea of what is the proper way of experiencing spirit."
>
> "The relationship provided a container for it [transformation]. Then I could survive and eventually move into thriving."

One aspect stood out strongly: the quality of appreciation, respect, and affection each has for the other:

> "Something very deep was my attraction to [my partner]. I sense her essence."
>
> "I take delight in seeing [her] in my environment; it makes me happy.
>
> "I appreciate I learn things I can't on my own."
>
> "Just appreciation . . . To see that unfold with a partner and share insights is wonderful.
>
> "I experience love, a deep sense of integrity inside myself from watching her."

The couples emphasized deeply intimate sharing and communication that transcends words and separateness:

> "A lot of that is communication. In our situation it has been inner communication as much as interpersonal"
>
> "Very often I write a love letter to [her] and put it under her plate. Every time she leaves me a note I save it. If I were to say what do I treasure, these are the moments."

"I'm committed to her seeing everything."

"We become one mind when we work together."

The experience of love had also changed over the years, gaining in selflessness and a quiet numinous quality:

"My experience of love has taken the form of her feeling her greatness, feeling her depth. The movement from self-love is to create energy—considering what I can do to help her feel good about herself and see her own greatness."

"I feel our hearts get to a place of communion and eyes filled with tears; we sit in these movies and hold hands.

"We spend lot of time not talking at all."

"An underlying recognition that we belong to each other."

With respect to sexuality, there was surprising agreement. Sex had been central to their early relationships and it still had its place, but increasingly it had transformed into a shared physical intimacy and closeness:

"Sexuality is so much bigger than usually defined. I like when we wake in the night and talk for a couple of hours and then go back to sleep. That is deep intimacy—often more than physical sex."

"Just want to hold each other even if there is no longer physical fire."

"Not as much as the years have unfolded—more early on in the relationship. We do cuddle, and sleep in the same bed."

When asked what attitudes were essential to their marriage, they offered a wide range of comments:

"Depth of honesty with oneself."

"Not to twist yourself out of shape in order to be liked by the other."

"Taking time regularly to put yourself in the other's place and understand what they feel."

"Compromise, flexibility, sense of humor, easy going energy."
"Patience, compassion, forgiveness."

All of the participants emphasized how important it is to live a conscious life, maintain a spiritual practice and work unceasingly to become the best person possible:

"Bring everything back to your own process, self observe, take responsibility for it, and work on it."
"Self responsibility and the desire to be the best you can be. To humble oneself completely."
"I feel that my own meditation life has continued. What I learn from you are things I would find in a prayer book but not notice before."
"We wouldn't have gotten together if [we] had not done our own work."
"I definitely feel that being together has helped us work out future karma, raising awareness, increasing the ability to not fixate on certain goals or outcomes. We can work together and assist each other. I feel really blessed being able to work our meditation practice both alone and together."

The fruits of the transformative relationship extend beyond the mundane and predictable into different realms. These couples experience small indescribable moments of transcendence:

"Our last stop in summer before bed is the balcony to see the stars in the dark . . . They are quiet moments, not a lot of activity. They don't come with a fanfare."
"One day [he] came down the steps and there was this strange little moment in which time stopped. They occurred all the way through."

One last comment from one of the participants: "Who would have *thunk* you could meet someone as a teenager and we would still be so close!"

Conclusion

Individuation is the pursuit of wholeness; love is the essence of wholeness. On the one hand is our personal drive to individuate—to find our individual meaning and purpose. On the other hand, in counterbalance, is our archetypal need for loving connection. Most Jungian literature focuses on one side of this balance, individual development. In this chapter, we suggest that the "complete" whole be recognized, in that individuation happens within the context of relationship.

Just as each soul must journey from unconsciousness through trials and difficulty toward ultimate transformation, so the quality of our relationships mirrors this evolution. Each immature relationship contains a kernel of potential. This seed may germinate into a mature partnership in which the members experience deep connection and contentment. Through grace, intention, and effort, some mature relationships further transcend their limitations to become sacred containers for spiritual growth—most often after many years together in the latter part of a lifetime.

In a transformative relationship, partners learn to face difficult truths about themselves. Friction between "dueling egos" is necessary for growth but ultimately must be sacrificed on the altar of a greater good, an ultimate potential. Wholeness becomes a harmony of "I" and "You," a transcendent and transformative unity. In the daily give and take, the meandering path of an evolving relationship, one observes a hidden hand directing the slow process of psychic growth—this we call individuation.

NOTES

[1] Thomas Merton, *Love and Living* (Orlando, FL: Harcourt, 1985).

[2] See C. G. Jung, "The Stages of Life," in *The Collected Works of C. G. Jung*, vol. 8, ed. and trans. Gerhard Adler and R. F. C. Hull (Princeton, NJ: Princeton University Press, 1960).

[3] C. G. Jung, "The Psychology of the Transference," in *The Collected Works of C. G. Jung*, vol. 16, ed. and trans. Gerhard Adler and R. F. C. Hull (Princeton, NJ: Princeton University Press, 1960), § 448.

[4] Frank Galati and Lawrence Kasdan, *The Accidental Tourist*, directed by Lawrence Kasdan (Warner Bros., 1988), DVD.

[5] C. G. Jung, "The Relations between the Ego and the Unconscious," in *The Collected Works of C. G. Jung,* vol. 7, ed. and trans. Gerhard Adler and R. F. C. Hull (Princeton, NJ: Princeton University Press, 1953), § 241, note 10.

[6] C. G. Jung, *Letters, Vol. 2, 1951–1961,* ed. Gerhard Adler, trans. J. Hulen (Princeton, NJ: Princeton University Press, 1976), p. 525.

[7] Martin Buber, *The Way of Man: According to the Teaching of Hasidism* ((New York: Routledge, 1965).

[8] Kristen Stewart, "The Health Benefits of Marriage," Everyday Health, Nov. 2010. Accessed September 22, 2013, at http://www.everydayhealth.com/family-health/understanding/benefits-of-tying-the-knot.aspx.

[9] Cory Bolkan, quoted in Paris Achen, "More People over 65 Find Marriage, Love," The Columbian, April 29, 2013. Accessed September 22, 2013, at http://www.columbian.com/news/2012/jul/29/ageless-romance.

[10] U.S. Dept. of Health and Human Services, Administration of Aging, "A Profile of Older Americans: 2012." Accessed September 22, 2013, at http://www.aoa.gov/Aging_Statistics/Profile/2012/docs/2012profile.pdf.

[11] See Achen, "More People over 65 Find Marriage, Love."

[12] Diana B. Elliott and Tavia Simmons, "Marital Events of Americans: 2009," U.S. Census Bureau, American Community Survey Reports, August 2011. Accessed September 22, 2013, at http://www.census.gov/prod/2011pubs/acs-13.pdf.

[13] Ruth Walker, M. Luszcz, D. Gerstorf, and C. Hoppmann, "Subjective Well-Being Dynamics in Couples from the Australian Longitudinal Study of Aging," *Gerontology* 57 (2011): 153–160.

[14] Plato, *The Symposium,* in *The Portable Plato*, ed. Scott Buchanan (New York: The Viking Press, 1948), pp. 143ff.

[15] Adolf Guggenbühl-Craig, *Marriage Is Dead—Long Live Marriage!* (New York: Spring Publications, 1977), p. 20.

[16] Joseph Campbell with Bill Moyers, *The Power of Myth* (New York: Anchor Books, 1988), pp. 6–7.

[17] Campbell, *The Power of Myth*, p. 8.

[18] Adapted from Roland Evans, *Seeking Wholeness* (Hygiene, CO: SunShine Press Publications, 2001), p. 107.

[19] Geoffrey Chaucer, *Canterbury Tales* (New York: Oxford University Press, 2011).

[20] See John A. Sanford, *The Invisible Partners* (New York: Paulist Press, 1980).

[21] C. G. Jung, "On the Psychology of the Unconscious," in *The Collected Works of C. G. Jung*, vol. 7, ed. and trans. Gerhard Adler and R. F. C. Hull (Princeton, NJ: Princeton University Press, 1953), § 78.

[22] C. G. Jung, "Marriage as a Psychological Relationship," in *The Collected Works of C. G. Jung*, vol. 17, ed. and trans. Gerhard Adler and R. F. C. Hull (Princeton, NJ: Princeton University Press, 1960), § 331a.

[23] See David Schnarch, *Passionate Marriage* (New York: Henry Holt and Co., 1997).

[24] See Thomas Lewis, Fari Amini, and Richard Lannon, *A General Theory of Love* (New York: Vintage Books, 2000).

[25] John Bowlby, *Attachment and Loss,* vol. 1, *Attachment* (New York: Basic Books, 1969).

[26] See P. Shaver and C. Hazan, "Adult Romantic Attachment: Theory and Evidence," in D. Perlman and W. Jones, eds., *Advances in Personal Relationships,* vol. 4 (London, PA: Jessica Kingsley, 1994), pp. 29–70.

[27] Mario Mikulincer, Victor Florian, Philip A. Cowan, and Carolyn Pape Cowan, "Attachment Security in Couple Relationship," *Family Process* 41, no. 3 (2002): 405.

[28] See Laura L. Carstensen, John M. Gottman, and Robert W. Levenson, "Emotional Behavior in Long-Term Marriage," *Psychology and Aging* 10, no. 1 (1995): 140–149.

[29] National Marriage Project, "The State of Our Unions: Marriage in America 2011," University of Virginia. Accessed September 27, 2013, at http://nationalmarriageproject.org/wp-content/uploads/2012/05/Union_2011.pdf.

[30] National Marriage Project, "Husbands Who Have the Happiest Marriage," University of Virginia. Accessed September 27, 2013, at http://nationalmarriageproject.org/wp-content/uploads/2012/12/NMP-Fact-Sheet-Husbands-1112.pdf.

[31] See Susan Turk Charles and Laura L. Carstensen, "Marriage in Old Age," in Marilyn Yalom and Laura Carstensen, eds., *Inside the American Couple: New Thinking, New Challenges* (Berkeley: University of California Press, 2002), pp. 236–254.

[32] Fran C. Dickson, "Aging and Marriage," in W. Kim Halford and Howard J. Markham, eds., *Clinical Handbook of Marriage and Couples Interventions* (New York: John Wiley and Sons, 1997), pp. 255–271.

[33] Marion Woodman, "Embracing the Dark," in Roger Housden and Chloe Goodchild, *We Two* (London: The Aquarian Press, 1992), p. 197.

[34] Woodman, "Embracing the Dark," p. 203.

[35] Guggenbühl-Craig, *Marriage Is Dead—Long Live Marriage!*, p. 122.

[36] Woodman, "Embracing the Dark," p. 205.

[37] *Ibid.*, p. 204.

[38] *Ibid.*, p. 206.

CHAPTER TWELVE

For Every Tatter in Our Mortal Dress
Stayin' Alive at the Front of the Mortal Parade

JAMES HOLLIS, PH.D.

> An aged man is but a paltry thing,
> a tattered coat upon a stick, unless
> Soul clap its hands and sing, and louder sing
> For every tatter in its mortal dress . . .
> —W. B. Yeats, "Sailing to Byzantium"

Yeats wrote those words when he was aged, in physical pain, and sick at heart for the many disappointments in his life. No young person is allowed to write such words. One can only say, "Wait a few decades, see what life brings you, and then we will see . . ." Such a pronouncement may sound like cynicism, even bitterness, but it is not. It is simple realism. Let me cite five exemplary paradoxes of the problem of aging in this troubled time between the gods.

1. In my youth, I was puzzled by a recurrent Greek adage: "Best of all is not to have been born; second best is to have died young." Early in life I found this thought almost incomprehensible, pessimistic, and antilife. Now I understand the wisdom, as well as the wry but futile hope of escaping life without its suffering. As Yeats elsewhere described the boundaries of our human condition: "Man is in love, and loves what vanishes. What more is there to say?"[1] So, reader, is that ancient advice offered us cynical, bitter, or realistic? How does it measure up to the totality of our experiences? Are we able, willing, to embrace the ominous fullness of this life which we otherwise desperately wish to prolong?

2. A writer once interviewed me on the subject of the second half of life for a national periodical published by a major interest group lobbying for richer senior living. She found her heuristic questions, and my responses, repeatedly edited and softened by the publisher, and irritatingly so. She became sufficiently heated and finally visited their headquarters to confront the editors. She found, to her surprise and dismay, that most of them were in their thirties. How could they really understand what it means to be in one's seventies or eighties? No wonder their cover articles were mostly focused on beautiful people like Harry Belafonte and Faye Dunaway. They could not, understandably, imagine themselves any way other than in their youthful conditions and states of mind.

3. In an earlier phase of professional life, when I was teaching an undergraduate course on the stages of life development, I asked my students to read the textbook with its quite illuminating examples and write an essay imagining their lives two units or cycles ahead of where they currently were. My silly thought was that perhaps by knowing something of the road ahead, they might be able to navigate its terrain a bit more consciously. How wrong I was! They read the material, which outlined the typical, even predictable issues and trials likely to arise for each stage, and they could accurately describe those issues. But when it came to imagining their lives in concrete settings or dilemmas similar to those described, they hit an imaginative wall, explaining only how they and their wonderful partners, and their lovely, devoted children, adroitly sidestepped these pitfalls and moved to an ever-increasing domestic,

professional, and philosophical bliss. This is one of the many reasons, and probably the most important, why I left college teaching in search of someone with whom to have a reality-based conversation. Yet the limits to the imagination of these youth are seemingly common to us all. It is not the limit of intelligence or good intentions. Rather, it is the limitation of an experiential framework and a constricted imagination governed by complexes, wishes, and the seductive modes of denial to which we are all subject.

4. A number of months ago, I was invited to be a luncheon speaker at a benefit for the gerontology program of a nearby medical school. I went expecting to find an assembly of gerontology students and professionals. Instead, I found a group of impeccably coifed, bedecked, bedizened, and bejeweled socialites. My talk addressed the greatest neurosis of our culture—the flight from aging and mortality and its concomitant deification of longevity through fantasies of health and cosmetic and surgical beauty. Not surprisingly, my remarks received the coolest smattering of applause. Apparently, the beautiful assemblage of spring lime and tangerine finery saw me as the ancient mariner with a dead bird around his neck. And how crazy must I be to say a disparaging word against longevity and health? (I am against neither, actually, but I did and still do question why we should live longer, and in service to what, other than a narcissistic, timorous ego. And I did and still do question why more of anything is somehow presumed superior to depth and purpose or the why of things.) As a reminder to all of us, I did offer Jung's observation that "flight from life does not exempt us from the law of age and death. The neurotic who tries to wriggle out of the necessity of living wins nothing and only burdens himself with a constant foretaste of aging and dying, which must appear cruel on account of the total emptiness and meaninglessness of his life."[2]

5. Adolf Güggenbuhl-Craig wrote a wonderful essay on old age and fools and did his best to disabuse us of any notion of "the golden years." He reminded us that the body falls apart, friends and family die, and most plans and expectations crumble. One thing remains regnant, however: the power to act like a fool and get away with it. After all, no one expects an aged person to be otherwise, especially in a youth-oriented, plastic, throwaway culture. Being a fool once again,

the oxymoronic wise fool, like the sophomore ("wise" + "moron"), is an opportunity, Güggenbuhl-Craig argued, to recover an original psychological integrity, playfulness, and an unfettered desire for exuberant life.[3]

So what, then, given our cultural *Sitz im Leben*, may I point to as a saving power for those who do not wish to go gentle into that good night, yet are not in denial of the nature of our nature, which is always naturing, always speeding us toward our mortal ends? My colleagues in this volume have so eloquently described so many problems and so many constructive approaches. Why should I—sharing a common condition of puzzlement over why we are here, what this life is about, and why we are apparently the only animal capable of reflecting upon its own dissolution and demise—have anything further to offer?

When the Dust Settles, With What Are We Left?

I do, however, have a modest assertion to leave with the reader. I believe that as long as we are curious, we are still alive. The body will continue to decline according to the ministries of fate, lifestyle, genetics, and a host of unimaginably converging forces. Yet, Yeats was surely right. For every tatter in our mortal dress, soul must compensate. Bluntly put, for every outer decline, failure of powers, environmental constriction, something within is challenged to grow apace. Amid the wreckage of history, the carnage of loss, the growing catalogue of grief, soul is summoned to grow. I believe, more today than ever before, that the quality of our lives will be a direct function of the magnitude of the questions we ask, questions we are summoned to pursue for ourselves. And we do have to ask them on our own because there is precious little in our culture that does not elevate and privilege the banal, the distracting, the trivial—all of which are affronts and diminishments to the soul. Of course, the sanguinary sea surge of aging and mortality are all the more troubling and unmediated in cultures that have lost their mythic connections to the gods and to those great redeeming rhythms of death and rebirth of which we are such a tiny part. Our ancestors may have longed for a reunion in another world with their lost brethren or understood themselves to be an ineluctable part of a great cosmic cycle in which life and death are one—all a part of going home. But most moderns experience their lives as fugitive egos, adrift, homeless, bereft, and disconnected from anything large or abiding.

In book after book, therapeutic hour after hour, I have asserted that the primary task of the so-called second half of life is the recovery of personal authority. As children and young adults, we are obliged to adapt to the circumstances of family, time, place, zeitgeist, and the sundry vagaries of personal fate into which we are thrust. The so-called first adulthood is spent enacting or fleeing from the messages we internalize from our phenomenological reading of life's text. One might summarize it this way: the agenda of the first half of life imposes adaptations of all kinds, and we all respond in our variegated ways to the demands, blows, challenges, and seductions of life. The second half, meanwhile, necessarily obliges sorting through the aftermath of choices and consequences: guilt, anger, recrimination, regret, recovery, and a summons to forgiveness of self and others. Thus the second half of life is usually less a chronological event, a desperate resolve, than a persistently compelling subpoena to sort through that immense internal traffic we all carry and to discern what is true for us.

Many of us know, and many more of us suspect, that there are no outer authorities anymore. Accordingly, among the plethora of cacophonous claimants upon our values and choices, we are left on our own to decide which ones are confirmed by our personal experience and which are confirmed by our autonomous internal resonance. Then we are called to find the courage and consistency to live these truths in the world. Sounds easy, but it is truly a lifelong project. To facilitate this process in individuals, myself included, I have devoted the second half of my life in the venues of therapy, classrooms, and books to raising questions and challenging people to grow up, to be accountable for these questions and work them through into more value-driven rather than neurosis-driven lives. (Jung pointed out that our private religions, the altars where we invest our most precious capital and spend most of our lives, is our daily service to our neuroses, namely, the "management systems" which temper our anxieties and solicit the satisfaction of our needs as best we can.) To continue this assignment life apparently brings each of us, let me share some of those questions here.

In his eloquent *Letters to a Young Poet*, Rainer Maria Rilke advised that his reader be patient toward all that was unsolved in his heart. The task is always to live our answers with courage and fidelity. But, Rilke reminds us, one is often not yet ready to live those answers. So the task is to live the questions faithfully until some distant day when we live our way into our answers.[4]

So it is, in the calculus of choice, the larger the questions, the larger the journey we get! As we all have learned, it is doubt rather than certainty that gets us an education, and it is doubt and questioning that gets us a more interesting life. Here are some questions which I think can, when lived with sincerity and personal integrity, lead to the enlargement of soul, even as the mortal tatters multiply.

Asking the Questions That Enlarge

"The meaning of my existence is that life has addressed a question to me . . . or conversely, I myself am a question."

—C. G. Jung, *Memories, Dreams, Reflections*

Where has fear blocked my development, kept me constricted, and still prevents me from being who I am?

Anyone reading this book is likely now old enough, wise enough, to recognize, ruefully, that by and large we have been our own worst problem through the years. We are the only ones present in every scene of our long-running soap opera and perhaps have reluctantly come to recognize that we often live in what Sartre called *mauvaise foi* or bad faith. Having acknowledged the necessity of adaptation, we grew defined by our strategies of conflict avoidance, sought the easier paths whenever possible, and surreptitiously transferred our dependencies to others: partners, organizations, ideologies. In our darkest hours, we admit to ourselves: cowardice, dependencies, lies and deceptions, and other forms of slip-sliding away. We all know places where we failed to "show up." We are haunted by times when we let others down in service to our own narcissism or fugitive motives. No wonder old age can be so difficult. Physical pain and diminishment is nothing compared to rereading the catalogue of personal shortcomings.

Well, the fat lady may be warming up just offstage, but it ain't over yet. As the noted American psychologist Yogi Berra said, "when you come to a fork in the road, take it!" Ask yourself where fear still blocks you. Having asked that question, whatever comes up on your personal screen is your new agenda. This does not mean that you have to take up skydiving or sell all and move to a monastery, though either might be right for a person here or there. It means that you decide that honesty with the world begins with honesty with yourself. It then means speaking truthfully with others rather than avoiding doing so. It means following that curiosity which lies at the heart of human nature wherever your physical and imaginative powers permit you to travel. In some cases, this will mean recovering the interest, the talent, the enthusiasm left behind. In other cases, it will mean risking doing what you wish to do with your precious time and energy whether it fits in with others, whether it is approved by others, and whether it is difficult or not. If we can hold to what is difficult to us, we will find that we are serving life not death, growth not aversive adaptation. And if not now, when?

What unlived life of my parents am I still carrying, and passing on to my descendants?

Jung's comment that the greatest burden of every child is the unlived life of his or her parents surely haunts all of us. In the face of a powerful outer exemplum, such as the parent/child dynamic, our most common tendency is to serve its message. Thus we may be blocked where our parents were blocked—in emotional freedom, in the capacity for risk, and in affirming our sexuality, personal passions, and enthusiasms. Or we may have spent our life in compensation for the shortfalls of the other. So, in saying we will not be like our mother or not live our father's life, we are still being defined by that other rather than by the natural source within us all. Or, finally, we will have devoted, and may still devote, our lives to an unconscious "treatment" plan, such as an addiction to numb the cleavage within ourselves, or a life of frenetic busyness, or a life of distraction. Our contemporary popular culture offers unparalleled distractions. People can stay wired, tuned in, numbed twenty-four hours a day, and more and more of us are doing precisely that. But someday soon we will be dead, and how will we have spent these last years, these last hours?

In addition, our internal blockages are passed on to our children, and they constitute a signal burden to them as well. We say we love our children, but are we sparing them the need to take care of our emotional lives? Are we dumping our unrequited needs upon them? Are we living through them, or their children—our presumptive, redemptive *simulacra*? And will our descendants, as a result, breathe a secret sigh of relief when they no longer have to carry us? Have we forgotten that they all are, even the estranged ones, still looking to us to provide the model, the mentoring? How we deal with our own aging, our impending death, our physical limitations, our losses, disappointments, and difficult hours are lessons they are absorbing day by day. With what courage, or lack thereof, we face our difficult and narrowing journey, with what immaturity and neediness we defer to others, with what wisdom we embody or fail to address, they are absorbing every day, whether we know it or not, and whether they now know it or not.

If we have lived small questions, and therefore small lives, they will too, or they will be forced to compensate for the life we shunned. If we did not step into our summons to grow up, how or why would we ever expect them to?

What, really, is my spirituality, and does it make me larger or smaller?

For many, the word *spirituality* is loaded with painful, regressive associations of religious dogma, guilt complexes and fear-based agendas. Yet, *spirit* remains the best word we have to describe that quickening of the soul and body that is the spark of life. What animates us, what drives us forward into life? That is to say, our spirituality is not what we say it is, but where we, in fact, invest our energies on a daily basis. Such investments are the true standard and only measure of our spiritual values.

How many of us can pass Freud's elemental test of spirituality? He noted over a century ago that most folks fill the immensity of the mystery of our cosmos with jury-rigged theologies replicating parental complexes, assuage the terrible uncertainties of life with shaky assurances, and, surprise, adopt theologies and practices which ratify neuroses or serve comforting narcissistic agendas. Our gods, in other words, sound surprisingly like us. How many of us can maturely examine our *imago Dei* (we all have one, whether conscious or not) and ask whether it leads us deeper into life and its unfathomable mysteries or helps us avoid the wonder and terror of uncertainty and mystery? How much mystery and ambiguity can we tolerate?

Such questions are not really about the mysteries of our universe. They are about us, our personal psychologies, and our relative psychological maturity. Until we recognize that our theologies and spiritual practices speak mostly about us, we will remain encased less in a spiritual respect for the mystery than in a shabby avoidance of it. The purpose of a mature spirituality is to live in depth, whether in the venues of loss and uncertainty or those of plentitude.

A mature spirituality is one that allows the old images to go because they were only that—images. The image is not the mystery. The mystery is the energy which informs the universe, which once animated those images, and which still courses through us. It is natural for ego consciousness to grab hold of the image, to fasten onto it in service to our various security agendas. But that energy will not be contained in the image, nor in our subsequent understandings and practices. By the time we have "fixed" the mystery, it is already gone. During my "individuation" exam at the Jung Institute in Zürich many years ago, one of the examiners said, solemnly, "my individuation began the day my God died." We all knew what she meant. Her *imago Dei* was no longer charged with energy, no longer numinous, and then she knew she had to grow up and take personal responsibility for the conduct of her journey.

The proper summons to ordinary consciousness then, is not to cling to what is already gone, but to abide the in-between, to embrace the wonder of the uncertain, and to remain open to the next venue in which the mystery might manifest. Sounds easy enough, but it is difficult to be strong enough to be that vulnerable. And yet, the energies of the universe will as they may, and shall pay no attention whatsoever to what we expect of them. The most religious statement I have heard on this matter is Jung's confession that he called God that which crossed his willful path and altered his conscious intentions for good or for ill. In other words, whatever radically reframes the ego's sense of self and world, whatever obliges us to come in naked humility before the other anew, is a spiritual

encounter. So, beware, then, of seeking religious experience. One might
in fact get one. (Is this why so many religious institutions and practices
protect one from religious encounter, and thereby insure a
diminishing, fear-driven, avoidant journey?)

Notice how respectful of mystery Jung's concept is. Notice how
it does not pander to fear or manipulate the concepts to fit personal
needs. Notice how it passes Freud's test by enlarging beyond narcissistic
self-interest and neurosis management to encounter the radical,
intractable otherness of the universe. Such an openness, such a
relinquishment of our puny power agendas may, in fact, prove worthy
of the word *spirituality*. It will ask of us so much more than that of
which we are comfortable. It will ask of us that we confess our smallness
in the face of the largeness of the mystery. But that is the only way we
can really respect the mystery and its sovereign autonomy. Such a
confession, while challenging the fear-based inflated ego is, in fact,
already a spiritual enlargement.

**Where do you refuse to grow up, wait for clarity before risking, hope
for external solutions, expect rescue from someone, or wait for someone
to tell you what your life is about?**

This is a particularly loaded question, a charged query, and yet
never have I had anyone ask me, in the context of a workshop:
"What do you mean?" and never has anyone paused long before
journaling in a personal response to these questions. Such a response
tells me that we all "know," and that we suffer both that "knowing"
and the stuckness which so often goes with it. If we really know,
why would we remain stuck? The answer is clear: it is not about
what it is about. That is to say, the stuckness is not about the
particular issue we confront, or which confronts us; it is about how
circuitry from that resistant locus reaches down to an earlier,
recalcitrant place, an archaic zone in our psyches which, when
activated, floods us with anxiety, whether we know it or not. We
naturally prefer stuckness to swimming in such discomfort as going
through it is required to get to the other side.

These questions all evoke shadow aspects of our psychic life,
namely, the encounter with that which threatens ego stability and
security, seems contrary to our values, or asks more of us than we figure
we can imagine. Thus, we privilege the status quo ante and indict

ourselves at the same time for so electing stuckness. We hate being stuck, but we hate dealing with the discomfiture getting unstuck will require even more.

When we unpack the clauses above one by one, we see that growing up means not only being conscious but also being accountable for doing something about what consciousness brings to us. Imagine that! Growing up would mean that we are out there on our own, and tremendously vulnerable. Yet we learned so long ago to adapt, avoid, rationalize, and precisely to defend ourselves against such exposure. This archaic defense mechanism has brought us this far, so we fear stirring up those lower powers if we can avoid them, even now fleeing in the face of accumulated consequences and troubling dreams.

The timorous ego naturally prefers clarity, certainty and the illusion of control, and it will even distort reality in order to obtain it provisionally, as we may surmise from the slippery spiritualities described above. Yet, life is a risk. Even as we admire those who historically set out upon tenebrous seas, filled with monsters of seduction and devouring appetites, most of us find it safer to hug the shore, safer to wait for certainty—a certainty that will never come— till the day someone pounds that last nail in our coffin.

In hoping for external solutions, we perpetuate our infantile dependency on parents or, far more subtly, parental surrogates. We may conduct the most responsible, productive outer lives, when measured against the materialist metrics of our meretricious times, and yet defer the summons to personal authority and the isolation and courage that requires. Simply to remind ourselves, personal authority means sorting through the immensity of inner and outer traffic, to "test the spirits" as the book of John (4:1) has it, and finding what is true for us, experientially and intuitively validated, and then the courage to live it in the world.

Similarly, the frightened, isolated child within each of us is still looking for someone to take care of us. Fortunately that person has finally arrived, long after we futilely sought such a person in our partners, our institutions, and our ideologies. That person is oneself. Better get used to trusting yourself, for you are the best you have, and will ever get. We look for someone else to explain life to us: a preacher, a politician, a friend, a parent, a therapist, an institution, a creed, a tradition. While all may be useful in partial ways, no one source will provide us with sufficient insight into this complexly changing world and into the incredibly labyrinthine layers of our own psyche. Besides, what is true for another, however sincerely transmitted, will seldom prove adequate to us. We cannot have someone else live our lives for us, though many parents try. We cannot ask another what one's own life is about, because they seldom have made much headway on figuring out their own journey, let alone ours. This does not mean that there are not many people out there perfectly willing to tell you how to live your life. But I do not count myself among them. As a teacher and a therapist, my job is to listen, offer ideas, examples, and so on, but most of all to ask you to figure it out for yourself and then live what you find into the world. And whatever you figure out for today will not apply a few years down the line, so better plan on going back to the drawing board from time to time. Your ego will not like this uncertainty, but in the end, it will not have a choice. Surely this is what Jung meant in *Memories, Dreams, Reflections* when he said that life has addressed a question to him, and that he himself is a question. What questions has life asked of you? What have you had to struggle with, to overcome, to understand? Where are you challenged to grow beyond your comfort zone? What question are you embodying? Your individuation process is your answer, so might we decide that it shall be the best we can provide.

Staying Alive

In 1978 I had finished my first year of studies in Zürich and was returning with my family to Luxembourg to catch the budget Loftleider flight back to the United States via Iceland. En route, while staying in a youth hostel in Paris, we heard the Bee Gees sing "Staying Alive" for the first time. My spirit was lifted, and I am lifted every time I hear it still. I think the appeal of that disco song is not the eponymous theme of perpetuating this ego. Rather, it quickens the spirit with its jaunty, in-your-face rhythm. It has, as they say in Philly, "attytood!" So, the spirit is found in the "attytood" we bring to this miserable, wondrous, and brief transit called life.

It is the troubling conundrum of our condition that the alternative to aging and dying is called "early death." It is perplexing and paradoxical to the ego state that we are forever speeding toward our own temporal dissolution. Accordingly, we have created sundry drugs, ideologies, and distractions to finesse this reality. But all of them are not the friend but the enemy of life. Plato observed nearly three millennia ago that the well-lived life demands the daily contemplation of death. He was not being morbid; that we might think so is rather the morbidity of our neurosis—our rejection of the gift of this paradox-driven life. Plato is rather asking for a more thoughtful journey, a more solemn, considered, value-driven, and dignified conduct of this precious, precarious life. As for death, it will come soon enough. Essentially, whatever we think about that telluric telos is essentially irrelevant. Either this ego consciousness is obliterated, rending all speculation, anxiety, and hope moot, or it is a transformation so beyond our imaginative powers that we cannot fathom its possibilities. All that will take care of itself. Meanwhile, the task is to live.

In the face of progressive physical diminishment, what we have as our continuing companions are our imagination and our curiosity. As long as they are present, we are alive, growing, and developing. Meanwhile, might we manage to stop whining and kvetching? As G. B. Shaw put it, let us affirm "being a force of nature instead of a feverish clod of ailments and grievances complaining that the world will not devote itself to making [us] happy." Let us risk letting go of our fearful, tenuous grip on life whereby, ironically, we remain enslaved to the fear of death. Let us embrace dying unto our previous life, and the fear which keeps us from the new, lest we die before we die. As Goethe put it,

> . . . so long as you haven't experienced
> This: to die and so to grow,
> You are only a troubled guest
> On the dark earth.[5]

NOTES

[1] W. B. Yeats, "Nineteen Hundred and Nineteen," in *Selected Poems and Two Plays of William Butler Yeats*, ed. M. L. Rosenthal (New York: Macmillan, 1962), p. 110.

[2] C. G. Jung, "The Sacrifice," in *The Collected Works of C. G. Jung*, vol. 5, ed. and trans. Gerhard Adler and R. F. C. Hull (Princeton, NJ: Princeton University Press, 1956), § 617.

[3] Adolf Guggenbühl-Craig, *The Old Fool and the Corruption of Myth* (New Orleans: Spring Publications, 2006).

[4] R. M. Rilke, *Letters to a Young Poet,* trans. M. D. Herter Norton (New York: W. W. Norton and Co., 1993).

[5] Johann von Goethe, "The Holy Longing," in *The Rag and Bone Shop of the Heart: Poems for Men*, ed. Robert Bly, James Hillman, and Michael Meade (New York: Harper, 1993).

CHAPTER THIRTEEN

A Jungian Approach to Spirituality in Later Life

LIONEL CORBETT, M.D.

I n this chapter I will enlarge on those factors that are particularly relevant to late-life spirituality, while at the same time providing some of the theoretical background which underpins the Jungian approach.

For Jung, the development of our spirituality is the quintessential task of later life and is essential for the full flowering of the personality. He felt there would be no evolutionary reason for aging unless it had some purpose for the species.[1] For Jung, our connection to the Self, or the intrapsychic God-image, becomes paramount after midlife. He also believed that it is important for older people to "make culture," or contribute to society, develop an inner life, discover undeveloped aspects of the personality, and continue to discover meaning.

In what follows, I draw the usual distinction between religion as an organized, historical institution and spirituality as the sense that life is meaningful or as a private form of connection to a higher power or to realities beyond the natural world. Or, spirituality can be defined simply as the capacity to experience mystery, beauty, awe, and the ability to affirm the value of life.

Spirituality after Midlife

Jung notes that after midlife (after 35), none of his patients in the second half of their lives recover unless they develop a religious attitude—not necessarily a commitment to a specific tradition or creed but rather a personal spirituality, an individual connection to sacred reality.[2] Herein lies the core of Jung's approach to spirituality at any time of life. For him, belief in a set of doctrines and dogmas is not enough, because belief in traditional ideas may fade or be eroded by painful life events. Particularly in the face of intense suffering, the teachings of the established traditions may seem like mere platitudes, whereas direct, personal experience of the sacred or the holy is indelible, leading to knowledge rather than belief alone. An authentic spirituality is therefore greatly enhanced by a personal experience of transpersonal reality, which for Jung means contact with transpersonal levels of the unconscious. It is important to point out Jung's insistence that we have no idea what the unconscious is. The term is only a placeholder which we use for the sake of convenience. Even the notion of the unconscious itself is, according to Jung, only a posit, a synonym for the unknown, and it should not be thought of as "an encapsulated personal system."[3] That is, we should not reify the unconscious.

Most important, for Jung, the experience of the transpersonal unconscious is indistinguishable from traditional accounts of the experience of the divine, even though strictly speaking we cannot say if God and the unconscious are synonymous. Whenever we believe we have experienced God, we do so by means of the psyche, as an image or symbol, and we cannot get out of the psyche because all of our experience is psychologically based. Thus, all our images of God (such as Christ or the biblical Yahweh) are psychologically conditioned. Jung believed that these images point to something, but we cannot directly experience what lies beyond the psyche because all our experience is mediated by the psyche. Therefore, we do not necessarily know the divine itself; we know only the way it appears to us via the psyche. Strictly speaking then, our image of God, which Jung refers to as the Self, should not be equated with the divine itself, although in practice most Jungians believe that an experience of the Self is an experience of the divine. The divine is then felt to be directly experienced within our subjectivity, rather than in some transcendent realm. It is important for Jung that one can have a direct experience of the Self in a way that is completely novel and unrelated to any traditional God-image. An important side benefit of this approach is that it abolishes conflict between competing religious traditions, since they all emerge from the same mythopoetic level of the psyche.

Numinous Experience

Most Jungians think of the Self as the divine essence or core of the personality, and one of the major developmental achievements of later life is the consolidation of a relationship with this level. We experience the transpersonal levels of the psyche or the Self in many ways. One of the most important happens to us in the form of numinous experiences. This word *numinous*, from the Latin *numen*, meaning a divinity, and also cognate with the verb *nuere*, meaning to nod or beckon, was used by Rudolph Otto in his famous *The Idea of the Holy*, first published as *Das Heilige* in 1917.[4] The word *numinous* therefore suggests divine beckoning or approval. Jung appropriated this term in his lectures on the psychology of religion in 1937 at Yale, and since then it has become a mainstay in all Jungian literature in the area of psychology and religion.

Otto, a Lutheran theologian, tried to capture the quality of religious experience by describing it as the *mysterium tremendum et fascinans*, a mystery that is tremendous and fascinating. There are several biblical examples of human contact with the *numinosum*. Two important such instances are Moses hearing the voice of God out of a burning bush and Saul on the road to Damascus. Saul sees a blinding light and hears Jesus's voice say, "Why do you persecute me?" The subject of such a direct experience of the holy is awestruck in the presence of something other than everyday reality, faced with an uncanny power beyond our understanding, an Otherness that defies explanation and adequate description. It is important to note here that whereas for Otto numinous experience implied the Christian God-image, Jung is much more interested in the emotional quality of the experience (mysterious, tremendous, fascinating, awesome, or dreadful) than its specific content, because numinous experiences may not be related to any Judeo-Christian theme. As the Jungian tradition has it, we cannot Christianize the objective psyche; it will produce numinous imagery from any religious or mythological tradition with no regard for the subject's preferences or personal history. Jung believes it is vital to pay careful attention to any manifestation of the *numinosum*, and this is, in fact, Jung's definition of religion. Partly because numinous experience does not respect traditional God-images, the mainstream religious traditions do not always value direct mystical experience; it may contravene received doctrine, for example, when Jesus appears to the individual in a numinous dream in the form of a woman.

A Numinous Dream about Aging

For Jungians, a numinous experience is an unmediated, direct experience of the holy, whether it occurs in the context of a traditional religious practice or not. For many of us, the dream is the most accessible mode in which numinous experience occurs. Here I would like to revisit (in an abbreviated form) a dream I reported some years ago, because it is not only numinous but also a unique initiation into the aging process. The dreamer was at the time a sixty-year-old woman who was very concerned about the prospect of aging. This kind of anxiety arises not only because we are concerned about the losses and physical decline of later life, but also because we have no socially sanctioned initiation into old age, which tends to be devalued in our culture. People may break down emotionally during any transitional period because of the uncertainty it can produce, and the transitional period into later life is no exception. At such time, the transpersonal Self may produce an initiatory, numinous dream such as the following:

> An authoritative male voice informs me that it is going to teach me about the process of aging. A black and white illustration appears before my eyes, which represents the rejuvenated Godhead. Underneath the diagram is the living head of a very old man. A connecting line is drawn from the old man's head to the diagram of divinity, which consists of an outer elongated square enclosing an inner circle. At the bottom of the circle is a crescent, convex upward. Out of the crescent arises

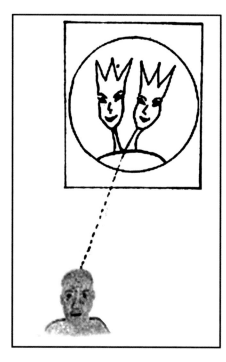

two heads on almost identical long necks. I know that they share the same body which is not shown. The voice explains that this is an abstract of the rejuvenated Godhead. The right head represents the male aspect of God and the left the female aspect. I want to know more about it, particularly about the feminine aspect of God, but the voice reminds me that this has been partly explained in a previous dream, and instructs me to focus on the old man. But I find the Godhead more interesting and I think to myself "God is one, two heads but one." At the same time, what I have learned in a previous dream flashes through my mind; the awareness that what I am shown here is not God as ultimate reality, which we are not equipped to understand, but either an oversimplified version of that reality or an aspect of divinity to which we can relate.

Figure 1: The Rejuvenated Godhead. Reprinted by permission of Open Court Publishing Company, a division of Carus Publishing Company, Chicago, IL, from *Betwixt and Between: Patterns of Masculine and Feminine Initiation*, edited by Louise Carus Mahdi, Steven Foster, and Meredith Little, © 1987 by Open Court Publishing Company. All rights reserved.

The two heads are in absolute harmony with each other. They look like ethereal spirits. Their facial expression is autocratic, blithe, somewhat curious and unemotional. The tops of their heads are shaped like an indented crown with three prongs that I can see on each head. The old man looks ordinary and earthy, with reddish skin. The voice explains that we still do not understand the process of aging, which is to enable the Godhead to rejuvenate. When we are born, God is old; when we grow old God becomes young, and when we die, God experiences re-birth. I am told that it is essential that particularly in old age we do not lose our connection to the Godhead, for otherwise we would deprive God our share in his rejuvenation, and may actually disturb the cosmic ecology. If we ignore the divine element, it sinks into itself and ceases to be conscious of itself. The voice goes on to say that belief in God constellates the inner child and thus furthers the process of divine rejuvenation. If, as we age, we lose touch with the inner child, we may simultaneously sever our ties to the divine. [5]

According to Jung, such dreams originate from the archetypal level of the psyche, which is the level that is the source of all religious traditions. This dream meets Otto's criteria for a numinous experience: it is mysterious, tremendous, and fascinating, although the content of the dream does not contain Judeo-Christian imagery. In fact, if anything, the image of an androgynous divinity contradicts these traditions' overly masculine image of God (although in the Kabbalah the divine has both masculine and feminine aspects, and in the Christian mystical tradition Christ has been depicted as androgynous).

The dream surprisingly tells us that the purpose of aging is the "rejuvenation of God," a completely unexpected and novel idea, which, however, proved to be reassuring to the dreamer, who no longer feels that aging is nothing more than a period of relentless decline toward death. She now has a sense that this phase of her life has a purpose. It is typical of numinous experiences of this kind to be so powerful that they have a healing effect. In fact, Jung writes that "the approach to the numinous is the real therapy and inasmuch as you attain to the numinous experiences you are released from the curse of psychopathology."[6]

The dream can be thought of as a collective or "big" dream, one that is relevant to society as a whole. At the same time, the dream is a revelation of the individual's personal myth; she has received a personal revelation, as distinct from participating in a collective revelation such as the receiving of the law on Mount Sinai. Part of the value of this experience is that it allows the dreamer to distinguish herself from the collective myth into which she was born, which is based on nationality, ethnicity, and collective conditioning. This realization frees her to discover her own deepest truth, rather than unconsciously participating in mass consciousness. Jung believed that one can only resist the influence of collective thinking if one's own individuality is well organized. For the individual to become conscious of his or her individual myth is of great value to the collective, since it provides us with individuals capable of critical thinking.[7]

The Self, Culture, and the Transformation of the God-image

The dreamer was raised in a tradition whose God-image is exclusively masculine, so this dream is an important corrective; one of Jung's major critiques of the Christian God-image was its exclusion of the feminine aspects of the divine. The dream indicates that we now need to imagine the divine in both its masculine and feminine aspects, and also—as indicated by the squared circle, an abstract image of the Self as totality—as neither masculine nor feminine.

Primordial numinous experiences of this type often need some kind of interpretation. Needless to say, the problem raised by the dream is that it is difficult to understand what is meant by the "rejuvenation of God," or what it could mean that when we are born God is old but gradually gets younger as we age and is reborn when we die. This sounds very much like a Zen koan. One way to look at this statement, instead of taking it as a literal account of divinity, is to see the dream as a comment on the Self, the image of God in the psyche, or the way the Self appears to us. For Jung, the Self may appear in the form of any traditional God-image: Christ, Zeus, Odin, or Yahweh are all local names for the Self. When we are born, we are immersed within the God-image of a particular tradition, which is old, but as we age, our God-image changes, sometimes radically, and in this way it becomes newer or younger.

The dream voice stresses the importance of maintaining connection to the inner child. This may correlate with the fact that in many traditions, including the mythologies of Jesus, the Buddha, Horus, and Krishna, the divine appears in the form of a child. All these appear in the form of divine children, usually in the context of renewal and regeneration. The dream suggests that as we age, we must cultivate a more childlike approach to the divine, and here we are reminded of Jesus calling on people to become like little children if they wish to enter the kingdom of heaven (Matthew 18:3, Mark 10:15, and verse 46 of the Gospel of Thomas). Perhaps this means that we must cultivate simple faith and trust instead of a dominant ego, in the way that a child relates to a parent.

This woman's God-image has been radically transformed by her dream, thus illustrating Jung's point that as our consciousness extends into the unconscious, we discover a "not yet transformed God."[8] This means that as we work on dreams such as this, we discover a God-image that challenges the image of God found in the tradition in which we were raised. Edward Edinger points out that such transformation of the God-image occurs as the Self incarnates (by becoming conscious) within human beings.[9] The idea of the incarnation of the Self means that the spiritual potentials of the Self, which are present at birth, gradually embody themselves and are increasingly lived out throughout the life cycle. These potentials act as a kind of spiritual blueprint for the developing personality.

In a personal letter Edinger wrote to me in 1987 about this dream, he says: "To me, the most important feature of the dream is that it informs the dreamer that she is a *partner* of God and a participant in the drama of divine transformation. This gives her suffering and sacrifice archetypal sanction and roots her in a living myth." The process of the transformation of the God-image belongs to a new myth (here used in the sense of a sacred story) which is emerging alongside our existing religious traditions. Each individual makes a contribution to this process.

In a series of books, I have described a variety of other ways in which numinous experience, or experience of the transpersonal unconscious, may occur.[10] These include: visionary experiences, which are dreamlike events occurring while the subject is awake, experiences through the body and through the natural world, and by means of creativity. None of these modalities are specific to later life, so the interested reader is referred to this literature.

The founders and saints of our religious traditions often reported direct numinous experiences, and on the basis of these accounts, huge superstructures of theology and interpretation evolved into our current religious systems. However, much of this institutional development was not based on direct experience of the transpersonal realm; it is theoretical or speculative, the opinion of church councils and the church hierarchy, often designed to maintain ecclesiastical authority. While these speculations may be of historical interest, since they are often based on <u>archetypal ideas such as the divine as a trinity</u>, they are not necessarily helpful during a severe life crisis, and old age is replete with such crises because of the inevitable losses we experience at this time. In contrast, direct experience of the holy is convincing without any need for theological confirmation. As a result of personal numinous experience, one has the sense that one is witnessed or supported by a divine presence, and this experience requires no particular denominational commitment.

Many researchers have found that spirituality and religious commitment in old age protect against loneliness and morbidity.[11] This effect is partly the result of belonging to a supportive community and is not necessarily the result of belief in the tradition's theology. Today, however, it is not unusual to find older people who have given up on the religious tradition to which they have belonged, because it does not work for them. Often, the spiritual teachings of the tradition have proved to be unusable because they do not correspond to the structures of the individual's personality. These teachings, such as "turn the other cheek," "do unto others," or the stress on forgiveness, offer good advice, but they only address consciousness; they ignore the unconscious, and one cannot implement and live a spiritual teaching that ignores one's character structure. The cardinal Christian virtues of <u>humility</u>, charity, love, and forgiveness are simply not possible if one's personality is grandiose or suffers from <u>fear, shame</u>, envy, or rage. As a result, it is not surprising that many people who consider themselves Christians simply ignore those teachings of Jesus that they cannot use, such as his emphasis on compassion for the poor. Some even turn his teachings on their head, for example, by stressing the importance of affluence even though Jesus preached the value of poverty. Many Christians pay lip service to the divine figures of the tradition but actually worship something else; they are purportedly Christian but pagan beneath the surface, as we saw in Germany in World War II.

We do not belong within a religious tradition if its sacred stories do not resonate with us, or if the tradition does not adequately address our suffering and has nothing convincing to say about the problem of evil. For many older people, the traditional Christian God-image found in the liturgy (such as the divine as a benevolent sky-father or shepherd) has become a meaningless metaphor with no emotional power. Sophisticated, high-end theology has not penetrated into the pulpit and does not reach the average churchgoer. Often, as Jung put it, theology "proclaims doctrines which nobody understands, and demands faith which nobody can manufacture."[12] For many people the politics of a particular institution—such as its attitude to women or homosexuality—have become increasingly abhorrent. Forced to turn away from a lifeless tradition, spiritually aware older people must therefore discover their own form of spirituality, their own sense of meaning and purpose, their own values, their own form of connection to the transpersonal dimension of reality, and their own attitude to death.

Individuation as a Spiritual Process

These developments are all components of the individuation process, or the full development of the personality, which goes on inexorably whether or not the older person consciously thinks in such terms. Individuation ideally comes to fruition in later life. For Jung, development is more than the result of the interaction of genes and the environment, as traditional psychology would have it, because the Self serves as a spiritual blueprint for the development of the personality. Our biography is spiritually determined, because individuation involves the embodiment of the potentials of the Self, which naturally happens more and more as we age. For Jung, this incarnation is an ongoing, spiritual process which occurs in everyone; it is not a once-and-for-all historical event as it is in the Christian story. However, the process of the incarnation of the Self invariably causes suffering as it differentiates elements of itself by becoming conscious within a human personality. Since the Self is the totality of consciousness, it can only divide into its constituent opposites within the psyche of a human being, who then experiences the tension of opposites such as good and evil. Although this process causes suffering, it is considered by many Jungians to be a service which humanity renders to the Self.

Suffering is an inevitable part of the process of incarnation because incarnation occurs through the experience of emotion, which is felt in the body. Our complexes are emotionally toned, and the archetype—the spiritual organizing principle of the personality—is at the center of the complex, so that when a complex is activated and we are emotionally aroused, the archetype is embodied. Accordingly, our suffering has a spiritual core, and attention to our complexes becomes a spiritual practice.

The Relativizing of the Ego

As we age, Jung believed that we increasingly discover that we are "the object of a supraordinate subject"—that is, we increasingly realize that the Self is aware of the ego, and the ego is not the essence of who we are.[13] As the jargon puts it, the ego or the empirical personality is increasingly "relativized," which means we discover that we live in relation to a wisdom that determines our destiny behind the scenes. This is a monumental realization, but the evidence is overwhelming when we see the astonishing accuracy of our dreams and synchronistic events. These are so closely tailored to our psychological structures it feels as if we are being directly addressed by an intelligence that understands us better than we know ourselves.

At the same time, we realize that, in Jung's words, "the experience of the Self is always a defeat for the ego," which is to say that we come to understand that we have much less control over the major events of our lives than we imagined.[14] There are transpersonal or spiritual dominants within the archetypal level of the psyche which radically affect us. Wisdom consists in getting to know which of these transpersonal forces are most significant to the individual and understanding how they manifest themselves in our lives.

For Jungian psychology, it is impossible to distinguish sharply between psychological and spiritual development in later life; the least one could say is that they overlap, and for many Jungians they are in fact synonymous. Jungian psychology therefore ignores the traditional distinction between psychology as a discipline only concerned with matters of this world and religion as attention to spiritual matters. Jung can seamlessly blend the spiritual and the psychological because for him the psyche is not purely personal; it has a spiritual or transpersonal dimension that is both the source of religious experience and also an important force within the life of the individual. The transpersonal unconscious is seen as a source of wisdom greatly superior to the ego, so whereas in earlier life one has to develop an adequate ego, the older person has to realize that the ego exists in relation to the Self, and a dialog is possible between them. To relativize the ego also means to give up one's grandiosity, omnipotence, the need to control others, the need for status, and the need for external sources of self-esteem. The hegemony of the ego decreases as we become more open to the demands of the Self, leading to spiritual maturation and more compassionate ways of relating to others.

There are other aspects of development in later life that are both psychologically and spiritually important. One has to develop wisdom, which includes the ability to be nonjudgmental when relating to others, the ability to maintain more than one perspective, to live with paradox, and to tolerate ambiguity. One has to broaden one's horizons beyond one's own ego concerns and those of one's own community, so that one is concerned with the cultural products of humanity as a whole.

The Issue of Meaning

One of the cardinal features of spiritual development at any age is the discovery of meaning in one's life, the feeling that life makes sense, without which one often despairs. This discovery becomes particularly important in later life, especially in the face of multiple losses and limitations, in order to avoid the sense that one's life has been nothing more than an inexorable struggle against an indifferent fate. We have little or no control over the losses which occur in old age, but we are free to discover meaning and to pursue our spirituality, which allows us to be less vulnerable to despair than would be the case if life seemed entirely meaningless. Because our culture does not ask about meaning in old age—society's interest is focused on the medical and social management of later life—the task of discovering meaning at this time, and the discovery of the purpose and value of aging, fall to the individual. There are no particular cultural norms that the individual can use.

In this context, meaning refers partly to the ability to discern a pattern, to make connections between otherwise disparate events in one's life so that they can be seen as weaving into a coherent theme which has moved through the course of one's life. We can discover this (often archetypal) theme as we tell the story of our lives. Storytelling in this way is a spiritual practice which helps us to discover who we are. Telling stories makes life events more meaningful than would be the case if we were to see events in isolation with no connection to each other. Telling a story often requires a life review, which may be painful for the elderly since it means looking at the discrepancies between their youthful fantasies and the way in which life actually unfolded. In this process, a good deal of grief may emerge as we look at disappointments and at goals that can never be met. But at least telling the story makes sense of a life, and telling such stories is an important means of connection to others and passing on whatever wisdom one has acquired.

Many spiritually oriented people feel that meaning is given to us by a larger intelligence. In that case, we feel that we have been guided to follow a particular pattern as if by a transpersonal calling, what Jung called a *spiritus rector*, or a guiding spirit (the Self) within the personality.[15] We then sense what Jung meant by the notion that each life has its own telos, or goal, and its own vocation that is given by the Self. For people with a more atheistic, existentialist bent, the most we can do is make our own meaning or project meaning onto our lives. In either case, when life is meaningful it helps us to affirm the value of life. Some people spend their lives finding meaning in the pursuit of acquisitions, power, or status—pursuits that are problematic when they are simply ways of shoring up a fragile sense of self. In old age, these pursuits not only become less available but they also are of reduced value; more important are relationships that matter, love and friendship, contribution to the future of the family or to future generations as a mentor, or the deepening of wisdom. A creative pursuit allows passion in one's life, while devotion to another person, to a cause, or to meaningful work may all allow transcendence of the self. Or one might discover that one's experience with suffering has enabled one to help others with similar difficulties. Erik Erikson's stress on integrity, the acceptance of one's life as it has been rather than succumbing to despair, is usually understood as a developmental achievement, but it is also spiritually important.[16] Without a sense that life has been worth living it is hard to come to terms with death, so that it is neither denied nor feared excessively.

Surrender and Acceptance in Old Age

One of the most important spiritual accomplishments is the development of the capacity for surrender in a situation in which we have no control over what has arisen. (Some spiritual traditions refer to this process as "letting go.") In a situation of suffering or disability in which all available measures have been tried, it is often a mistake for an elderly person to continue to insist on independence and mastery. Instead, radical acceptance and exploration of the meaning of one's situation may be far more valuable. The heroic attitude is appropriate for the first part of life, as the ego is developing. But the last part of life requires an antiheroic attitude, a growing submission to the larger reality which is symbolized and spoken of by Jung as the Self.

For those elders who are committed to a traditional religion, surrender to a difficult situation may mean acceptance of what they experience as the divine will, in whatever way this is imagined in their tradition. This process not only fosters their connection to the transcendent dimension, it also has important effects on personality development, since it allows relief from struggle and a sense of peace. Surrender means accepting one's limitations and vulnerabilities and allowing mature dependence on others—sometimes for the first time— and it fosters the capacity for relationship, sometimes to new heights. Surrender may require that we let go of a lifelong need to control one's life and to control others. This work is especially difficult for individuals with a narcissistic character structure for whom grandiosity and control are defenses against painful emptiness. It is also difficult for people who lack basic trust or for those who cannot contain painful emotions. Surrender is also difficult because it has cultural connotations of failure in a society that values autonomy. But when surrender is possible, it is spiritually and psychologically transformative. One becomes a witness to the world as well as a participant. What we lose biologically, we can gain psychologically and spiritually. The spiritually valuable aspect of loss in later life is the possibility it allows for letting go of the dominance of the ego and for releasing us from the demands of social conventions. Without minimizing the painful aspects of aging, at least some older people can compensate for loss by developing a closer connection to the Self and a spirituality that sees their life in the context of life as a whole, as part of a chain of being. If they are fortunate enough to participate in a tradition that teaches reincarnation or the continuation of the soul after death, such doctrines are comforting.

Conclusion

It may seem that Jung's approach is rather idealized or too prescriptive, but it is not confined to Jung. The Swedish sociologist Lars Tornstam has a similar approach. He believes that well-being in later life depends on the discovery of meaning and purpose, combined with a desire for communion with an entity greater than oneself. He describes this process as "gerotranscendence," a shift in the person's perspective from material concerns to a more transcendent view of reality, often accompanied by an increase in life satisfaction.[17] It is important to acknowledge here the erroneous implication that transcendence implies detachment from our ordinary physical, embodied existence. Many of Tornstam's research subjects reported that they felt that they were part of a chain of generations and part of the larger unity of life, with increased interest in everyday experiences— as if, I suggest, they experience transcendence within the ordinary. Also consonant with Jung, they became aware of shadow aspects of their personality of which they had previously been unconscious.

Jung's approach to later life receives some support from the world's folkloric traditions. In Allan Chinen's study of fairy tales with older protagonists, he found that stories of the elders from several cultures tend to focus on transpersonal tasks.[18] These tasks transcend individuality because they belong to our existence as part of the totality of the world. Often these protagonists are transformed by encounters with the numinous, which takes them beyond the ego. These elders reach a stage at which they can free themselves from social conventions and develop a state of spontaneity that makes them in a way innocent and childlike—which reminds us of the dream reported above.

Our spirituality by definition has to come to terms with death, whether or not this includes belief in the survival of some kind of consciousness after death. The reality of death makes us ask what our life means and what really matters to us. The prospect of death provokes less anxiety when we do not cling to the ego, so that death becomes a form of transcendence in its own right. Lifton and Olson have suggested various modes of death transcendence. In the biosocial mode, we perceive ourselves as part of our children and culture, which gives a sense of continuity. In the creative mode, our work and other projects with which we are identified allows a sense of transcendence. The religious mode allows belief in the immortality of the soul, while the nature mode makes us feel part of the processes of nature.[19] The mystic, who has actually experienced connection to or union with the transcendent dimension, has an assured sense of transcendence. Whether these attitudes—or adherence to any religious doctrines—are seen as defensive or not is a matter of personal commitment. But the elder who adopts one of these or some analogous approach is able to prepare with some equanimity for the inevitability of death. This preparation requires enough psychological work to feel a sense of completion, so that Jung was able to say that we go into analysis so we can die.

For Jung, the exploration of the inner world is a spiritual practice in its own right, and certainly in old age this exploration can become far more important than responding to the demands of society. This emphasis of Jung corresponds to the experience of many older people who value contemplation more than activity in the world. Jungian psychology therefore has a great deal to offer older people who wish to develop a personal spirituality without adherence to any specific tradition. By paying attention to the manifestations of the objective psyche, for example, in dreams, we gain access to the same source which gives rise to traditional religions, but we discover our unique relationship to this level—

with no need for any institution or hierarchy. During this process, some older people might discover symbolic material which suggests that they belong in the tradition in which they were raised. But with a Jungian approach, they are able to understand this imagery without being literal and without submission to an official interpretation. Many others prefer to free themselves from all traditions and "stand before the Nothing out of which All may grow."[20] This approach may in fact be the next stage in our religious evolution—a new myth of God, based on a new God-image, what Edinger called the New Dispensation, a new way in which divine grace enters the world.[21]

NOTES

[1] C. G. Jung, "The Stages of Life," in *The Collected Works of C. G. Jung*, vol. 8, ed. and trans. Gerhard Adler and R. F. C. Hull (Princeton, NJ: Princeton University Press, 1960), § 787.

[2] C. G. Jung, *Modern Man in Search of a Soul* (New York: Harcourt, Inc., 1933), p. 229.

[3] C. G. Jung, "Archetypes of the Collective Unconscious," in *The Collected Works of C. G. Jung*, vol. 9i, ed. and trans. Gerhard Adler and R. F. C. Hull (Princeton, NJ: Princeton University Press, 1959), § 46.

[4] Rudolph Otto, *The Idea of the Holy* (New York: Oxford University Press, 1952).

[5] Lionel Corbett, "Transformation of the Image of God Leading to Self-Initiation into Old Age," in *Betwixt and Between*, eds. Louise Mahdi and Steven Foster (La Salle, IL: Open Court, 1987), pp. 374–375.

[6] C. G. Jung, *Letters, Vol. 1*, ed. Gerhard Adler, trans. R. F. C. Hull (Princeton, NJ: Princeton University Press, 1973), p. 377.

[7] C. G. Jung, "A Psychological Approach to the Trinity," in *The Collected Works of C. G. Jung*, vol. 11, ed. and trans. Gerhard Adler and R. F. C. Hull (Princeton, NJ: Princeton University Press, 1958), § 285.

[8] C. G. Jung, *Letters, Vol. 2*, ed. Gerhard Adler, trans. R. F. C. Hull (Princeton, NJ: Princeton University Press, 1973), p. 314.

[9] Edward Edinger, *The Creation of Consciousness* (Toronto: Inner City Books, 1984).

[10] Lionel Corbett, *The Religious Function of the Psyche* (New York: Routledge, 1966); *Psyche and the Sacred* (New Orleans, LA: Spring Publications, 2007); and *The Sacred Cauldron: Psychotherapy as a Spiritual Practice* (Wilmette, IL: Chiron, 2011).

[11] J. S. Levin and L. M. Chatters, "Religion, Health and Psychological Well-Being in Older Adults," *Journal of Aging and Health* 10, no. 4 (1998): 504–531.

[12] Jung, "A Psychological Approach to the Trinity," § 285.

[13] C. G. Jung, "The Relations between the Ego and the Unconscious," in *The Collected Works of C. G. Jung,* vol. 7, ed. and trans. Gerhard Adler and R. F. C. Hull (Princeton, NJ: Princeton University Press, 1953), § 405.

[14] C. G. Jung, *Mysterium Coniunctionis,* vol. 14, *The Collected Works of C. G. Jung* (Princeton, NJ: Princeton University Press, 1970), § 778.

[15] C. G. Jung, *Aion,* vol. 9ii, *The Collected Works of C. G. Jung* (Princeton, NJ: Princeton University Press, 1960), § 257.

[16] Erik H. Erikson, "Identity and the Life Cycle: Selected Papers," in *Psychological Issues,* vol. 1 (New York: International Universities Press, 1959).

[17] Lars Tornstam, "Gerotranscendence: The Contemplative Dimension of Aging," *Journal of Aging Studies* 11 (1997): 143–154.

[18] A. B. Chinen, "Fairy Tales and Transpersonal Development in Later Life," *Journal of Transpersonal Psychology* 7 (1985): 99–122; and A. B. Chinen, "Forms of Transcendence in Later Life, *Journal of Transpersonal Psychology* 18 (1968): 171–192.

[19] R. J. Lifton and E. Olson, *Living and Dying* (New York: Praeger, 1974).

[20] C. G. Jung, "The Spiritual Problem of Modern Man," in *The Collected Works of C. G. Jung,* vol. 10, ed. and trans. Gerhard Adler and R. F. C. Hull (Princeton, NJ: Princeton University Press, 1964), § 150.

[21] Edinger, *The Creation of Consciousness.*

~ BIBLIOGRAPHY ~

Achen, Paris. "More People over 65 Find Marriage, Love." *Columbian*, April 29, 2013, http://www.columbian.com/news/2012/jul/29/ageless-romance.

Administration of Aging, U.S. Dept. of Health and Human Services, *A Profile of Older Americans: 2012*, http://www.aoa.gov/Aging_Statistics/Profile/2012/docs/2012profile.pdf.

Allport, Gordon. *Becoming: Basic Considerations for a Psychology of Personality*. New Haven, CT: Yale University Press, 1955.

Armstrong, Karen. *The Battle for God: A History of Fundamentalism*. New York: Random House, 2000.

Baltes, Paul B. "On the Incomplete Architecture of Human Ontogeny: Selection, Optimization, and Compensation as Foundation of Developmental Theory." *American Psychologist* 52, no. 4 (1997): 366–380.

Baltes, Paul B., and Margaret M. Baltes. "Psychological Perspectives on Successful Aging: The Model of Selective Optimization with Compensation." In *Successful Aging: Perspectives from the Behavioral Sciences*, ed. Paul B. Baltes and Margaret M. Baltes. Cambridge, England: Cambridge University Press, 1990.

Bernstein, Jerome. *Living in the Borderland*. New York: Routledge, 2005.

Bertalanffy, Ludwig von. *General System Theory: Foundations, Development, Applications*. Rev. Ed. New York: George Braziller, 1968.

Black, H. K. "'Wasted Lives' and the Hero Grown Old: Personal Perspectives of Spirituality by Aging Men." *Journal of Religious Gerontology* 9 (1995): 35–48.

Blazer, Dan G., and Celia F. Hybels. "Origins of Depression in Later Life." *Psychological Medicine* 35, no. 9 (2005): 1241.

Blythe, Ronald. *The View in Winter*. Norwich: Canterbury Press, 2005.

Booth, Wayne. *The Art of Growing Older: Writers on Living and Aging*. Chicago: University of Chicago Press, 1992.

Bowlby, John. *Attachment and Loss*, vol. 1, *Attachment*. New York: Basic Books, 1969.

Bowling, A., and P. Dieppe. "What Is Successful Aging and Who Should Define It?" *British Medical Journal* 331 (2005): 1548–1551.

Bowling, A., and S. Iliffe. "Psychological Approach to Successful Ageing Predicts Future Quality of Life in Older Adults." *Health and Quality of Life Outcomes* 9, no. 1 (2011): 13–22.

Brandstadter, Jochen, and Klaus Rothermund. "Self-Percepts of Control in Middle and Later Adulthood: Buffering Losses by Rescaling Goals." *Psychology and Aging* 9, no. 2 (1994): 265–273.

Buber, Martin. *The Way of Man: According to the Teaching of Hasidism*. New York: Routledge, 1965.

Buettner, Dan. *Blue Zones: 9 Lessons for Living Longer from the People Who've Lived the Longest*. 2nd ed. Washington, DC: National Geographic Society, 2012.

Butler, Robert N. *Why Survive? Being Old in America*. Baltimore: Harper and Row, 1975.

Byock, Ira. *The Best Care Possible*. New York: Penguin Group, 2012.

———. *Dying Well: Peace and Possibilities at the End of Life*. New York: Berkley Publishing Group, 1997.

Cambray, Joe. "The Place of the 17th Century in Jung's Encounter with China." *Journal of Analytical Psychology* 50, no. 2 (2005).

Campbell, Joseph, with Bill Moyers. *The Power of Myth*. New York: Anchor Books, 1988.

Carstensen, Laura L., John M. Gottman, and Robert W. Levenson. "Emotional Behavior in Long-Term Marriage." *Psychology and Aging* 10, no. 1 (1995): 140–149.

Centers for Disease Control and Prevention. "Ten great public health achievements—United States, 1900–1999." *Journal of the American Medical Association* 281, no. 16 (1999): 1481.

Chinen, A. B. "Fairy Tales and Transpersonal Development in Later Life." *Journal of Transpersonal Psychology* 7 (1985): 99–122.

————. "Forms of Transcendence in Later Life." *Journal of Transpersonal Psychology* 18 (1968): 171–192.

Chiriboga, David A. "Comments on Conceptual and Empirical Advances in Understanding Aging Well through Proactive Adaptation." In *Adulthood and Aging: Research on Continuities and Discontinuities,* ed. V. Bengtson. New York: Springer Publishing, 1996.

Cohen, Gene. *The Mature Mind: The Positive Power of the Aging Brain.* New York: Basic Books, 2006.

Cohen, Gene, Susan Perlstein, Jeff Chapline, Jeanne Kelly, Kimberly Firth, and Samuel Simmens. "The Impact of Professionally Conducted Cultural Programs on the Physical Health, Mental Health, and Social Functioning of Older Adults." *The Gerontologist* 46, no. 6: 726–734.

Cole, T. R. "The 'Enlightened' View of Aging: Victorian Morality in a New Key." *Hastings Center Report* (1983), pp. 34–40.

————. "The Prophecy of *Senescence*: G. Stanley Hall and the Reconstruction of Old Age in America." *Gerontologist* 24 (1984): 360–366.

Cook, Elizabeth, and Tina Picchi. "The Temenos of Palliative Care." *Psychological Perspectives* 56, no. 2 (July 2013).

Corbett, Lionel. *Psyche and the Sacred.* New Orleans: Spring, 2007.

————. *The Religious Function of the Psyche.* New York: Routledge, 1996.

————. *The Sacred Cauldron: Psychotherapy as a Spiritual Practice.* Wilmette, IL: Chiron, 2011.

————. "Transformation of the Image of God Leading to Self-Initiation into Old Age." In *Betwixt and Between,* ed. Louise Mahdi and Steven Foster. La Salle, IL: Open Court, 1987.

Edinger, Edward. *The Creation of Consciousness.* Toronto: Inner City Books, 1984.

Eliot, T. S. *Four Quartets.* In *Collected Poems 1909–1962.* New York: Harcourt, Brace and Co., 1963.

Elliott, Diana B., and Tavia Simmons. *Marital Events of Americans: 2009.* U.S. Census Bureau, American Community Survey Reports, August 2011, http://www.census.gov/prod/2011pubs/acs-13.pdf.

Erikson, Erik H. "Identity and the Life Cycle: Selected Papers." In *Psychological Issues*, vol. 1. New York: International Universities Press, 1959.

Erikson, Erik H., and Joan M. Erikson. *The Life Cycle Completed.* New York: Norton, 1998.

Erikson, Erik H., Joan M. Erikson, and Helen Q. Kivnic. *Vital Involvement in Old Age.* New York: Norton, 1989.

Evans, Roland. *Seeking Wholeness.* Hygiene, CO: Sunshine Press Publications, 2001.

Featherman, David L., Jacqui Smith, and James G. Peterson. "Successful Aging in a Post-Retired Society." In *Successful Aging: Perspectives from the Behavioral Sciences*, ed. Paul B. Baltes and Margaret M. Baltes. Cambridge, England: Cambridge University Press, 1990.

Fisher, B. J. "Successful Aging, Life Satisfaction, and Generativity in Later Life." *International Journal of Aging and Human Development* 41, no. 3 (1995): 239–250.

Flood, M. "Successful Aging: A Concept Analysis." *Journal of Theory Construction and Testing* 6, no. 2 (2002): 105–108.

Forster, E. M. *Commonplace Book,* ed. Edward Connery Lathem. New York: Holt, Rinehart, Winston, 1969.

Frankl, Viktor E. *Man's Search for Meaning.* Boston: Beacon Press, 2006.

Freedman, Marc. *The Big Shift: Navigating the New Stage Beyond Midlife.* New York: Public Affairs, 2011.

———. *Encore: Finding Work That Matters in the Second Half of Life.* New York: Public Affairs, 2007.

Freud, Sigmund. *The Future of an Illusion,* ed. James Strachey, trans. W. D. Robson-Scott. New York: Anchor Books, 1964.

———. *A Phylogenetic Fantasy: Overview of the Transference Neuroses,* ed. Ilse Grubrich-Simitis, trans. Axel Hoffer and Peter Hoffer. Cambridge, MA: Belknap Press, 1987.

———. *Totem and Taboo,* trans. James Strachey. New York: W. W. Norton, 1950.

Galenson, David W. *Old Masters and Young Geniuses: The Two Life Cycles of Artistic Creativity.* Princeton, NJ: Princeton University Press, 2006.

Geller, Sondra. "Sparking the Creative in Older Adults." *Psychological Perspectives* 56, no. 2 (July 2013).

Gerteis, Margaret. *Through the Patient's Eyes: Understanding and Promoting Patient-Centered Care.* San Francisco: Jossey-Bass, 1993.

Goldsmith, M., and Frida Kahlo. "Abjection, Psychic Deadness, and the Creative Impulse." *Psychoanalytic Review* 91, no. 6 (2004): 723–758.

Gould, Stephen Jay. *Ontogeny and Phylogeny.* Cambridge, MA: Harvard University Press, 1977.

Gordon, R. R. "Death and Creativity: A Jungian Approach." *Journal of Analytical Psychology* 2, no. 2 (1977): 106–124.

Guggenbühl-Craig, Adolf. *Marriage Is Dead—Long Live Marriage!* New York: Spring Publications, 1977.

———. *The Old Fool and the Corruption of Myth.* New Orleans: Spring Publications, 2006.

Halford, W. Kim, and Howard J. Markham, eds. *Clinical Handbook of Marriage and Couples Interventions.* New York: John Wiley and Sons, 1997.

Hanna, Gay, and Susan Perlstein. "Creativity Matters: Arts and Aging in America." Monograph published by the Americans for the Arts, September 2008.

Havighurst, Robert, Eva Kahana, and Boaz Kahana. "Evaluating a Model of Successful Aging for Urban African American and White Elderly." In *Serving Minority Elders in the 21st Century,* ed. May L. Wykle and Amasa B. Ford. New York: Springer Publishing, 1999.

Hemingway, Ernest. *The Old Man and the Sea.* New York: Scribner, 1952.

Heschel, Abraham Joshua. *I Asked for Wonder,* ed. Samuel Dresner. New York: Crossroad, 2001.

———. *The Sabbath.* New York: Farrar, Straus and Giroux, 1951.

Heschel, Abraham Joshua, and Elizabeth Kea. *Amazed by Grace.* Nashville: Tomas Nelson, 2003.

Hill, John. *At Home in the World.* New Orleans: Spring Journal, 2010.

Hillman, James. *The Dream and the Underworld.* New York: Harper and Row, 1979.

———. *The Force of Character and the Lasting Life.* New York: Random House, 1999.

Hogensen, George. "The Self, the Symbolic and Synchronicity: Virtual Realities and the Emergence of the Psyche." *Journal of Analytical Psychology* 50, no. 3 (2005): 271–284.

Hollis, James. *Finding Meaning in the Second Half of Life*. New York: Gotham Books, 2006.

———. *The Middle Passage: From Misery to Meaning in Midlife*. Toronto: Inner City Books, 1993.

———. *What Matters Most*. New York: Gotham Books, 2009.

Housden, Roger, and Chloe Goodchild, eds. *We Two*. London: Aquarian Press, 1992.

Institute of Medicine. *Crossing the Quality Chasm: A New Health System of the 21st Century*. Washington, DC: National Academy Press, 2001.

Ivey, Bill, and Steven J. Tepper. *Engaging Art: The Next Great Transformation of America's Cultural Life*. New York: Routledge, 2008.

Jeffri, Joan, et al. "Above Ground: Information on Artists III: Special Focus on New York City Aging Artists." Study for Research Center for Arts and Culture, Teachers College, Columbia University, 2007.

Johnson, Steven. *Emergence: The Connected Lives of Ants, Brains, Cities, and Software*. New York: Scribners, 2001.

Jung, C. G. *Aion*, vol. 9ii, *The Collected Works of C. G. Jung*. Princeton, NJ: Princeton University Press, 1960.

———. "Archetypes of the Collective Unconscious." In *The Collected Works of C. G. Jung*, vol. 9i, ed. and trans. Gerhard Adler and R. F. C. Hull. Princeton, NJ: Princeton University Press, 1959.

———. "Letter to Pere Lachat." In *The Collected Works of C. G. Jung*, vol. 18, ed. and trans. Gerhard Adler and R. F. C. Hull. Princeton, NJ: Princeton University Press, 1950.

———. *Letters, Vol. 1*, ed. Gerhard Adler, trans. R. F. C. Hull. Princeton, NJ: Princeton University Press, 1973.

———. *Letters, Vol. 2, 1951–1961*, ed. Gerhard Adler, trans. J. Hulen. Princeton, NJ: Princeton University Press, 1976.

———. "Marriage as a Psychological Relationship." In *The Collected Works of C. G. Jung*, vol. 17, ed. and trans. Gerhard Adler and R. F. C. Hull. Princeton, NJ: Princeton University Press, 1960.

———. *Memories, Dreams, Reflections*. New York: Pantheon Books, 1973.

———. *Modern Man in Search of a Soul*. New York: Harcourt, Inc., 1933.

———. *Mysterium Coniunctionis*, vol. 14, *The Collected Works of C. G. Jung*. Princeton, NJ: Princeton University Press, 1970.

———. "On the Psychology of the Unconscious." In *The Collected Works of C. G. Jung*, vol. 7, ed. and trans. Gerhard Adler and R. F. C. Hull. Princeton, NJ: Princeton University Press, 1953.

———. "A Psychological Approach to the Trinity." In *The Collected Works of C. G. Jung*, vol. 11, ed. and trans. Gerhard Adler and R. F. C. Hull. Princeton, NJ: Princeton University Press, 1958.

———. "The Psychology of the Child Archetype." In *The Collected Works of C. G. Jung*, vol. 9i, ed. and trans. Gerhard Adler and R. F. C. Hull. Princeton, NJ: Princeton University Press, 1959.

———. "The Psychology of the Transference." In *The Collected Works of C. G. Jung*, vol. 16, ed. and trans. Gerhard Adler and R. F. C. Hull. Princeton, NJ: Princeton University Press, 1960.

———. "The Relations between the Ego and the Unconscious." In *The Collected Works of C. G. Jung*, vol. 7, ed. and trans. Gerhard Adler and R. F. C. Hull. Princeton, NJ: Princeton University Press, 1953.

———. "The Sacrifice." In *The Collected Works of C. G. Jung*, vol. 5, ed. and trans. Gerhard Adler and R. F. C. Hull. Princeton, NJ: Princeton University Press, 1956.

———. "The Soul and Death." In *The Collected Works of C. G. Jung*, vol. 8, ed. and trans. Gerhard Adler and R. F. C. Hull. Princeton, NJ: Princeton University Press, 1960.

———. "The Spiritual Problem of Modern Man." In *The Collected Works of C. G. Jung*, vol. 10, ed. and trans. Gerhard Adler and R. F. C. Hull. Princeton, NJ: Princeton University Press, 1964.

———. "The Stages of Life." In *The Collected Works of C. G. Jung*, vol. 8, ed. and trans. Gerhard Adler and R. F. C. Hull. Princeton, NJ: Princeton University Press, 1960.

———. "Synchronicity: An Acausal Connecting Principle." In *The Collected Works of C. G. Jung*, vol. 8, ed. and trans. Gerhard Adler and R. F. C. Hull. Princeton, NJ: Princeton University Press, 1960.

Kaplan, Hillard S., and Arthur J. Robson. "The Emergence of Humans: The Coevolution of Intelligence and Longevity with Intergenerational Transfers." *PNAS* 99, no. 15 (July 23, 2002): 10221–10226.

Kauffman, Stuart A. *Reinventing the Sacred: A New View of Science, Reason, and Religion.* New York: Basic Books, 2008.

Kaufman, M. Ralph. "Old Age and Aging: The Psychoanalytic Point of View." *American Journal of Orthopsychiarty* 10, no. 1 (1940): 73–84.

Kaufmann, Yoram. *The Way of the Image: The Orientational Approach to the Psyche.* New York: Zahav Books, 2009.

Kent, Mary, and Rose Li. "The Cuts and Aging: Building the Science." Paper prepared for the National Endowment for the Arts, Office of Research and Analysis, 2013.

Kim, Jaegwon. *Supervenience and Mind.* Cambridge: Cambridge University Press, 1993.

Kohut, H. "Forms and Transformations of Narcissism." *Journal of the American Psychoanalytic Association* 14 (1966): 243–272.

Krull, Marianne. *Freud and His Father*, trans. Arnold Pomerans. New York: Norton, 1979, 1986.

Laidlaw, Ken, and Nancy A. Pachana. "Aging with Grace." *APA Monitor* 42, no. 10 (2011).

Langs, R. *Beyond Yahweh and Jesus: Bringing Death's Wisdom to Faith, Spirituality, and Psychoanalysis.* Latham, MD: Jason Aronson, 2008.

———. *Death Anxiety and Clinical Practice.* London: Karnac Books, 1997.

———. *The Evolution of the Emotion-Processing Mind: With an Introduction to Mental Darwinism.* London: Karnac Books, 1996.

———. *Freud on a Precipice: How Freud's Fate Pushed Psychoanalysis over the Edge.* Latham, MD: Jason Aronson, 2009.

———. *Fundamentals of Adaptive Psychotherapy and Counseling.* London: Palgrave-Macmillan, 2004.

———. *Love and Death in Psychotherapy.* London: Palgrave-Macmillan, 2006.

Lazarus, Richard S. and Susan Folkman, *Stress, Appraisal, and Coping.* New York: Springer Publishing Company, 1984.

Levin, J. S., and L. M. Chatters. "Religion, Health and Psychological Well-Being in Older Adults." *Journal of Aging and Health* 10, no. 4 (1998): 504–531.

Lewis, Thomas, Fari Amini, and Richard Lannon. *A General Theory of Love.* New York: Vintage Books, 2000.

Lifton, R. J., and E. Olson. *Living and Dying.* New York: Praeger, 1974.

Maslow, A. *Toward a Psychology of Being.* New York: Wiley, 1998.

McCarthy, Kevin F., Elizabeth Heneghan Ondaatje, Laura Zakaras, and Arthur Brooks. *Gifts of the Muse*. Santa Monica: RAND Corporation, 2004.

Melia, S. P. "Solitude and Prayer in the Late Lives of Elder Catholic Women: Activity, Withdrawal, or Transcendence?" *Journal of Religious Gerontology* 13 (2001): 47–63.

Merton, Thomas. *Love and Living*. Orlando, FL: Harcourt, Inc., 1985.

Mikulincer, Mario, Victor Florian, Phillip A. Cowan, and Carolyn P. Cowan. "Attachment Security in Couple Relationship." *Family Process* 41 (3, 2002).

Moody, H. R. "Getting Over the Denial of Aging." *Hastings Center Report* 37, no. 5 (September 2007).

Morowitz, Harold J. *The Emergence of Everything*. New York: Oxford University Press, 2002.

Nakashima, Mitsuko, et al. "Decision Making in Long-Term Care: Approaches Used by Older Adults and Implications for Social Work Practice." *Journal of Gerontological Social Work* 43, no. 4 (2004): 405–434.

National Endowment for the Humanities. *Framing a National Research Agenda for the Arts, Lifelong Learning and Individual Well-Being*. Washington, DC, November 2011.

National Endowment for the Arts. "The Arts and Human Development." White paper, Washington, DC, 2011.

National Marriage Project at the University of Virginia. *Husbands Who Have the Happiest Marriage*. http://nationalmarriageproject.org/wp-content/uploads/2012/12/NMP-Fact-Sheet-Husbands-1112.pdf.

———. *The State of Our Unions: Marriage in America 2011*. http://nationalmarriageproject.org/wp-content/uploads/2012/05/Union2011.pdf.

Neugarten, Bernice L. "Age-Sex Roles and Personality in Middle Age: A Thematic Apperception Study." *Psychological Monographs* 72 (1958): 1–33.

———. "Personality Change in Later Life: A Developmental Perspective." In C. Eisdorfer and M. P. Larson, eds., *The Psychology of Adult Development and Aging*. Washington, DC: American Psychological Association, 1973.

Otto, Rudolph. *The Idea of the Holy*. New York: Oxford University Press, 1952.

Pecukonis, Edward, Otima Doyle, and Donna L. Bliss. "Reducing Barriers to Interprofessional Training: Promoting Interprofessional Cultural Competence." *Journal of Interprofessional Care* 22, no. 4 (2008).

Pew Research, "'Nones' on the Rise." *The Pew Forum on Religion and Public Life*. October 9, 2012.

———. "The Return of the Multi-Generational Family Household." *Social and Demographic Trends*, 18 March 18, 2010.

Phelan, Elizabeth A., and Eric B. Larson. "Successful Aging: Where Next?" *Journal of the American Geriatrics Society* 50 (2002): 1306–1308.

Phelan, Elizabeth A., Lynda A. Anderson, Andrea Z. LaCroix, and Eric B. Larson. "Older Adults Views of 'Successful Aging'—How Do They Compare with Researchers Definitions?" *Journal of the American Geriatrics Society* 52 (2004): 11–26.

Plato, *The Symposium*. In *The Portable Plato*, ed. Scott Buchanan. New York: Viking Press, 1948.

Plotkin, Bill. *Nature and the Human Soul: Cultivating Wholeness and Community in a Fragmented World*. Novato, CA: New World Library, 2008.

Poon, Leonard W., Sarah H. Gueldner, and Betsy M. Sprouse. *Successful Aging and Adaptation with Chronic Diseases*. New York: Springer, 2003.

Portmann, Adolf. "Metamorphosis in Animals: The Transformation of the Individual and the Type." In *Man and Transformation: Papers from the Eranos Yearbooks*. Princeton, NJ: Princeton University Press, 1972.

———. *New Paths in Biology*. New York: Harper and Row, 1964.

Rilke, Rainer Maria. *Letters to a Young Poet*. New York: W. W. Norton, 1993.

Rowe, John W., and Robert L. Kahn. "Successful Aging." *The Gerontologist* 37, no. 4 (1997): 433–441.

Ruch, Willibald, Rene T. Proyer, and M. Weber. "Humor as a Character Strength among the Elderly." *Zeitschrift fur Gerontolgie und Geriatrie* (February 2010).

Sadler, Euan, and Simon Biggs. "Exploring the Links between Spirituality and 'Successful Aging,'" *Journal of Social Work Practice* 20, no. 3 (2006): 267–280.

Sanford, John A. *The Invisible Partners*. New York: Paulist Press, 1980.

Schnarch, David. *Passionate Marriage*. New York: Henry Holt and Co., 1997.

Schulz, Richard, and Jutta Heckliausen. "A Life Span Model of Successful Aging." *American Psychologist* 51, no. 1 (1996): 702–714.

Schur, Max. *Freud, Living and Dying*. New York: International Universities Press, 1972.

Seung, Sebastian. *Connectome: How the Brain's Wiring Makes Us Who We Are*. Boston: Houghton, Mifflin, Harcourt, 2012.

Solecki, Ralph S., Rose L. Solecki, and Anagnostis P. Agelarakis. *The Proto-Neolithic Cemetery in Shanidar Cave*. College Station: Texas A&M University Press, 2004.

Stewart, Kristen. *The Health Benefits of Marriage*. Everyday Health, November 2010. http://www.everydayhealth.com/family-health/understanding/benefits-of-tying-the-knot.aspx.

Thomas, William H. "The Search for Being." *AARP Bulletin*, November 2004.

———. *What Are Old People For? How Elders Will Save the World*. Acton, MA: VanderWyk and Burnham, 2004.

Tornstam, Lars. *Gerotranscendence: A Developmental Theory*. New York: Springer, 2005.

———. "Gero-Transcendence: A Meta-Theoretical Reformulation of the Disengagement Theory." *Aging: Clinical and Experimental Research* 1 (1989): 55–63.

———. "Gerotranscendence: The Contemplative Dimension of Aging." *Journal of Aging Studies* 11, no. 2 (1997): 143–154.

U.S. Department of Commerce, Bureau of the Census. *The Next Four Decades: The Older Population in the United States: 2010 to 2050*. Online report, May 2010.

Vaillant, George E. *Aging Well: Surprising Guideposts to a Happier Life*. New York: Little, Brown, 2003.

von Goethe, Johann. "The Holy Longing." in *The Rag and Bone Shop of the Heart: Poems for Men*, ed. Robert Bly, James Hillman, and Michael Meade. New York: Harper, 1993.

von Franz, Marie-Louise. *On Dreams and Death,* trans. Emmanuel Xipolitas Kennedy and Vernon Brooks. Boston: Shambhala, 1986.
———. *The Puer Aeternus.* Salem, MA: Sigo Press, 1970.
Walker, Ruth, Mary Luszcz, Denis Gerstorf, and Christiane Hoppman. "Subjective Well-Being Dynamics in Couples from the Australian Longitudinal Study of Aging." *Gerontology* 57 (2011): 153–160.
Watson, Burton. *Chuang Tzu: Basic Writings.* New York: Columbia University Press, 1964.
Wheelwright, Jane Hollister. "Old Age and Death." In *Betwixt and Between,* ed. Louise Mahdi and Steven Foster. La Salle, IL: Open Court, 1987.
Whitmont, Edward C. "The Destiny Concept in Psychotherapy." *Journal of Jungian Theory and Practice* 9, no. 1 (2007).
Wilkstrom, Britt-Maj. "Older Adults and the Arts: The Importance of Aesthetic Forms of Expression in Later Life." *Journal of Gerontological Nursing* 30, no. 9 (2004).
Whyte, David. *Midlife and the Great Unknown: Finding Courage and Clarity through Poetry.* Sounds True, 2003, compact disc.
Woodman, Marion. *The Crown of Age.* Sounds True, 2003, compact disc.
———. "Embracing the Dark." In *We Two,* ed. Roger Housden and Chloe Goodchild. London: Aquarian Press, 1992.
Yalom, Marilyn, and Laura Carstensen, eds. *Inside the American Couple: New Thinking, New Challenges.* Berkeley: University of California Press, 2002.
Yeats, William Butler. *Selected Poems and Two Plays of William Butler Yeats,* ed. M. L. Rosenthal. New York: MacMillan, 1962.
Yeung, Danni Y., Carmen K. M. Wong, and David P. P. Lok. "Emotion Regulation Mediates Age Differences in Emotions." *Aging and Mental Health* 15, no. 3 (2011): 414–418.

~ ABOUT THE CONTRIBUTORS ~

Joseph Cambray, Ph.D., is president of the International Association for Analytical Psychology. He was a faculty member at the Center for Psychoanalytic Studies at Harvard Medical School, a member of the Editorial Advisory Board for the *Journal of Analytical Psychology*, and a member of both the New England Society of Jungian Analysts and the Jungian Psychoanalytic Association of New York. He is author of *Synchronicity: Nature and Psyche in an Interconnected Universe* and coeditor, with Linda Carter, of *Analytical Psychology: Contemporary Perspectives in Jungian Analysis*. He has published numerous papers and book chapters and regularly lectures on the international circuit. He has a private practice as an analyst with offices in Boston and Providence, Rhode Island.

Michael E. Carbine, M.A., writes on issues related to Jungian psychology with a special focus on the application of Jungian ideas to the field of aging. After a forty-year career in Washington, D.C., as a business writer and publishing executive, he began working in Southern California as a policy and program developer in the aging services field. He began studying Jungian psychology while working on a master's degree in religion and psychology at the University of Chicago Divinity School. He was coproducer of the March 2012 symposium at the Library of Congress entitled *Jung and Aging: Bringing to Life the Possibilities for Vibrant Aging*, sponsored by the Library of Congress and the Jung Society of Washington.

Michael Conforti, Ph.D., is a Jungian analyst and the founder and director of the Assisi Institute. He has been a faculty member at the C. G. Jung Institute–Boston and the C. G. Jung Foundation of New York, and he served for many years as a senior associate faculty member in the doctoral and master's programs in clinical psychology at Antioch New England. A pioneer in the field of matter-psyche studies, Conforti is actively investigating the workings of archetypal fields and the relationship between Jungian psychology and the new sciences. He is the author of *Threshold Experiences: The Archetype of Beginnings* (2007) and *Field, Form, and Fate: Patterns in Mind, Nature, and Psyche* (1999, revised edition 2003).

Lionel Corbett, M.D., trained in psychiatry at the University of Manchester in England and as a Jungian analyst at the Jung Institute of Chicago. Prior to his training as a Jungian analyst he practiced medicine as a geriatric psychiatrist. His primary interests are in the religious function of the psyche and in the development of psychotherapy as a spiritual practice. Corbett is a core faculty member at Pacifica Graduate Institute and the author of *Psyche and the Sacred: Spirituality Beyond Religion*, *The Religious Function of the Psyche*, and *The Sacred Cauldron: Psychotherapy as a Spiritual Practice*.

Melanie Starr Costello, Ph.D., is a licensed psychologist, historian, and Zürich-trained Jungian analyst in private practice in Washington, D.C. She earned her doctorate in history and literature of religions from Northwestern University. A former assistant professor of history at St. Mary's College of Maryland, Costello has taught and published on the topics of psychology and religion, medieval spirituality, and clinical practice. She is author of *Imagination, Illness and Injury: Jungian Psychology and the Somatic Dimensions of Perception*, a study of the link between illness and insight.

Roland Evans, M.A., trained as a clinical psychologist in the United Kingdom and taught for many years at Naropa University in Boulder, Colorado. He has a private practice specializing in counseling for mature couples and older men and is author of *Seeking Wholeness: Insights into the Mystery of Experience.*

Gay Powell Hanna, Ph.D., M.F.A., is executive director of the National Center for Creative Aging (NCCA), an affiliate of George Washington University. NCCA provides professional development and technical assistance, including service as a clearinghouse for best practices, research, and policy development to encourage and sustain arts and humanities programs in various community and health-care settings. Hanna holds a doctorate in arts education with a specialization in arts administration focusing on service to people with disabilities from Florida State University and a master of fine arts in sculpture from the University of Georgia. A contributing author to numerous articles and books, Hanna is noted for her expertise in accessibility and universal design.

James Hollis, Ph.D., is the author of fourteen books, cofounder of the C. G. Jung Institute of Philadelphia and Saybrook University's Jungian Studies program, director emeritus of the Jung Center of Houston, vice president emeritus of the Philemon Foundation, and an adjunct professor at Saybrook University and Pacifica Graduate Institute. He resides in Houston, Texas, where he conducts an analytic practice.

Robert Langs, M.D., is a classically trained psychoanalyst who has forged a new, adaptation-centered paradigm of psychoanalysis in which trauma, death anxiety, and universal archetypes play a central role. He is the author of forty-seven books and more than two hundred refereed journal papers and book chapters. His most recent books are *Beyond Yahweh and Jesus: Bringing Death's Wisdom to Faith, Spirituality, and Psychoanalysis* and *Freud on a Precipice: How Freud's Fate Pushed Psychoanalysis over the Edge.* He is currently in private practice in New York City.

Kelley Macmillan, Ph.D., M.S.W., is clinical assistant professor at the University of Maryland School of Social work. He earned his degree in social work from Indiana University and his doctorate, with a focus on gerontology, from the University of Kansas. He works in the areas of health and aging and with social service agencies to develop services that build on new practice opportunities, such as patient-centered medical homes, transition care teams, and multisite field placements, and in programs serving older adults. He has served on numerous associations and committees and has published many articles and book chapters on the provision of services to aging adults and those with mental-health issues.

Mary A. McDonald, M.D., is a geriatrician serving in the home-care practice of the Division of Geriatric Medicine at Washington Hospital Center. She is medical director at the Washington Home and Community Hospice. She is also associate professor in the Department of Family Medicine, Division of Geriatrics, at Howard University College of Medicine. McDonald has published articles and chapters in geriatric medicine.

Aryeh Maidenbaum, Ph.D., is a Jungian analyst and director of the New York Center for Jungian Studies. He is a former faculty member at New York University, where he taught courses in Jungian psychology for many years. Among his publications are "The Search for Spirit in Jungian Psychology," "Sounds of Silence," "Psychological Types, Job Change, and Personal Growth," and *Jung and the Shadow of Anti-Semitism*, and he is a contributing author to *Current Theories of Psychoanalysis*, edited by Robert Langs.

Jerry M. Ruhl, Ph.D., is a clinical psychologist, executive director of the Jung Center of Houston, and a faculty member at Saybrook University's Graduate Studies Program in Jungian Studies. He is coauthor of three books with Robert A. Johnson, including *Living Your Unlived Life* and *Contentment: A Way to True Happiness*. Ruhl sees patients in private practice, facilitates dream groups, and presents seminars nationally.

Leslie Sawin, M.S., is a planner and program designer developing educational programs that bring Jungian ideas to the general public. She is currently co-program director at the Jung Society of Washington and directs the society's community-based efforts. She earned a master's degree in health policy and management from the Harvard School of Public Health and is currently enrolled as a certificate candidate in the Jungian Studies Program at Saybrook University. Her community-based programs include ongoing Jungian program development with the Library of Congress.

∼ Index ∼

electronic health records (EHRs), 114–115
Eleusinian feast of Thesmophoria, 162
Eliot, T. S., 81
emergentism, 46–50, 56
emotional support, 116–118
emotion-processing mind, 81
emotions, in older people, 24
Encore Chorale (Washington, DC), 130
engagement, 140–143
entelechy, 66
environmental movement/crisis, 171–172
Erikson, E. H. and J. M., 24–25, 32, 130, 228
Eros, 74, 165
    related to death, 152, 156, 160–161
evil, problem of, 224
evolution, 45

F
fairy tales, study of, 229
faith traditions. *See* religious traditions
fear, 206–207
    of death, 213. *See also* death anxiety
fear and anxiety, during health crises, 116–117
femininity, stereotypes, 27
food security and nutrition programs, 92
Forster, E. M., 173
Freud, Sigmund, 44–46, 77–79
    elemental test of spirituality, 208, 210
Friedman, Marc, 133
fundamentalism, religious and political, 153

G
Galenson, David, 124–125
Gandhi, 34
Geller, Sondra, 94, 97

generativity, 160
generosity, 189–190
George Washington Institute for Spirituality and Health (GWISH), 99
geriatrics, 138
gerontology, 44, 90, 94, 203
gerotranscendence, 25, 30–31, 229
Gerteis, Margaret, 110
God, viii, 62, 190, 216, 220, 231
    rejuvenation of, 221
God-image, 215–218, 221–222, 224, 231
    transformation of, 222
Goethe, 213
good, and evil, 225
Gould, Stephen Jay, 46
grandparenthood, 89
Gray Panthers movement, 28, 133
graying of America, 53
great round of life, 156
Greek mythology, 158, 160–161, 184–185
Green House Project model, 112
Guggenbühl-Craig, Adolf, 184, 191, 203–204

H
Haeckel, Ernst, 45
Hall, G. Stanley, 44–46
Hanna, Gay Powell, 96–97
health
    behavioral, 112
    mental and spiritual, vii, 20
    physical, 20, 108, 130
health care and medical services, barriers, 92
health care and wellness services, 91
health-care delivery systems, 98–99, 108, 110, 113, 119–120, 139
health information exchange, 115

skilled nursing facilities, 113
Smith, Maria Ann, 125
social capital, 133
Social Security eligibility, 89
social service professionals, 90, 94,
    101, 117, 119
social services delivery, 93, 110, 119–
    120
social work, 94
Songwriting Works, 131
soul, 165, 204
soul mates, 184
spirit, and nature, 166, 168
spiritual ancestry, 54–57
spiritual attitude, 74
spiritual development, 33–34, 182,
    225–226.
    See also psycho–spiritual
    development
spiritual direction, 65
spiritual life, 62
spiritual maturation
    and aging, 152
    and death, 163–164
spiritual vitality, 154
spirituality, 16–17, 24, 29–31, 33–
    34, 48, 63–64, 94, 98–99, 145,
    154, 182, 208, 210, 224, 226,
    229–230
    of aging, 165
    central to human development,
        152, 155
    connection to creativity, 124
    important to Jungians, ix
    in support and wellness programs in
        hospitals, 99
    late-life, 215, 223
    mature, 158, 165, 209
    not a predictor of successful aging, 33
    personal, 216
    and psychology, 154–155
    role in maturation, 46
spiritus rector, 227

Stagebridge Senior Theatre, 132
Stern, William, 44–45
story making and storytelling, 95–96,
    172, 227
substance abuse, late-onset, 92, 97
suffering, 12, 31, 91, 99–100, 116,
    153, 159, 202, 216, 225, 228
suicide, 92, 97
supervenience, 56
surrender, in old age, 124, 164, 181,
    228
symbol, 167
symbolic function, 154–155, 168
synchronicity, 55–57
systems theory, 46–47, 49

T
Taoism, 52–53
Tennyson, Alfred, "Tithonus" (poem),
    158–159
Thanatos, 160–161
Thomas, William H., 169
TimeSlips, 131
Titchener, Edward, 44–45
Tithonus, 158
Titian, 34
Tolstoy, Leo, 89
Tornstam, Lars, 31, 229
transcendence, 62–63
transcendent function, 51
transformation, 168
transition, 156–158, 163–164, 218
transpersonal Self, 14, 31
transportation, for the elderly, 92
trauma, and aging, 81–82
trigger decoding, 81–82
Tyler, Anne, *The Accidental Tourist*, 181

U
unconscious, 11, 32, 36, 79, 184, 216
    transpersonal, 222
University of the Third Age, 22

CPSIA information can be obtained at www.ICGtesting.com
Printed in the USA
BVOW05s0551280414

351789BV00005B/29/P